MOTHER
IS IT
WORTH IT?

MOTHER
IS IT
WORTH IT?

Rusley Turner

Matador
9 Priory Business Park,
Wistow Road, Kibworth Beauchamp,
Leicestershire. LE8 0RX
Tel: 0116 279 2299
Email: books@troubador.co.uk
Web: www.troubador.co.uk/matador
Twitter: @matadorbooks

ISBN 978 1838590 734

British Library Cataloguing in Publication Data.
A catalogue record for this book is available from the British Library.

Printed and bound in the UK by TJ International, Padstow, Cornwall
Typeset in 11pt Sabon MT by Troubador Publishing Ltd, Leicester, UK

Matador is an imprint of Troubador Publishing Ltd

This work is dedicated to MAMA, the heroine of the piece, hoping that she would forgive me for publishing all the funny, rude and down to earth parts of her story.

Chapter One

The warm September day was sinking into a slumber as twilight deepened to nightfall. A faint tang of autumn mists mixed with wet peat drifted from the dark woods behind the house. In front of us black velvet mountains reached up into the translucent, deep-sea sky – speckled with myriad crystalline, winking, stars – and the 'wheep' of a curlew echoed back from the saltings in an otherwise silent world.

An owl flew slowly past – within twenty feet of us. A breath of wingbeat and a glimpse of a pale intense face, as this ghost of a creature was momentarily silhouetted against the heavens.

It settled in the oak tree by the top gate, thought for a moment, then let forth a shriek. Another one answered from deep within the woods.

The stillness was broken by the swish of the sea. Someone was rowing a boat up the coast – the creak of the oars against the rowlocks in a steady rhythm – slowly decreasing until it was lost in the darkness.

Bats flickered through the dusk on their erratic, noiseless flight – will-o'-the-wisp creations adding to the unreal quality of the night.

Brian leaned forward to put another log on the open barbecue fire. The dried bark burst into flame and burned with a comfortable yellow flame, illuminating our faces – relaxed and at peace. Our meal was over and we were replete with food and the atmosphere of tranquillity.

Four years ago, in 1982, we left settled jobs in the prosperous home counties and moved to this enchanted spot on the coast of Wales where the clear Irish Sea washes up to the immutable Welsh mountains. We exchanged regular salary cheques for the doubtful income from a small sheep farm. We also exchanged the noise, the traffic jams, the smoky atmosphere and the expensive housing, the rates and many other urban characteristics for the silence of the open spaces, the clean air, the warmth of a supportive village community and the relatively uncomplicated life of the satisfied human being.

On our arrival, newly emerged from the suburban rat race, it was sheer bliss to be able to ignore the clock – to make up our day's work only as our inclination, or the weather, dictated. It was difficult to believe that an irate employer would not want an explanation for that odd hour spent idling in the rock pools at the top of the beach or merely sitting in the sun contemplating one of the most spectacular views in Britain from the front door of our new home.

There were some initial disadvantages of course. The tiny farmhouse – a toy town home – lay snuggled in woodland, a stone's throw from the beach. A fairy-tale place – the sort of home where Snow White and the Dwarfs would be found. But it was also dark, damp and chill on the inside. So we had blasted and hewn the solid rock from the side of the hill and had built a light, warm, spacious extension to house our middle-aged hopes and also Mama.

Mama, Brian's mother, is something special. For many years she has suffered with Alzheimer's Disease or Senile Dementia. Not the sort that causes silence or emptiness in a mental home, but the jolly, devil-may-care sort that sings and laughs a lot and is ungoverned by any need to conform to what is known as polite behaviour.

But many of her eccentricities and aberrations are scarcely noticeable in the general disorder that was, and still is, for much of the time, normal life for us. If Mama has a fancy to wear two hats on her head and meanwhile laugh herself to stitches at some private joke, then I am glad she is enjoying herself. If she wails – she can no longer talk – I will often join in, to serenade the sheep, or the dogs, who will sometimes lift their noses skywards, and howl their mite too. There is something quite therapeutic in this sort of thing. Although I cannot emulate Mama's bold attempts on some loud and seemingly discordant classical work, I will happily wail out one of the old hymn tunes, a sea shanty or something from a 1920s musical.

The local wildlife, some of whose members had watched our initial endeavours with apprehension, soon turned us to good account and settled back to resume their lives with, in many cases, an improved range of food and shelter. I am sure the birds, the badgers and the small mammals eat as much poultry cereal as the hens, and the constant piles of building materials make a temporary home for many a passing soul. When I moved an old tarpaulin that had lain unattended for several months, it housed a grass snake, at least half a dozen assorted frogs and toads, and innumerable creepy-crawlies.

As the snake lives on a diet that includes frogs, it was understandable that it should choose this site, but were the frogs suicidal or did they not know that the snake was there?

Such Pickwickian intellectual debates have replaced issues that formerly occupied my mind. The terms of the latest Finance Act are now a matter of supreme indifference. It is no longer necessary for me to burn the midnight oil to keep abreast of the complexities of the constantly changing fiscal legislation. My present existence makes me more likely to be concerned about what the tide is doing. Have I time to go and collect that big log which arrived on this morning's tide, before it is washed away again? And whether I have sufficient food, in all the necessary different forms, to supply the hungry hordes that haunt the farmyard or manage to get their legs under my kitchen table.

The farm animals have added another dimension to our existence. We knew little of the art of farming when we arrived here but, by degrees, and aided by a stalwart Welshman who has coerced and bullied us into shape, we have stocked the farm with breeding ewes. Sadly, our mentor will tell you that they are not like the ewes on the average Welsh farm. They are distressingly tame with distinct characters that amuse, interest or enrage, depending on their respective specialities. There are shy ones, sly ones, greedy ones, bossy ones, aggressive ones, rebels, hooligans, comedians, gentlemen, good mothers, bad mothers and some who will give you a thumping butt on the bottom when your back is turned if the mood takes them.

As I write this in May 1986, the future looks relatively comfortable. We feel able to cope with the vagaries of farm life and with Mama. So has our move from the conventional rat race been a success? Nothing, absolutely nothing, would tempt me back to the suburban life. There are perhaps hot summer evenings when, instead of enjoying a good soak in the bath with a cooling drink in my hand, I find myself down in the hay meadow – embraced by the warm smell of dried grasses – aching limbs as each armful is hoisted on to the top of the hay cart – hair full of dust and scratchy bits in my bra – but oh so content with life.

Perhaps, too, we were lucky in that our responsibilities to Mama – her own name for herself as speech became a difficulty – had forced us quite early on to seek jobs where at least some of the duties could be carried out at home so that one of us could take over the caring role. Thus the transition was not as great as it might have been since we have both continued to work on a part-time basis in the same line of business as before. And this has produced an income to supplement the meagre amounts from the farming enterprise and from our small campsite. Coupled with that we had no responsibilities for dependants apart from Mama. While I think many families would enjoy and benefit from this type of existence, I do not think it is sensible to expect to be able to make an adequate living from the land alone. But those who have yearnings for the outback and the will to work – although it doesn't usually seem like work – should move heaven and earth to muster the wherewithal and *do* it.

Chapter Two

Back in the misty depths of time when I was a teenager, there was a local lad who had caught my eye and whose attention I was anxious to catch in return. In fact, we'd known each other for donkeys' years. In a utility liberty bodice – buttoned down the front – and with long suspenders reaching down to thick hand-knitted black stockings and a pair of navy blue fleecy knickers with long legs under a black gymslip, I had been obliged to sit near Brian in the school dugout during a wartime air raid – my gas mask in place, to add the final thrill. True I was only about eight at the time – and Brian, at ten, wasn't, or shouldn't have been, aware of the passion-provoking nature of my underwear. But all this was forgotten as adolescence advanced, and from being rather a bore, boys became interesting, even exciting, creatures, especially to a girl with no siblings.

Whether my persistence paid off – or perhaps there was a lack of other likely candidates, I don't know – but I did succeed in attracting a response, and throughout our teens, Brian and I knocked around together – walking, riding our bikes, fishing and generally being a pain to our parents.

When he was eighteen, Brian entered an engineering apprenticeship with Vickers-Armstrongs, the aircraft firm, at Weybridge in Surrey – some twenty miles away from our homes in Farnham. This was a great worry and I spent many hours with a pair of those old-fashioned curling tongs, trying to beautify myself in order to ward off any possible opposition from among the new friends Brian was making. He met a great many people from all different walks of life and one of them, a fellow apprentice called Terry Collins, was to have a major effect on our lives. Unlike Brian, he was one of a group of apprentices selected to go on an Outward Bound course to be held at Aberdovey in Mid Wales.

He came back full of tales of his adventures – of the beauty of the country, the people with their own language and interesting culture, the wild open mountains, the forests, the lakes. He eulogised about it for months. I shouldn't think Vickers made much profit from their labours for ages afterwards – they seemed always to be talking of Wales and its wonders. Brian's imagination was fired – so too was mine when the details were passed on to me – and Wales became a Mecca for us – a distant, as yet unattainable goal. But we promised ourselves that one day…

The years passed. I settled to be a very humble bank clerk in what is now Barclays Bank Trust Company. Brian and I got engaged when we were nineteen and twenty-one, and married two years later in 1958.

Our first home was a converted Norfolk Broads auxiliary sailing boat. It had been a thing of luxury in the heady

1920s but was now old and tired – hence in our price range. As a home it left a lot to be desired. The accommodation was cramped and the decks leaked like a sieve when it rained, but we did have fun with it. Life afloat was mad, frightening, hilarious and damp. Who else has had to spend the first night of their honeymoon struggling to keep the love nest afloat, because the gland that was supposed to seal the propeller shaft where it passed through the hull had loosened, allowing river water to flood into the bilges? Then up to the floorboards. Then over the floorboards, to threaten the wedding frillies packed in a suitcase and a paper carrier containing a cooked chicken, some tomatoes and a lettuce – the latter items intended as the basis for a romantic candlelit dinner. At three in the morning Brian was still struggling with the leak, and I'd hacked the chicken into workmanlike hunks that we ate with our fingers by the light of an oil lamp, as we debated what we had better do. Fortunately Brian was able to repair the leak but it was typical of life afloat. The unexpected, expensive, physically exhausting, or uncomfortable, challenge was always being offered.

Nowadays every Tom, Dick and Harriet seems to be able to afford a car as soon as they're eighteen, but in the late fifties cars were a considerable luxury and we'd been married for over a year before we were able to join the motoring elite. Even then, our car was ancient and moody. Periodically bits fell off it and Brian welded or riveted them back on. But with the ready optimism of youth, we weren't to be deterred from making the long journey westward to Wales as soon as the holiday period commenced.

Money, as always, was in short supply and with little more than a £5 note, a borrowed tent, and a car full of tools and equipment to cover almost every contingency, we set off. After the best part of a day of bouncing over pre-motorway roads in our 1934 Morris 12, it became apparent to me that Wales was a good deal further off than I had envisaged. I knew perfectly well that it was about 250 miles, but with little experience of travel, I had no conception of just how far that was. It was long before the days of the MOT test and I can still remember looking through the hole in the floor by my feet and watching the tarmac creep past as we ground up the hills in bottom gear – and then rush madly along as we hurtled down the other side. It took us nearly twelve hours to reach Wales, but it was well worth it.

That first holiday was idyllic. Five days of camping by the lake at Tal y Llyn for 2/6p a night – a lot in those days – climbing Cader Idris and walking the hills. Exploring remote paths through fairy-tale woodlands, by turbulent mountain streams, over ancient stone bridges, and up steep valleys to bleak, windswept, open moors.

I remember cooking boiled eggs on a meth spirit stove as the sun crept over the mountain; washing in, and drinking, the water from the stream; lying on a windblown hilltop amongst the coarse grasses and the wild flowers; feeling at complete peace with the world. To us, Wales was indeed a magic place. Recollections of that holiday kept me going through many a long hour at work for ages afterwards.

We returned to Wales many times during those early years of our married life – usually on a shoestring with a borrowed tent – the journey becoming easier as we managed to afford a better car. Apart from the obvious beauty of the scenery – the space, the silence, the unspoiled woods and streams – Wales is full of legend and romance. Its history is full of colourful characters and events. In this part of Wales – probably the last to suffer the doubtful advantages of industrial development – so many of the ordinary people have a natural culture that is difficult to define. Their innate poetry and imagination seem less blunted by the canned entertainments of our present day. They recite their heritage in the language of the hearth and sing their hearts out for the sheer joy of hearing the familiar sounds. It is so good that this enthusiasm is still alive and bearing up very well.

I had been something of an embarrassing afterthought in my parents' lives, as they were both in their forties when I arrived – their only child. Looking back at old photos, I think they must have regarded me with bemused interest while I was a toddler, but as I grew up, we had rather an uneasy relationship. My father was in the Navy and away at sea for most of my early childhood and my mother was left on her own with this awkward, often difficult, child. Mother had spent many happy years abroad in the sun and had enjoyed an active social life. To be confined to the home in cold, wet, wartime Britain, with an unattractive child for company, no nice clothes and few social events, was hard for her. Poor things – they must have been sadly disappointed with their ugly duckling. I was useless at all the things they prized – a nervous bundle of inferiority with just a hint of the hooligan.

Brian too was an only child with a sadly ailing father who died shortly after we were married. Brian's mother naturally needed a great deal of moral and practical support in her widowhood and she spent a great deal of time with us. It became our habit to take her on holiday each year. Where else but to Wales?

By the time we were in our mid twenties, my parents were approaching their seventies and they too were beginning to need some practical support, so originally we took all three of them on holiday together, plus Mama's dog. This always proved to be a disaster as the two mothers could never agree about anything except that Princess Margaret should have married Group Captain Peter Townsend, and one or two other similar matters that did not concern either of them at all.

My mother would corner me in the kitchen of our rented cottage and complain that Brian's mother pampered her dog and that it smelt – contentions I privately agreed with, but could not admit to. In turn, Brian's mother, who prided herself on calling a spade a spade, would tell my mother roundly that her shoes were obviously unsuitable for a country holiday and that hats were best kept for church. If I suggested a picnic lunch, one of them would agree while the other would think it looked like rain and suggest we had a restaurant meal. If my mother offered to take us out for a drink and a bar snack, Brian's mother would be feeling off colour and refuse to eat anything. In reply, Brian's mother would buy a luscious box of fresh cream cakes and my mother would refuse to have one. Before every outing there was a great deal of deliberation as to whether we should, or should not, take mackintoshes and umbrellas, even if there was a cloudless blue sky and a good weather forecast. We could never move out of the cottage without first having heard the latest forecast.

I'm sure there are many people who know just what I mean. In reality we were all quite close and fond of one another but it didn't stop the mothers having a verbal swipe at each other from time to time – and I too sometimes found myself talking and acting in a way that was quite foreign to my nature – at least I hoped it was.

After several years of such annual events, my mother decided to take her unsuitable shoes and her hats to stay in a hotel at Torquay, so the annual pilgrimage was reduced to four and a dog, and was so much easier to cope with.

But even these problems did not dampen our enthusiasm for Wales. We used to hire a cottage at Dinas Mawddwy – an enchanting spot some miles to the east of Dolgellau. The cottage was long and low – it seemed almost to have sunk into the ground. It was surrounded by a large garden with a wide tumbling mountain stream curling round almost to encircle the little homestead. The mountains reared up on all sides, with banks of rhododendrons on the near slopes – a typical chocolate-box scene or the sort of thing you see as a mural in a back-street fish and chip shop in downtown suburbia. We always seemed to have good weather and my recollections are of eating our breakfast in the garden where an ancient wooden table and bench had been provided, the bees humming amongst the clover and the creeping buttercups, a slight rustle of breeze moving the dry grasses making the seed heads hissle and bow their plumed pennants, the guggle and bubble of the everlasting stream, and Mama scolding her dog for getting his feet wet yet again.

Then, in the evenings – our skin tingling with sun and sea – we sat on the old garden seat with a salad supper – perhaps a sherry or glass of wine too – and soaked up the stillness and the peace. The nights always seemed mild and clear with a lollipop moon bathing in a blue velvet sky. We must have had bad weather sometimes but I can never recall it.

Year after year we stayed at Dinas and we grew to know that part of Wales quite well. We particularly loved the Dovey and Mawddach estuaries – and their changing colours. Sometimes a symphony of grey in different shades, like a Chinese watercolour – perhaps with a sea mist casting a mysterious shadow through which glimpses of a mountain outline could be caught. At other times brilliantly lit with unrealistic greens, blues and browns – like a gaudy poster. And every range of light and shade in between.

We loved the little grey stone towns of Dolgellau and Machynlleth, and the seaside town of Barmouth with its small harbour backed by the steep rock on which the stone houses squeezed and jostled for room, served by flights of stone steps and narrow flagged alleyways, their stout, weather-beaten faces to the west winds.

It was on one of these holidays that my father was taken ill. He was a marvellous old boy. He managed to hide his pain and discomfort until the day before we were to return home. On that fateful Friday evening he had a violent haemorrhage and it was with much anxiety that we drove him home the following day. He proved to have bowel cancer. He survived an operation but it left him weak and dispirited for many months.

Within a year, my mother had also been diagnosed with cancer, again successfully treated, and Brian's mother had started to show signs of forgetfulness and confusion. The annual Welsh holiday with the parents had to be abandoned and life was never quite the same again.

Clearly we had to be within easy reach of the family, and to have somewhere to entertain and cope with them, so we sold our boating home and bought a cottage near Guildford, only some fifteen miles from Farnham, where the parents continued to live.

The next few years passed in a welter of family matters. My father had another major operation and was ill, on and off, for nearly five years. My mother recovered from her cancer very slowly indeed. We had been very disappointed with the hospital care she received following her operation. Six weeks after the surgery, she was losing ground very rapidly and in a desperate effort to halt the slide, we discharged her from hospital, against medical advice, and cared for her at home. She was so ill we felt we had nothing to lose, but it was the most frightening and heart-searching period of my whole life.

There was little support from the medical brigade as we'd had the temerity to remove Mother from their care. So we coped on our own with help from a retired district nurse who called every day and who should have been given a valuable medal. I took unpaid leave from the bank and inch by inch we winched mother back to health. It was a long, arduous business with many a temporary slide backwards, but eventually she could sit up in bed, could even feed herself, could begin to read the newspapers and we began to feel we were winning. She learned to walk again – slowly, painfully – three or four steps a day with Brian and I on each side. Then on her own with a walking frame and then without a walking frame, merely steadying herself against the furniture. Finally she felt ready to attempt an assault on the stairs to her own bedroom – her biggest ambition at that time. With the constant need to be on hand, we had originally set up a bed for her in the dining room of her home, and she'd lived in that room for many months. But her own bedroom, with all her clothes and pots and potions, became a great goal, which was instrumental in encouraging her to walk further. I remember sitting on her bed with her on the day she finally made it. We were both weak with the worry and the effort – but oh so happy.

At this stage, my mother was seventy-one. She lived for another ten years – to enjoy herself and lead a life of superior quality.

Brian and I should have been very happy at this period in our lives. We had good health, a good marriage, good jobs and were surrounded by good friends. Brian's employers had gone through several changes to become the British Aircraft Corporation, but Brian didn't seem very content with his work. So much time and money seemed to be spent on projects that foundered before they were put into production. Several of his older colleagues had apparently never worked on a project that had lasted long enough for even a prototype to be built. To spend the working day making modifications and amendments to detailed drawings which they knew would be abandoned shortly afterwards was soul destroying. It was also worrying that so much time and money seemed to be poured into this apparently bottomless pit without even the liklihood of furthering knowledge or research – it was just painstaking and totally unproductive.

So he left that august company and went to work as production engineer for a local firm that built loudspeakers. The difference was dramatic. If they didn't get their product out each week, then the firm would not survive, so Brian found himself working very hard to help keep their production line moving. At the end of the week he could see the boxes of speakers ready for dispatch to customers and he would know that the firm would stay in business for another week or so at least.

There seemed to be few chiefs to support the number of Indians in the establishment. The company had two branches in the London area and this one in Surrey but it all seemed to be very low in technology after the British Aircraft Corporation.

Brian found himself building machines to improve the method of production one minute, ferrying somebody who had been taken ill back to their home the next, unblocking the ladies loo, mending the tea urn in the canteen, and a thousand and one other assorted jobs, none of which would ever have come his way at the British Aircraft Corporation. He found it refreshing to have such a direct impact on what went out of that factory at the end of the week – being a part of the relatively small team directly responsible for how the firm stood in the marketplace.

I had left Barclays Bank Trust Company too. In spite of qualifications, all undertaken in my own time at my own expense, they were not prepared to take their female staff seriously. Younger, unqualified lads were taken on, paid a higher salary and offered a cheap mortgage. So I had transferred to a local firm of chartered accountants and did some of their tax and investment work, which gave me experience of accountancy practice. Two years later I had moved to another firm of accountants and was in charge of their tax department – a demanding and overpowering job that had little moral satisfaction since it principally involved devising schemes to help the already rich become even richer, or avoid as much tax as was possible. Those years turned my hair white and gave me an outsize stress problem, but it also gave me an insight into what I wanted from life. I wanted time. Time to lie on my stomach on the grass and watch a square foot of soil to see the creatures I was sharing this planet with. Time to hide in a bush and watch the great tits teach their fledglings to fly. Time to watch the patterns the clouds make. Time to offer a listening ear to cries from the rest of the world. I seemed to have spent so much time sorting out my own problems that little had been spared for the difficulties of others, many of whom were even less able to cope with their burdens than I was with mine.

Brian too felt this need to have more time to devote to other things. He was keen to spend more time on the small trailer boat we had bought to replace our original boating home – to fish, to sail, and generally mess about in the boat or, more accurately, boat about in a mess.

So we had planned to retire as early as possible and buy a small property somewhere on the water, hopefully in Wales. For the moment, while we still had to have an eye on the parents, this was out of the question, but I can remember sitting in smog-laden traffic jams on my way to work, promising myself that better days would come.

And indeed, they did come.

In 1977, my mother and father came to stay with us for a few days. Father had been poorly for several weeks but with no identifiable illness. One of his old pals had died early in the year and, since that time, Father seemed uninterested and unprepared to go on living. So four days into the visit, at the age of eighty-one, he died – apparently from pneumonia.

Mother – also eighty-one – did not wish to continue living at their old home so she moved into our spare bedroom. Her house was sold, her furniture put into store, and we set about applying for planning permission to build her a small flat within our home. This took nearly a year and the long-awaited day when she was to be reunited with her goods and chattels as they were retrieved from store saw her in a sorry way. A stroke two days previously had rendered her speechless and with paralysis of the right arm and leg. She tried so hard to survive but unfortunately another stroke on the morning of the great day took her into unconsciousness and she died as her dearly loved, and long-awaited, bits and pieces were being carried into what had been intended as her new home.

It was all rather shattering. For so long we had been in harness – our lives had been inextricably bound up with the requirements of the family, not just our immediate parents but five other elderly relatives who had no one else to turn to in their old age – and now our only commitment was to Brian's mother who would certainly need to come and live with us as time passed.

We had learned a few things, however.

I knew I couldn't share a home with Mother-in-law unless she had an entirely self-contained unit with a door that could be closed, and locked if necessary, dividing her part of the house from ours. The months during which my mother had lived with us had contained many difficult moments largely through a lack of privacy on both sides. It was clear that Brian's mother was starting to suffer with a mental disorder and, from experience, I could see that if she came to live with us, it would be vital to have separate apartments. Mama spent a great deal of time with us as it was. Time when she would turn out my fridge at three o'clock in the morning to leave the contents on the draining board where the cats subsequently had a field day with a half-eaten joint of beef. Time when she turned out the bathroom cupboard and left the contents strewn all over the floor. And many more similar times.

The extension we had built for my mother would not adapt into a separate unit so clearly we would have to move house. By this time Brian's employers had sold off the Surrey works of the business and extended their premises in London. Brian had remained at the Surrey branch to work for the new owner but he was also building special-purpose machines for the group in London. The new owners of the Surrey branch were, however, proving difficult to work for, and as Brian was keen to go back to his old job, which was now in London, and his former employers were keen to have him, it seemed sensible for him to do so. We would then buy a bigger house somewhere within reach of the North London premises of the company, and Mama would move in with us.

The new home was near Dunmow in Essex, an old, rambling, rather isolated house with ample room for all three of us.

Meanwhile, Mama's doctor, who was temporarily living next door to her in Farnham, was adamant that she was in urgent need of supervision for twenty-four hours a day. We later realised that she had a penchant for getting up at 4am on summer mornings and ringing his doorbell, or removing his milk from the crate, or wandering around his garden to peer through his windows, so his insistence that we take her under our wing as soon as possible was not entirely disinterested.

We phoned her twice every day and saw her two or three times a week, and whenever we saw her, or rang her, she seemed to be coping, albeit in a muddled way. But this seems to be the hallmark of people with mental troubles. Invariably they are stimulated to behave in quite a normal fashion when there is activity or someone arrives, so it was not apparent to us that Mama was as poorly as she really was. Coupled with that, Mama most definitely did not want to move. She had lived in that house for forty years and would not leave it until she was 'carried out feet first'. The police were telling us fibs. She hadn't been lost in Sainsbury's at all. Likewise, the fire brigade hadn't broken into the house because she'd lost the door key. They must have been referring to someone else. It had to be rather delicately put to her.

We were asking her to join us as the house we were buying was rather big and would need a lot of looking after. It would be fun – she could come out in the car more often. Maybe she would feel like making some of the mince pies for which she'd been famous – a treat not seen for several years now. We *needed* her.

She would agree one minute, disagree the next, and forget the minute after. So we took matters into our own hands, arrived on her doorstep with a furniture van, bundled her into the car, her goods and chattels into the van, and life with Mama began.

Chapter Three

The new house was a lovely old sixteenth-century timbered property. It was easy for Brian to whiz down the M11 to North London, and big enough to accommodate us all in comfort.

It had been four separate farm cottages but the previous owners had converted it into one roomy, if draughty, house. The four separate units were still clearly definable, however, and Mama was to have most of number one. This consisted of a bed-sitting room, a small kitchen with a door leading into our kitchen, a bathroom, and a south-facing sunroom with lots of glass and a door to the garden so Mama could come and go as she pleased. And she did please a great many times each day, as we knew from the bell we had installed to tell us when the door was opened.

She spent hours brushing and pampering the current canine – a black long-haired affair called Fred, while we oversaw her domestic arrangements, provided her meals, cleaned her flat and attended to her laundry. We had fitted out the little kitchen with a sink unit, an electric cooker, a fridge and various cupboards, thinking she might even be able to prepare herself simple meals. She'd lost a great deal of weight before she moved in with us and it was clear that she had not bothered to feed herself properly. But I had anticipated that I would leave her basic essentials like bread, butter, cheese, cakes and biscuits, and that she would get herself small snacks without reference to us.

This proved to be a vain hope. Mama would wrap the bread up in a brown paper bag and take it out into the garden to leave it under a bush, or she'd flush it down the loo, or break it into small pieces and put it in a vase. Cakes and biscuits were given to Fred, hidden under the wardrobe, squashed down the back of the radiator or disposed of in any one of many other hiding places!

She became increasingly confused with long periods of crying interspersed with flares of temper. She was rarely happy.

Playing with Fred as a child plays with a doll offered the greatest solace. She brushed and combed his hair for hours at a time, dressed him up in woollies, hung necklaces around his neck and pinned brooches on the coat she made him wear, whatever the weather. He really was the most long-suffering animal and never showed any resentment. They clung to each other like two waifs.

But when visitors called or there was some other activity going on, she could invariably rally her mental resources and appear almost normal. For the first year or so many of our visitors didn't realise she was ill. She had a stock of half a dozen phrases to trot out. 'I wonder what sort of Christmas we'll have this year,' or 'I'm worried about my old friend May as I haven't heard from her for a long time,' or 'I feel cold today.' Sometimes this latter one came on a sweltering hot day, but she seemed to know it was wrong and would correct it by adding, 'in spite of the weather'.

Sometimes she would start on a long, complicated story about a friend or former neighbour. This would have endless ramifications and would incorporate entirely irrelevant bits of family gossip. If she fancied she was not being taken seriously, the story would cease abruptly to be followed by tears or a burst of temper.

I am certain there were many occasions when she knew she was ill.

We tried to talk to her about it as first we wanted to help her, if help were possible, and secondly, we wanted her to know that we would still love and want her even if she was mentally ill. I knew she had a personal knowledge of the unfortunate stigma attached to mental problems. She had often spoken, in earlier days, of the years when her grandfather had lived in her childhood home; of the horror of the neighbours as he had screamed and fought with her parents. Eventually Grandfather had been 'put away', but the episode had not been put away from Mama's memory and I wondered if this recollection ever obtruded to worry her.

It was difficult to talk to her as she tended to deny that anything was wrong. If we persisted, she would generally cry, and the crying got more and more distressed as we continued to try and help. On odd occasions when she clearly knew she was in a muddle, the most effective help was to squeeze her hand and make a little joke to pass the moment off.

After our move to Essex we had taken her to see the local doctor who had been very sympathetic but was unable to offer any practical help. There was no question of any assessment to see if medical help could be given, or of visits to a day centre where she might have been observed and perhaps a therapy given. It was entirely up to us how we coped – or, indeed, did not cope.

With strangers, she was quite talkative. She would chat easily to the policemen who regularly extricated her from her more adventurous activities. She had taken to wandering off if our eyes weren't constantly on her. She would walk quite a distance – sometimes only in her undies – and then tell a farrago of nonsense to anyone who tried to help.

Her imagination seemed to know no rein, and as she really appeared quite normal at first sight, most people accepted her stories as the truth.

Eventually the Essex police and the local residents got to know her quite well. Whereas we'd previously scrambled into action to scour the countryside when we knew she was missing, we arrived at a point where we could almost rely on somebody phoning to tell us she was on the wander and in what direction she was heading.

Perhaps it seems we should have monitored her activities more carefully but it was extraordinarily difficult. There were times when we just couldn't be with her. Brian would be at work in London and I would be working in the office at home when the phone would ring. I would answer it and be temporarily out of earshot of Mama's front doorbell. In the meantime, Mama would have disappeared. There were so many other similar occasions.

If we locked her in, she would either shout until released or try to climb out of the window – not an easy business as both the unbolted opening windows were quite high with quite a drop to the ground on the outside. All the remaining windows in Mama's part of the house had been secured to stop her escaping out of them.

She was quite crafty too. She came to understand that opening her front door brought us on the scene. Generally, she forgot, but on the odd occasion, she did remember, and this caught us out several times.

I would be mowing the grass with both her door and her unbolted sitting room window in view. She would take this opportunity to climb through her bathroom window and lower herself onto the ground on the far side of the building – out of my sight. The variations were endless, as can be imagined. Night-time brought its own problems. She had a bell which rang in our bedroom so she could call us if she needed us. This bell also told us when she had opened her outside door so we knew when she left the house. It sometimes rang ten times in a night, or so it seemed. Sometimes it didn't ring.

Early one October morning I made the early tea, prepared Mama's tray with her biscuits, her drink and her cleaned, soaked dentures – unlocked the connecting door between our two kitchens and called to her as I carried in the goodies. There was no reply. Her outside door was locked with the key hanging on the piece of chain in the usual place – but no Fred and no Mama. It is quite frightening to go into premises expecting to find someone there and find it empty. It seemed almost sinister. The bathroom window was swinging on its hinges but a glance through it did not show me the familiar hurrying figure. It was barely seven o'clock – only just daylight.

I rushed upstairs to our bedroom and broke the news. Brian was out of bed in a trice – dragging on his jeans and his woolly. I was similarly pulling on my clothes – and we were off in the cars in a cloud of dust. We combed the village slowly – looking in all the gardens – some people were no doubt still in bed. Boldly we looked in back gardens, greenhouses, sheds – but there was no sign of Mama.

I returned home to phone the police. Brian decided to drive slowly eastward and check the smaller lanes that led to a tiny airfield. There was sometimes early morning traffic in that direction and someone may have seen Mama, may even have given her a lift.

The police were helpful and promised to contact the hospital in case she had been taken there. It hadn't occurred to me that maybe she had been involved in an accident but immediately I thought of the fast, busy trunk road, the A120, which passes within half a mile of the house.

I got back into my car and drove four miles in each direction along the A120 without result. I turned northwards. It was deep open country – many hundreds of acres of bare fields interspersed with tiny lanes overhung with trees and the occasional large house with closed gates. She could be anywhere. Anger set in. I rehearsed the comments I was going to make when we did find her. We would have to have a different system – a tighter regime. Those windows would have to be sealed up totally. She could stew in that flat if it was hot.

I parked the car in one place and climbed through the hedge. This field was full of a winter cereal. Trying to avoid the plantlets, I climbed up to a small rise which gave a view of many miles of autumn landscape. Several public footpaths crossed the country at this point but there was no sign of Mama.

By now it was after half past eight. She could have been out for hours – maybe lying in a ditch. She'd have to go into a home – we could no longer cope with her. Tears streamed down my face. I got back in the car and drove on slowly towards the next village – more than a mile from home as the crow flies, several more by road. The little school bus was in front and I followed it into the village street where a collection of mums with youngsters stood waiting. Amongst this small group stood Mama – in her blue cotton nightie and blue slippers, with no coat or even a cardigan and with Fred, looking bewildered and apprehensive, at her feet. She looked unutterably small and frightened and vulnerable. All anger totally evaporated. I rushed across the road and hugged her. I don't think I've ever been so pleased to see anybody before or since. Even writing about this event upsets me still. I suppose I felt a sudden overwhelming lack of confidence to cope – that we'd let Mama down – and was this perhaps tinged with self-sorrow – not a helpful emotion.

The problems with the care of a senile patient are magnified since you become responsible for them as they have no conception of responsibility for themselves. They may look and sound quite normal for much of the time, but this merely adds to the difficulties.

It is surprising that we weren't drummed out of the village as Mama seemed to have caused havoc in almost every household. No washing line was sacred, and many gardens were stripped of their flowers. One lovely old couple who lived in a bungalow on the edge of the village were extremely frightened to find this distracted-looking character trying to get into their kitchen. Mama had found an old key and was trying to unlock their back door. When this failed, she tried their front door. Very sensibly they phoned the police and once again Mother was ferried home in a taxi with a blue light on the top.

There were amusing occasions too. The previous owners of the house had been in dispute with the Inland Revenue. One day a man arrived, knocked on Mama's outside door, and asked to speak to Mr Marshall. Mama was apparently quite chatty – told him she lived alone in the house, denied all knowledge of a Mr Marshall and sent him on his way. Neither Brian nor I were aware of this visit.

Back in the office, the man from the tax office reported this response but his boss was unsympathetic. 'They're having you on, boy. That's probably his wife. Get back and have another go.'

So back he came a few weeks later – found Mama in the lane – and demanded to know the whereabouts of Mr Marshall. Perhaps he tried a more aggressive attitude and this sparked Mama off into an aggressive reply as she told him roundly to 'Clear off.'

Nonplussed, he did clear off but on the insistence of the Department, was back on the doorstep again, a week or so later. This time he was not proposing to take 'No' for an answer.

He was again assured that Mama lived in the house quite alone – no one had lived in the other part for many years.

He was doubtful. As Mama closed the door and retreated into her sitting room, he decided to take a look for himself. So he wandered around the outside of the house, peering through the ground-floor windows.

Brian – in his machine shop in the garden – suddenly noticed this intruder ambling along, trying our front door, shading his eyes to peer through the sitting-room window, then on to the dining-room window.

His ire was raised. Out he went – quietly – to stand in the middle of the path. Just as the visitor stepped back off the flower bed on to the concrete, they came face to face.

Brian is unable to recall his exact words, which is just as well as they were probably unprintable, but the poor little man nearly had an apoplectic fit. All was soon explained however and the tale ended happily over a cup of tea.

It seemed odd that we had not heard him on his two previous calls. Perhaps Mama had spoken to him through her open window or maybe he was not near enough to the microphones in her rooms for us to hear the substance of the conversation over the listening system. If we had briefly heard a man's voice, we would have assumed that it was the radio. Mama chatted to herself or to Fred all day long, often with the radio on as well, so her voice would not necessarily have alerted us that a visitor had called. But this sort of thing was very worrying.

We also had ludicrous situations with people who tried to deliver things. Mama's part of the house was at the front where callers arrived first, and as she tended to go out to meet anyone who was arriving, she had a chance to concoct some story to amaze, frighten or put off anyone with a parcel or a message for us. It was particularly worrying, as relief postmen or callers who were unaware of her difficulties would often give her the post or parcels for us. There were many occasions when we would find the post some days later, perhaps hidden in an old biscuit tin or under the cushion on her chair, and there must have been times when we didn't find it at all.

So there we were in Essex with a spacious house, ideal for our purposes, lovely country all around, Mama under our roof and all set up to make life as enjoyable as possible, having regard to our circumstances.

At this stage Mama was in her early seventies and physically very well indeed, so would probably go on for many years. With this in mind, we had enlarged the house to give us a new front entrance, a new dining room and a new bedroom with bathroom attached. We'd also bought a paddock and had settled ourselves down for an extended stay. Because of the need to keep Mama in hand, Brian was working at the London factory for only two days a week and building his machines in the workshop at the back of the house for the other three weekdays. I was working for two days a week with a local firm of accountants and we had a lovely lady who came on those days to help in the house and to assist Brian with Mama.

Then... Brian read an advert in the property section of a boating magazine:

FOR SALE
75 ACRE FARM ON WELSH COAST

The telephone number gave us a rough idea of the locality – it was in the area we loved most. It seemed silly to bother to ring – we had only just finished the mammoth reorganisation of the Essex house. How could we possibly uproot the household and move to the far side of the country?

We did ring.

The vendors sent us the details and a photo. The little white farmhouse, framed with dark pine woods, looked like something from a fairy story The views of the sea and mountains were stupendous. We talked about it, on and off, for days. Neither of us could forget it and yet it seemed such a foolhardy idea. Quite out of the question... surely?

We'd had trouble in finding someone to care for Mama when we felt the urgent need to go away for a day or two. None of the local residential homes for elderly people were able to oblige so we'd not had a holiday since she came to live with us. But we had found a couple of sets of people who were prepared to take her on for two or three days at a time by living in our house and continuing with the regime we had set up for her. I provided vast lists of instructions and somehow or other they always managed to hold out until we got back. Generally, it was only a matter of three days at the most. For people who were not used to Mama and her ways, a very long time indeed.

Out of the blue, the young couple who had stood in for us for a long weekend the previous summer actually rang one evening and offered to Mama-sit for another long weekend, since they wanted to earn some cash for their holiday. The coincidence seemed uncanny.

So we came, and saw – and marvelled.

At the top of a wooded hill the little farmhouse lazed in the warm spring sunshine. A mass of daffodils nodded golden heads as we wandered down the track to the tiny harbour, only a stone's throw from the house. The sea was gin-clear. It sucked gently at the stones on the slipway and lapped at the rocks bordering the far side of the harbour. Several old oaks hung over the water and in their shadow we could see mullet, some nearly two feet long, drifting along in the shallows.

The mountains on three sides had a rain-washed freshness and a pair of buzzards, circling overhead, flung their shrill cries into the blue haze.

The scent of bog oak burning in the Rayburn cooker in the kitchen of the homestead drifted down from the solid square stone chimney, mixing with the salt air and the tang of the seaweed washed up at the top of the tide line.

It was timeless – a dream – removed from reality – and we wanted it desperately.

The rest of the land was interesting too. It was partly wooded with tiny beaches separated by rocky outcrops. At low tide, small cliffs of lichen-covered rocks with pools full of mussels dropped away to miles of golden sand with warm shallow lagoons full of cockles.

Inland, the soil was dark and rich – an old peat bog or raised mire from which the peat was still dug. It had a lonely, eerie feeling. Ducks rose out of the small pools that interspersed the bog, and birds, strange to us, whirred a warning of impending danger as Brian and I struggled over the soft, uneven ground.

We spent the whole day exploring the farm – getting more and more depressed. The farmhouse was enchanting from the outside but small, damp and dark on the inside. Life would be difficult for the two of us but with Mama as well… No, it was out of the question.

Coupled with that, it was not cheap, and we'd need to spend a fortune on it: to rebuild the house, to put the fences and farm buildings in order, not to mention the roadway, the hedging and the ditching.

No. It was a great shame – but maybe something similar would be available later in our lives when we were ready to move to our retirement home.

But we both knew it was very unlikely.

It was a very depressing drive home. The news of the start of the Falklands War was announced as we drove through Birmingham, adding to the gloom.

For the next week we talked of little else. Apart from the difficulty of moving Mama, what could we do for a living? We were in our mid-forties, too young to retire. It was obvious that the farm would not support us. The land was not suitable for agriculture and would make only poor grazing for unfussy sheep. We had both worked all our lives in our different spheres but would this sort of work be available in Wales?

It is only fair to say that we did have some financial resources: we'd had two salaries coming into the household, my parents had left me their funds and, as I had worked in the financial market for many years, we had made some provision for the future. Furthermore, Mama had sold her house and still had the capital, which produced an income, so our financial responsibilities to her were not as great as they might have been. But we were by no means sure that this was going to be sufficient to stand the sort of outlay we could see would be necessary as well as keep us in the basic essentials of life for the rest of our days.

We are fortunate in that we can live on very little. In the early days of our marriage, we were obliged to and, although at the time it was hard, it has stood us in good stead ever since.

We talked the financial angle over very carefully, debated the economies that could be made if necessary and decided that, taking that aspect alone, it was worth the risk. After all there must be some jobs we could do even if we couldn't find the work we were trained for. Brian loves tinkering with outboard motors and could perhaps do something in the boating line. I'm useless at housework but a dab hand with a garden fork and can knock up a passable Victoria sponge. Surely somebody would need a gardener or a cook if I could not find the work for which I was trained.

But there remained the problem of Mama. We both felt that we must make efforts to enjoy our own lives, at the same time as coping with Mama. After all, the caring could well go on until we were also old. Coupled with that, if our own interests were widened, the caring requirement would not assume such all-consuming proportions. We were most anxious that caring for Mama should not become the dominant issue in our lives. To this end we had tended to widen our range of hobbies.

But if we were able to change our lifestyle totally – to spend our lives in the manner of our choice – while at the same time maintaining our responsibilities to Mama, then would this not be the answer? The more we considered it, the more sensible it seemed. Furthermore, she was becoming very difficult to control at times and it was so much easier to cope if we were both at hand.

I remember one day when Brian was in the London factory and a man had arrived on our doorstep with a pressing need to sell me a solar heating panel. As with many salesmen, he was reluctant to take no for an answer, so we had engaged in verbal badinage for some fifteen minutes or before he departed.

I had left Mama ensconced in a chair in her sitting room with Fred comfortably settled on her lap. We'd just had a cup of tea and she had seemed quiet and sleepy.

As I shut the front door on the salesman, I happened to glance outside and there was Mama, having got out of the window, scuttling off down the lane in the pouring rain in her slippers and with no coat. She carried her shopping bag, which I later discovered contained her clock, her radio, Fred's dish and two spoons. Fred himself trotted at her heels on a lead. I set off after her, but she refused to come back to the house. I took her arm, but she shook me off. I took it again, more forcibly. She screamed, flung the bag down and gave me a violent push. She then sat down in the mud and refused to budge. Fortunately, our neighbour drove up the lane some minutes later and between us we managed to get her home, all of us very wet and in top fluster.

She had developed great cunning and an almost superhuman strength. I was a hefty eleven stone and five feet-eight whereas Mama was quite a fragile nine stone and five feet two, but there were a number of occasions when she had almost been able to overpower me. Usually this was when I was in a vulnerable position, squatting by her to put her shoes on or in a similar precarious state. It was barely credible that such a small frame could summon up such strength.

Brian and I both had these battles of will with her and I can remember Brian literally carrying her back from one of her excursions – feet kicking, arms flaying the air, and voice raised, to put it nicely.

We tried very hard to be gentle and passive but there were times when it was extremely difficult to stay calm and unaffected by these scenes. But there were also lighter moments. Sometimes, for no apparent reason, Mama would start to laugh. She would be absolutely convulsed, tears streaming down her face as she rolled about in her chair with merriment. There is something infectious in laughter. Within minutes Brian and I would also be rolling about in a fit of the giggles without having the least idea why.

But the difficulty of controlling Mama's activities was much eased if we were both at hand. She very rarely made a scene unless it was a one-to-one confrontation. If we both appeared and reasoned with her, she would invariably give in like a lamb. So, from a practical point of view, it would make life easier if we could both be at home for most of the working day.

We would have to find some suitable accommodation for her for the first few months though, until we could build a new house, or at least extend the existing farmhouse. This was a major factor in the whole scheme. We most definitely could not take the poor old soul into that damp, dark, cramped house, however enchanting it looked from the outside. Perhaps a light, spacious, warm static caravan, with all mod cons, would prove to be the answer for a short time. It could be left in the farmyard, very close to the house, with all our existing listening aids.

Brian's responsibilities to his employers, who had been very good in many ways, were another problem. He found it difficult to talk about our project to his immediate superiors. I suppose he felt they would try to talk him out of it and he didn't want to be dissuaded. So we decided to make a serious offer for the farm before he spoke to them. There was always the possibility that the scheme would not proceed.

The offer was duly made and, after a bit of haggling, accepted. It was a frightening, exciting time.

We put the Essex house on the market just as the Falklands campaign was at its height. Suddenly we were at war and I suppose we all wondered where it was going to end. We had hardly any viewers and no sign of an offer, even a poor one.

As the summer advanced, panic began to set in, for we'd committed ourselves to the purchase of the farm and we could see that we'd have two properties on opposite sides of the country and a colossal overdraft. But to our enormous relief a buyer did turn up and the sale of the house in Essex was concluded within ten days of our completion of the purchase of the farm.

Brian had by this time explained our intentions to his employers and resigned. Happily, they agreed to give him various projects to build and, for the moment, he was to continue to maintain some of the machines he had already built and installed in the London factory. This meant he would drive to London every month or so for a couple of days. It would also mean he would still have something of a stake in the great big outside world; his intellectual capabilities would still be required, and he would keep his technical knowledge and interests up to date.

This was very pleasing to me, as I had wondered if he would miss the company of his working colleagues, the chat and banter of his life in the factory. With this offer, however, he would be in frequent contact over the phone and actually on the premises every few weeks. As Treasurer in our marriage, it also pleased me that there would be something coming in to swell the financial kitty.

So it was all go for our journey westward. The old American settlers must have felt much as we did – we were journeying into the unknown and we proposed to take with us as much as possible to cover almost every conceivable eventuality.

Brian has always been a hoarder. We had innumerable ancient TV sets (the spare parts were always useful) and masses of other bits and pieces he had collected over the years. He looked at it ruefully and agreed that some of it would have to go to the dump. Sadly, he loaded it onto the road trailer, tied it down, and off it went.

Two hours later he arrived home. Far from being clean and empty, the trailer was almost full of items he had found on the dump that would be invaluable to us in our new life – or so he assured me. We had merely exchanged one load of junk for another. I forgave him as he had also picked up about fifty pottery flower pots – most of them not even chipped – but I could see it was useless to embark on this sort of enterprise again.

Having dismantled my parents' house in 1977 and Mama's home in 1979, we had a vast pile of clutter that was of little practical use. But I too am a hoarder and anyway I didn't feel it would be right to get rid of it. We still had suitcases of my mother's clothes, some of them dating from the twenties, and many of her personal things, which I felt I ought to keep. Most of the contents of Mama's house had been strictly functional but there were still Grandmama's dinner services and a welter of domestic paraphernalia that we'd kept in case Mama ever recovered sufficiently to ask for it. This was in addition to our own accumulation from twenty-five years of married life.

There was no doubt – it would all have to go with us and be stored in a barn when we got to Wales, at least for the first few months, so it had to be packed in a storable condition with each box clearly marked to show what it contained. We'd bought a large static caravan for Mama, and as it was already fully furnished the contents of her flat were to be stored at the farm as well.

I scoured the local supermarkets for cardboard boxes and soon we had a formidable pile packed and ready for the move – without any appreciable reduction in the pile still to be packed. We unpacked the first lot, packed smaller things inside larger things, and repacked it. Then we got more experienced at what would fit into where, so we unpacked some for the second time and repacked it, yet again.

Finally all but the items needed right up to the point of departure were packed and we were ready to make our entry into our new life.

With help from two friends, Brian had piled all his heavy machinery into a huge van, borrowed for the occasion, and had delivered it to our new home the weekend prior to the main move. He'd loaded it all, including a lathe weighing over half a ton, and had driven it to Wales one day, unloaded it and then driven back to Essex the next day. So he was pretty tired.

Pickfords turned up just after eight in the morning two days later and four men worked until after six in the evening, packing all our worldly goods into this huge pantechnicon. Mama's fridge had looked innocent enough when they came to quote for the move – they weren't to know, at that stage, that with our improved packing technique, it weighed nearly a hundredweight.

Poor Mama was deprived of her furniture at midday and then installed in the back of the car, with Fred and all her immediate necessities about her. Brian had spent a lot of time packing everything in carefully so she had ample room, but periodically she'd get out of the car when no one was looking and start to lug all her goods and chattels back indoors again. 'Twas a merry party.

Just after nine o'clock on the evening of 14th September 1982 we made our final exit from the suburban world. Brian had Mama and Fred, plus a mass of things Pickfords were unable to find room for, and was towing the road trailer, which he'd filled with a strange accumulation of old junk that he suddenly fancied he couldn't do without. I had three very frightened cats in their cages, plus a mass of things to cover our first few days, as Pickfords were not due to arrive for seventy-two hours.

It was a memorable journey. We were both extremely tired; rain turned to hail which was succeeded by fog. The news of Grace Kelly's death came over the radio as we laboured north westward along the M1.

As we penetrated the wilds of Wales, our headlights picked out small animals scuttling across the road. We seemed to be the only human beings abroad – it was like a dream.

Fatigue makes the mind see odd things. For much of the last part of the journey I thought I could see a large white horse running along the road by the side of the car. It must have been the car lights reflected off the stone walls – but it seemed natural in the unreal quality of the night.

It was a moment of great joy when we turned off the main road into the lane that leads to the farm at 4.20 in the morning: tremendous relief at having arrived safely, but more than this, there was the conviction that we were starting on a great adventure and that it was right for us.

The first thing we saw as we drove along the farm road through our newly acquired fields was a large white horse gazing at us in absolute amazement.

Chapter Four

Before we settled down to sleep for what was left of the night, I couldn't resist looking in the chicken house for eggs. It was very quiet as I padded over the farmyard – everything was still and the air smelled of pine woods and wet earth. The hens briefly unpacked their heads from under their wings and blinked in the torchlight before settling back to their slumbers. There, amongst the hay in the nest box, was one dark brown egg.

The following days were particularly happy. We could relax after months of tension. The weather was gorgeous – a September calm. We couldn't do a great deal as our gear was still on its way, so we explored the farm buildings, literally almost on the beach, and we made plan after plan for the future. Suddenly it was as if we were just starting out on life – everything was new and exciting. For the first time in our adult lives we were at liberty to forget the clock – we could eat when we chose, could dress as we pleased and make our own list of priorities. Even Mama's requirements did not seem so all-consuming.

We had inherited a wether, or neutered ram, called Lucky, and the fifteen chickens, and I was worried about how Mama's little dog and our three cats would cope with these additions to the household.

Fred, the dog, was virtually tied to Mother. She either carried him about or kept him on a lead – but there would no doubt be occasions when he could make good an escape if he chose, and I wondered about the safety of the chickens if he was loose.

The chickens ranged free about the farmyard. The hen house door was opened every morning and they would get up and start their day when they felt ready. Soon after breakfast I would go out and call them. They would be scattered amongst the bracken at the edge of the wood or under the rusting farm machinery, scratching up the leaves or the peat mould, examining the soil very carefully and pecking greedily at any choice morsel that had been uncovered. When they heard their corn being tipped into the bucket in the barn they immediately left their occupation of the moment and rushed towards the feeders, often being sprinkled with cereal in their enthusiasm for their breakfast. When this had gone, they would resume their former explorations – only returning to the hen house for half an hour to lay their eggs. After the egg-laying, they did a bit of boasting – clucking notice of the arrival for several minutes – before returning to their excavations amongst the undergrowth. At tea time I would go and feed them again, and as daylight started to fade, they put themselves to bed, squabbling briefly over who should roost on which part of which perch in the hen house, before settling their ruffled feathers to their satisfaction, and preparing for sleep. Later in the evening, we would go out and close the door to keep them safe from the foxes. All hens should have such a life.

The three cats had met chickens before and were reliable enough, but their previous experience had not shown them how to deal with a large woolly bundle of trouble that could charge at a frightening speed if the mood took him. Lucky, the neutered ram, was very tame and considered himself a dog. He had been brought up with a dog and had a lot of the characteristics of the canines – so I could see that the cats may well put him in that category and act accordingly.

Our senior cat was a large grey tabby called Merry – a very conventional fireside cat, devoted to his home and always apprehensive if out of it. Even the periphery of the garden was foreign territory to Merry. He spent a lot of time worrying about the timing of the next meal, what it would consist of, and how big the helpings would be. Just occasionally, he would have a burst of energy and, with eyes blazing, hurl himself round the walls of the bath. He did not care for dogs, and to stake a claim to his home, he would spray the area around the cat flap in the back door, a smelly business that seemed to worry him almost as much as it did us.

Robertson, our number two cat, was a marmalade and a real bovver boy. He was stocky, compact and as tough as old boots with loads of confidence. Never a cat fight took place in our locality without him being in it – usually as one of the principals. He would have Lucky taped immediately. We'd watched similar confrontations before. Large dog bounces up. Robertson assembles his adrenalin. Just as dog gets within reach of that smirking ginger face, his nose is delicately etched with fine tracery from two sets of feline claws. When dog opens his eyes – no sign of cat.

Lucky appeared to spend most of his day hanging around the house and I could see that Robertson would also derive amusement from sitting on a wall, or one of the ancient bits of machinery, just out of Lucky's reach, and swearing furiously at that ragbag of tangled wool as it passed beneath him. But Robertson also had a tendency to spray around the doors if a dog was about, so the cats' reaction to Lucky was a matter of modest concern.

None of the cats regarded Fred as a dog – probably because he spent most of his time in Mama's arms.

Leo, our small Siamese puss, was enchanting. He represented the one bit of class in the whole of our establishment. Delicately built with elegant movements, he knew full well how beautiful he was, and traded on it shamefully. He had a great urge for the dramatic. With arched neck and exaggerated body movements, he would posture at an imaginary foe. His face would contort to look as awful as possible and his body would be rigid. The most bloodcurdling yowls accompanied this little display. When he was satisfied that he had repelled the enemy and impressed the onlookers, he would relax and climb on a chair. He had a mind of his own and would turn a deaf ear to anything he didn't wish to hear. He was also a thief and would answer back when rebuked – but he was also the one to climb on your lap when you happened to be down at heart and he rarely failed to utter a greeting when we met. I was sure he would not care for Lucky, but he would certainly outpace him.

In the event, my worries were unfounded as Fred took not the slightest notice of the chickens and the cats not the slightest notice of Lucky, nor he of them.

We'd formed no definite plan of action for the farm prior to the move, but clearly we had to do something about the house pretty quickly as Mama couldn't stay in the caravan indefinitely. For the moment it worked very well. She spent all day with us, either sitting in a chair near where we were working, or, if we were out on the farm somewhere, she sat in the car nearby and watched. She very rarely tried to escape from the car. It was possible to do most of the jobs we had on hand at that time *and* have an eye to Mother. This, generally, had not been possible previously. She thoroughly enjoyed watching us pull down an old shed or sort out our clutter and store it in the barn. She could see us for most of the day. In the past, Brian had been either at work or in the workshop at the back of the house, while I had been at work or working in the house. It had not been possible to have her with us for such a large proportion of the day. But now she was with us as we worked, at mealtimes and in the evenings. If it was wet it was a bore to have to cart all our food over to the caravan and eat it there, but Mama seemed happy enough and didn't appear to be suffering from the move. She had no idea where she was, or indeed, who she was, but she would invariably trot out some quite reasonable answer if you asked her these sorts of questions.

As I've already said, in the past it had been impossible to lock her in to her quarters as she would shout and hammer on the doors until released. Monitoring her movements by the bell on her door had worked up to a point, but there were many occasions when she would open and close that wretched door every minute or so. When we were trying to work as well, it was well-nigh impossible to check her actions every single time it rang. She was so full of energy and enterprise that it was very difficult to keep abreast of her activities. Our new doctor had, however, prescribed a sedative at night – not that she knew she was taking it – and thus she slept soundly, and we were able to lock her in without fear of her rousing the farmyard at 2am.

We had detectors to transmit any problems in the caravan (one of the advantages of Brian's involvement with the electronics industry), but by and large, the nights were trouble-free, so we too could enjoy an undisturbed sleep – the first time for many months. There was one disadvantage though. The sedative ensured a quiet night – but it was also a wet one. Incontinence became a fairly regular event.

The first priority then was to review the farmhouse. To see if it was possible to improve and enlarge it to accommodate all three of us.

Unfortunately, this proved to be something of an architect's nightmare. On the west side there was sheer rock some fifteen feet high. Indeed, the house had been built into this rock. In one downstairs room there was a rocky outcrop in the corner at the base of the wall.

On the north side there was a drop of about six feet down to the farmyard. The farmyard was narrow at this point – just a driveway – on the far side of which was the barn.

Hard on the east side was the farm road leading to the outside world and on the east of the roadway was a rocky hillock rising steeply from the road. The south side, the front, had some few feet of garden and then the land dropped away steeply towards the sea.

It was not practical to extend the north, east or south elevations and extremely difficult to extend westwards.

We called in various firms who knew about this sort of thing and they all suggested building a completely new structure somewhere else on the farm. The existing building was apparently constructed of poor quality building stone, picked up, or quarried on the site, some 250 years before. It split or shattered very readily and rainwater had already permeated through the walls and oozed up through the tiles on the floor. Furthermore, the chimneys needed to be lined and the roof needed to be replaced, so all in all, it seemed sensible to build a new house somewhere else on the farm.

We went and had a chat with the council. Was it likely that planning permission would be granted for a new house somewhere – *anywhere* – on the seventy-five acres we owned?

The answer seemed to be a very definite 'No'.

We had another review of the situation and called in a few more experts. One firm suggested demolishing the existing house with all its problems and rebuilding a new one on the site.

We knocked this idea around for a while but it didn't really appeal. The building was old and quite attractive, even if difficult to live in, and it seemed sacrilege to raze it to the ground. Coupled with that was the possibility that we could destroy the only dwelling on the farm, and the planning people could refuse to allow us to rebuild a new home.

There was also a suggestion that the shell of the building should be retained and the interior gutted and then rebuilt. But this too seemed impractical.

Panic was beginning to set in and Brian went into town for a bottle of Scotch.

We reverted to the first plan – an extension would have to be the answer. That rock on the west side would have to go.

So, we got in touch with a local contractor who knew about removing rock. He brought in several other experts. They clambered over it, scratched bits off it and generally looked very unhopeful.

It seemed that they were divided on how much would need to be removed and how well it would respond to blasting.

We were worried about the blasting as the house literally stood on the rock. If the blasting shattered the seam extending under the west wall then, short of sky hooks, the house would probably fall down anyway.

Throughout this trying time, Mama sang hymns to herself and chatted to the dog.

We had also made an addition to the ménage – menagerie would be more apt.

While we were on a flying visit to the farm in the months before we actually moved in, I had been in a local shop and had got into conversation with a man who kept pigs. A lot of local people knew that the farm had been sold and they were interested to know who was to take over. Consequently, we found it very easy to get into conversation with complete strangers.

We had already discussed the economics of keeping a couple of pigs for fattening and although Brian had rather vetoed the idea, when our new-found friend offered to keep us two weaners from his next litter, I had returned no definite answer. We'd left it that we'd be in contact again as soon as our move had taken place. So, after we'd been in residence for a few days, I rang the pig chap to say that we thought it advisable to wait until we were more organised before embarking on a pig-keeping venture.

Fortunately, he'd forgotten all about our original conversation but promised to come and look us up quite soon.

Whether it's the language problem or my bad hearing, I don't know, but the next day he turned up with three piglets which he'd apparently had great difficulty in obtaining, and which we found impossible to refuse. Muttering under his breath about this unnecessary waste of time, Brian set about converting a stable into a pied-à-terre for our new charges and thus we started keeping pigs. My abiding recollection of those first few weeks is that of constantly hauling huge cauldrons of boiled vegetables and cereal down the steep hill to Mesdames Filet and Tenderloin and their brother, Gammon Steak. Pigs eat far more than anybody can possibly ever imagine.

A couple of months had passed since we moved in, and still we hadn't made any progress on the building front.

It took courage to make a final decision to blast that rock out, and with it perhaps half the house. It was impossible to estimate how the seams would shatter – how resilient the underlying rock would prove to be. At best, the rock would split and shatter relatively easily, right down to the base of the cottage wall, and there would *not* be a fault running through the rock where it supported the house. At worst, the top few inches of relatively soft, easily shattered rock, would give way to resilient, hard, unyielding material, and this would have a seam extending under the house. The variables were great and this applied to the cost of the operation too.

We talked it over with the contractor. He suggested we allow him to bring over some of his heavy gear and to have a prod or two at the rock to see just how much could be removed without blasting. Once the top few inches had been scratched off and the site properly exposed, there was more chance of making an accurate assessment of the problem. It was even possible that quite a substantial amount of rock could be removed with the heavy digging gear, and the blasting operation could be reduced to a minimum. Even if very little rock could be taken off with the digger, then we would at least have a better indication of the likely outcome of the full blasting programme and we could proceed, or we could abandon it, as the situation dictated. This was a relatively modest operation from the financial point of view too – although we knew it could well prove to be abortive expenditure.

In view of the cost, it also seemed sensible to approach the council to see if they were prepared to entertain the possibility of an extension to the house, as clearly if this was not likely to be permitted, then we were barking at the wrong tree.

So off went the builder to the council and back came the response that they would entertain the possibility of an extension. It was the first real step in the right direction.

So, one November morning a long low-loader lorry crept along the farm road and delivered a vast orange thing with arms and legs all over the place.

For some reason this orange machine was called Claud (among other things), and as the low-loader couldn't deliver him to the site, he had to be offloaded at the foot of the hillock and then drive himself a trackway up through the undergrowth.

It took nearly a day for Claud to get within reach of the site – but it was worth it, as the following day gave the first hint of success. The general structure of the rock did not appear to be as resilient as had been anticipated. Furthermore, the faults in the grain gave the impression that damage would probably not occur to the existing west wall of the house if the blasting did proceed. So yes – we would go ahead with the blasting programme as soon as the contractors could fit us in.

By now it was the middle of November, and soon after eight on a cold, wet night of impenetrable blackness, there came a thunderous knocking on our back door. I opened it gingerly to reveal in the lamplight two very wet, dishevelled characters with enormous packs on their backs, standing like refugees in the rain.

'Where's the campsite?' demanded the spotty one with glasses.

We stood there looking blankly at each other.

'Which campsite are you looking for?' I asked tentatively.

'This one, of course,' returned Spotty/Glasses.

'Where are you from?' I enquired. There was a home for naughty boys not very far away, and I wondered if they were escapees.

'We're from the Outward Bound Centre, but we've lost touch with the main party. We were due here at six o'clock – it's all been booked.'

That settled it. Nobody had spoken to either of us about camping, so clearly, they were due somewhere else – where the rest of the party would have arrived and were probably worried. Our neighbouring farmer had a campsite and we knew that cadets and scouts often stayed there – so it seemed fairly obvious that they should be on the adjacent farm.

We showed them the way and off they went.

An hour later there was another thunderous knocking on the door.

This time it was six wet, dishevelled characters with packs on their backs.

'Can you direct us to the campsite please, and have two campers arrived already?'

We explained what had happened. Off they went in the sleet.

An hour later, there was yet a third hammering at the door. The six outward-bounders stood there in the mud looking footsore and weary.

'We can't find our two mates, or the campsite next door. Three of us have foot problems. Can we camp here for the night?'

It was nearly eleven o'clock. Clearly, they could go no further that night. They all came in and sat in a steaming group around the Rayburn to drink mugs of tea and eat a cake I had made that afternoon and which should have lasted a week.

We hung their wet clothes over the stove and suggested they bed down in the cowshed for the night. The cowshed was watertight and full of straw bedding – some of it rather suspect as Lucky also slept there, but they didn't seem to mind.

The kitchen was awash with mud from their boots and puddles of water that dripped from their clothes.

We wondered what we ought to do about their two colleagues. Apparently, they had their own tents, sleeping bags and food, so were equipped to survive – but we wondered if we should have alerted the Outward Bound Centre in spite of the assurances of the party leader.

I had a miserable night worrying about them, and was very relieved the following morning to find the original two had camped just a few yards from the house, having given up the attempt to find their appointed camping place.

All eight were reunited, and after a round of tea and toast by the Rayburn, they set off in much better shape to walk up to the main road, where they were to be collected and taken back to the centre.

Nothing like this had ever happened in any of my previous homes.

At the beginning of November, the blasting contractor phoned us and announced that he was about to start our little job. I rather resented the 'little job' and resolved to bear it in mind should we be presented with an excessive bill. To me it was a very large job indeed, but I suppose if you are used to blasting out routes for motorways and similar contracts, then a job lasting for only a few days, and involving the removal of a mere two thousand tons of rock, must seem like child's play.

So we hired a compressor to drill the charge holes, a JCB to assist Claud by scooping out the spoils after each charge was fired, and a big lorry to carry the rock away – all with their respective operators – and blasting started – not all of it from the contractors.

Chapter Five

For some years prior to our arrival, the land had been let to another farmer who had grazed his stock there during the summer. When we'd made a brief visit to the farm, in the July before our move, we'd found cows, horses and sheep cheek by jowl with a girl guide camp, some caravanners and a group of outward-bounders. The grass had almost disappeared in places, and the animal droppings made it inadvisable to walk in sandals.

We didn't therefore want to let the land, but clearly we'd have to do something, as Lucky and the two horses who lodged here couldn't cope with all the grass – and there was no possibility that we could get the mower over all of it on a Saturday morning. I particularly wanted the wild flowers to flourish, so just a few of something seemed a good idea.

I've always been rather frightened of cows and horses, but sheep didn't seem as if they could offer any physical violence. So we spoke to a local farmer we had come to know, and he arranged the purchase of twenty-two very elegant Welsh Mountain ewes. We also managed to borrow a ram to serve them so that lambs would arrive in the spring.

It's fashionable now to be interested in self-sufficiency – growing your own food, making your own clothes from materials you have produced, and so on. Undoubtedly many aspects of that way of life are worthwhile. But we were both in our mid forties and it was foolhardy to expect our ageing bodies to cope with the hard physical work demanded by a full self-sufficiency programme. If you have a family of strong, willing children, who won't desert the post, then maybe more things are possible and practical. We had no army of muscle power behind us, however, apart from paid labour, and it was clearly silly to set up a situation where the work became an excessive burden that killed us within a couple of years. We were prepared to work hard but we also wanted to enjoy our new life – to have time to pursue our interests. For years I'd grown our vegetables and had spun fleeces on a spinning wheel Brian had built from a kit. I'd knitted our woollies and baked much of our basic food. We'd kept bees with a spectacular lack of success and we'd been involved with many other aspects of self-sufficiency to a greater or lesser degree. These existing lines would be bolstered up with home-produced eggs, lamb and pork, but this would be the limit of our adventures into the realms of DIY sufficiency.

There was no evidence of a kitchen garden anywhere in the vicinity of the house and a few prods with the garden fork showed that the soil was only a few inches deep. The underlying material was solid, unyielding bedrock.

At the foot of the knoll on which the house and the woods stood, there was a field that looked promising. It was obviously wet but the soil looked dark and rich.

Furthermore, an eight-foot garden cane could be pushed into it with very little effort. It had been used for grazing for many years but had originally formed a part of the old peat bog.

I started to dig a deep bed, some three feet wide. The soil was peaty and very acid but with a correction of manure and lime, it should be ideal for vegetables that could tolerate some acidity. It was very hard work, but by double-digging a distance of six feet a day, the bed – some sixty feet long – slowly emerged. It looked quite professional. The soil was nicely broken down into a tilth and it was piled up in the middle of the bed to resemble one I had seen on the gardening programmes on TV. I wheeled barrowloads of old stable manure down and heaped it on – almost (but not quite) rubbing my hands with satisfaction.

Then the chickens found it. They'd never seen such an exciting bill of fare. They scratched and pecked to their heart's content, until there was a depression where the soil should have been piled up.

I scraped all the soil back onto the bed and laid dead branches on it. They loved that even more – the snack bar-cum-sandpit now had perches.

I conceded defeat and abandoned further digging until we could either fence a suitable area of the field or contain the chickens in a hen run.

I'd never considered the matter before, but sheep really are wild animals. Our ewes had beetled off to the far side of the farm and took fright if we went within a hundred yards of them.

While I didn't expect them to be tame, I felt slightly aggrieved that they were so totally ungrateful for the effort I was making to welcome them.

At the time, I think we felt we had a sensible approach to animals but looking back, it is clear that we still had the suburban attitude, which tries to humanise them.

The boundary fences were in a very poor state and I was worried that our ewes would stray on to our neighbour's land. They had colonised an area of the farm where the fence was almost non-existent and we could see it was only a matter of time before they pushed under the stretch of rusty barbed wire that passed as a fence, dividing our neighbour's land from our own. So, yes, we'd have to renew all the boundary fences – a long laborious job that Brian didn't feel able to tackle. We rang a local farmer who had been most kind with help and advice and asked him to suggest someone to do the job. He suggested a local lad whom I will call Dai Gwyn and brought him over to meet us. It was the start of a very good friendship as Dai has been a tower of strength in umpteen different ways. The success of the farm and the building project has, to some extent, been due to his efforts.

Dai worked out how many rolls of wire we would need and how many fence posts and strainers. We ordered the lot and Dai and his henchman Arthur set about making us sheep-proof.

But at this point, the blasting was occupying my mind to the exclusion of almost everything else. If you happen to enjoy a really good fright, which has the added spice of costing a great deal, then it's just the thing to give you a whale of a good time.

Mama exchanged her hymns for First World War army songs – now only partially recognisable – and was beginning to add a long drawn-out wail at the end of every phrase. At times, this got me to the point where I would join in, and we'd warble in unison – me in falsetto and Mama in contralto. Occasionally we'd change places and Mama would take the soprano ripieno and I would do the bass. I was surprised to find I could do quite a passable impression of Paul Robeson. Sometimes Mother would stop in mid phrase and give me rather a square look. This wasn't too bad but when the postman caught us in mid chorus one morning, it was difficult to know what to say.

The blasting contractor had arrived with the compressor and sundry other bits of gear and had set all his equipment out. He carefully explained the seriousness and danger of the job – the need to keep the gelignite under cover at all times, the signal system as the charge was about to be fired, and various other precautions.

My knees, already wobbly, were showing signs of declining to hold me up at all, and I was obliged to visit the bathroom with undue frequency.

We, in turn, had explained where the water main was buried and the course of the sewage pipes and the electric and telephone cables.

And blasting started.

Gelignite George explained to the man on the big orange machine where he wanted to place the first charge.

The man on the orange thing swung one of the orange arms in that direction. On the end of the arm was a thing like a gigantic tooth. He lowered this tooth into the ground and scratched around for a bit. Then he raised the arm — and up came the water main into an interesting-shaped piece of modern sculpture that gushed forth water about four feet above the ground.

Ten minutes into blasting and work had stopped.

We are assessed for our water charges on a meter basis, which means that all water we use is clocked up on a meter. Once every six months a man comes to read the meter and we are then sent a bill for what we've used. We were therefore *paying* for all that water gushing out of the pipe and turning the yard into a rich mud soufflé.

We had never actually established the whereabouts of the tap to turn the water main off. Indeed, the former owners had not known either and it was suspected that it was buried when the sea wall on the far side of the farm had been rebuilt. The meter itself was also on the far side of the farm, some half a mile away and, on the spur of the moment, Brian decided he would have to go and see if it was possible to turn the supply off at the meter. There was no possibility of driving the car across the land and to go by road meant a mile and two sets of gates out to the main road, then two miles along the main road, then back through two sets of gates down towards the coast.

It would be quicker to run over the boggy, craggy farm path. Carrying a selection of tools, Brian set off, while we sat and watched the fountain.

Thirty minutes later Brian returned — no means of turning the water off anywhere on the line.

Hurried consultation. Brian and I started digging like two frantic moles upstream of the sculpture — and found the pipe. Brian quickly made a fitting, sawed through the pipe, and capped it off. The fountain subsided.

But we now had no water for the house.

Work recommenced. Hours and hours of drilling, with the compressor adding an accompaniment.

Eventually one charge hole was deep enough and the charge was laid. We all took cover – the five-second signal was given, followed by an earth-shattering explosion.

Huge clods of earth and boulders shot up into the air and rained down in a cloud some hundred feet from the scene. The chickens set off in a squawking herd down the lane, and the three cats moaned in fear.

Mama enjoyed it enormously. She and I, with the cats, had witnessed the proceedings from a comfortable seat in her caravan, well out of range, and with a grandstand view of the excitement.

After the fallout, we emerged from our hiding places to goggle at the outcome. I couldn't see anything more exciting than a smallish hole but apparently the rock had cracked and Claud, the big orange machine, could extract the broken material to expose the next level to be blasted.

It was hoped that we'd do two blasts a day. While the excavator dug around and dragged out what it could, Gelignite George got going on the next hole.

The second blast wasn't quite as bad. We knew what to expect but it did crack the walls of the manhole through which the sewage pipes passed.

At the end of the first day, as the men went home, all seemed devastation. The kitchen floor was covered in mud, we had no water in the house and Brian had banned all visits to the loo. He hastily constructed a standpipe in the yard so I could at least draw water – even though it meant taking the kettle or a bucket out across a sea of mud to collect it. Unfortunately, we hadn't a hose clean enough to pipe it directly into the kitchen.

He also made a temporary repair on the brickwork in the manhole but we couldn't use the loo until the cement had set.

Day two into blasting saw the complete demise of the manhole. The grain in the rock in that area didn't run as Gelignite George had anticipated and the sewage pipes ascended into the air in a burst of coloured brickwork. Brian had rushed into town early in the morning to buy a new hose and had made a makeshift water supply to the kitchen sink, but we were now minus a loo for an indefinite period.

It was a wet cheerless grey day – the lorry had carved huge tracks in the lane and the yard looked like a tank training ground. As the men left, late in the afternoon, Brian again went into town and returned with a bottle of Scotch and a Porta Potti. Armed with these comforts we started day three.

This dawned with a biting east wind, which threatened frost. Some washing I had painstakingly done in the kitchen sink and hung out to dry was caught by the fallout from one of the blasts, and one of the windows in the barn was smashed to smithereens by flying debris, cascading fragments of broken glass all over the piles of boxes and stored furniture.

By late afternoon the frost had set in and the water supply to the kitchen through the new hose had solidified.

Days four, five and six passed in much the same way, with disasters of a greater or lesser magnitude every hour or so.

By day seven we were left with the large rocky outcrop on which the west wall of the house sat, and which continued to rise up to a height of five or six feet on the outside of the house.

Clearly we would have to have a passageway from the old house to the proposed new wing, and therefore, there would have to be a hole, at least, made through this rock. Claud, the big orange thing, had managed to flatten an area of some thirty-six feet wide by sixty feet long but we were left with this big rock that divided the proposed new wing from the old house.

The men felt it should be possible to get some, if not all, of the blockage out, to leave a clear flat platform to the west of the old house, but it all looked extremely dangerous to me.

But Gelignite George was apparently used to this sort of thing. He told us lots of stories of previous, very difficult, situations that had turned out well, so it seemed silly not to have one more go at that rock.

We agreed. The charge was laid – and fired – and the whole of the middle section of the west wall of the farmhouse blew into one of the downstairs rooms, leaving much of the rock on the outside, in place. At least the wall – three feet thick – was still roughly in position but some fifteen inches to the east of where it had been previously, and with large cracks through which I could see, from the inside, the workmen surveying the damage from the outside.

Big debate. Was the whole of the west wall going to fall, leaving the roof unsupported? Should it be an insurance job? Did it matter even – if we were going to build on to that wall anyway?

We put in some props to support the upstairs floor and the men went home.

That night we sat like refugees in our battered home and decided to call it a day with the blasting. Somehow or other we'd get over the problem of the remaining rock.

Next day off went all the men with their machines. As the heavy JCB lumbered off down the lane, the driver had a momentary lapse of concentration and took to the grass verge. Under that grass verge were the sewage pipes leading from the house down to the septic tank. Some forty feet of that ceramic pipework was now in dozens of small pieces about two feet underground.

The main contractor was very concerned at all the problems we'd suffered. Before he took Claud away, he came and moved some of the spoils still left from the blasting and made a flat car park at the end of the yard, where previously there had been a soft, muddy patch of ground. He also brought a load of small stone to cover this car park, and he offered to lend us, free of charge, his road roller to press it all down.

Unfortunately the roller had a fault in its gearbox, but this had been explained to us. However, when Brian started it up to experiment with how it worked, it smartly reversed into his car, pushing in the number plate. This really was the final straw, but for some reason, it left me helpless with merriment. I can still remember Brian's look of outraged horror and resignation as he turned the engine off and went to inspect the latest bit of damage.

Gelignite George told us afterwards that he'd used eighty-five kilos of gelignite and we'd moved over two thousand tons of rock. We did understand that it was impossible to know how the rock would shatter and that, all in all, we had emerged from the ordeal tolerably well.

We did have a level platform on which to build an extension although it was some three feet higher than the ground floor of the old house and it did have a big rock in just the wrong place. This would have to be turned into some sort of feature in the link block between the old cottage and the proposed new wing, but there was now sufficient space to make a passageway, at least, from the old house, to the hoped-for new extension.

We lost no time in summoning the architect, and explaining what we wanted to do. It was hoped that he'd translate it into something the council would find acceptable, since he had an intimate knowledge of what was, and what was not, likely to be permitted.

We felt we may as well start with our ideal and then give way on whatever the council found fault with. So, we had a lengthy meeting and off went the architect with lots of notes and sketches. In view of our urgent need to house Mama in a more civilised manner, he had promised to give it his immediate attention.

After a couple of weeks we rang him to ask how the plans were going. He was not available.

A day or so later, we rang again. He was still not available. We spoke to his secretary. The plans were 'in hand' and would be with us 'very shortly'.

We rang again – and again – and again.

When we were on the point of asking somebody else to prepare the plans, the drawings arrived by post, and bore no relation whatever to the conversations we'd had, and the sketches the architect had made when he was with us.

We rang him again and he agreed to have another go. Within a week we had some plans that were in line with what we wanted. He rehashed them once more and finally they were submitted to the council – who deliberated for some weeks and then turned them down.

While all this was going on, Dai, with his pal Arthur, had made a start on the fencing. It seemed to be the first constructive job and it was pleasurable to get my wellies on and walk over to see what progress they had made.

Almost all the local Welsh people spoke their own language and I found this fascinating to listen to. Arthur was particularly Welsh with few English characteristics. He was, and still is, a quiet, shy man – well versed in the ways of the country and the things that live in it. He was in demand at lambing time to catch the foxes that would otherwise take the lambs. Any farmer with a fox problem was quick to get on the phone and ask for Arthur's help at any time of year.

This hunting bears no relation to fox hunting as most of the country see it – large horses, mainly upper-crust people dressed up in funny clothes, with menials offering alcohol to those exalted figures sitting on the saddles. Arthur's hunting was conducted with a selection of farm dogs, all of which appeared friendly and well-behaved and played their own part in the drama.

Sam, the lurcher, was a big grey job – rather like a greyhound but with long shaggy hair. He provided the speed in the chase but had no ability to scent the fox and only joined in when the other dogs had picked up the trail. Even then he was only used if the fox was out on open ground and the hounds could not catch him.

The three little terriers were used to check the fox's den, or any likely nooks and crannies where a fox may have been lying up. Peg, the mother terrier, had a malformed leg but ran very happily on the other three, with the fourth joining in now and again. She was an intelligent little thing and knew to avoid a badger's earth, since she would stand little chance in an underground confrontation with a badger. She also knew perfectly well where I kept the biscuits and would ask for a titbit in the most delightful way – rolling off the beg position as her wayward leg let her down.

Her two sons hadn't yet learned to distinguish between fox and badger and to avoid them entering an earth that might contain a badger, they were tied together with a short chain on their collars. I was worried about this at first, but they were well used to it and could run flat out with a sort of internal radar telling one when the other one wished to stop. Then there were the five hounds – a mother and her four pups. While searching for the scent, their tails were down in the normal position but once they'd caught a sniff of the quarry, their tails went up and wagged furiously, and they started to bay.

After all this performance, the fox was invariably shot by one of the guns accompanying the hunt and it was all over very quickly. There were no points of protocol in this type of hunting. Even so, I hated it, but what else was to be done? Beautiful as they are, foxes are a great problem if they become too numerous. It is most upsetting to see a fox after a lamb with the ewe trying desperately to protect her baby, usually without avail.

But to get back to our two helpers. Apart from being the local huntsman, Arthur was a shepherd and during the slack season he also repaired the dry stone walls and did odd fencing jobs, hence his appearance at our farm. As with many people who spend their time with sheep, he was extremely quiet. For the first year or so of our acquaintance, his entire English vocabulary appeared to consist of 'Schew' or 'Schew Schew', if he was particularly moved about something.

Dai was much more anglicised since he had spent some time in England and he was much less reticent. He too was a shepherd, but he also did a lot of building and repair work for local farmers as well as fencing jobs and anything else that turned the odd bob or two. He proved to be very useful to us – as builder, shepherd, translator of doubtful Welsh phrases and in so many other ways. He was slightly built with a mop of curly hair and a deferential manner that was most unusual. I was always 'Mrs Turner' to my face and 'the Missus' if he was talking to Brian. Most of the time he very decorously went about his business on the farm, but just occasionally he would lose his temper with his dog. Glen was a young working sheepdog and still learning his trade. Sometimes he got in a muddle with the commands and would drive the sheep in the wrong direction. Dai was beside himself on these occasions and roared abuse in fluent downtown Welsh.

Or again, if one of the cats trod on his newly laid concrete before it had set, and he thought I was out of earshot, he would shower epithets on the luckless mog – such epithets ceasing abruptly if I opened the window to enquire into the matter.

He knew everyone locally and could advise on who was related to whom (and what their father died of), and where things we needed could be obtained. This was so useful in this area of scant population.

But all this was for the future. As we hurtled towards that first Christmas in Wales – then into the new year – we battled problem after problem, but never for one moment regretted our move.

Chapter Six

By this time it began to seem as if we were making a single-handed attempt to clear the national debt. What was more, all the expense appeared inescapable and we had little to show for it. The new fencing had been finished and it was pleasing to know we were stock-proof, but in almost all other ways, the farm looked less well than when we had taken it over. We'd spent a lot of cash and we hadn't even finished the demolition on the building site, let alone started to construct anything.

Nonetheless, we loved it. The practicalities of life were sometimes onerous – there were generous amounts of mud everywhere, the water situation was difficult, as were the toilet facilities – but it was all well worth it.

Life here has an unreal quality – like something from a dream. The house sits on its hillock, nestling in the dark woods, but through an opening in the trees, there is the sea, fringed by forests, from which rise the lofty crags of a mountain range.

For much of the time there is complete silence – nothing moves, and – the rest of the world seems a long way away.

Indeed, it *IS* a long way away, as it is nearly a mile out to the main road, and that is only sparsely used.

At night, owls hoot from point-blank range. It is dark and mysterious. On moonlit nights, the clean, unpolluted air enhances the silver light shining over the mountains, the woods and the sea. It is like a stage set or a cheap market picture.

On the other hand, the weather can show its teeth. The winds shriek and roar and the seabirds scream. The air is salt and fresh and the beaches littered with debris. However low I may have been feeling at the constant barrage of problems, my spirits could not help but revive as I squelched along the shoreline – struggling against the wind howling through my thermals – to inspect any peculiarity that may have been washed up.

Robertson, the marmalade cat, spent most of his waking hours on the beach. We could tell the state of the tide by his movements. If he was asleep on the pile of rolled-up carpets on the landing, then it was high tide. During those first few months he was so obviously perplexed by the tides. Had it been low tide every morning, he could have understood it – but the tide moves on so that it became low tide at lunchtime, and then afternoon. He grew to be particularly fond of the small soft-shelled crabs. It was annoying that he'd stuff himself full of bits and pieces on the beach and then come and be sick on the kitchen floor. He never seemed to learn. I would watch him fishing in the rock pools with immense dedication – several times to be cut off by the tide. But he would swim ashore and would, as an alternative, make a thorough inspection of a pile of seaweed, to chew off the tasty bits. He grew very plump and his coat, previously always rather sparse, became thick and luxurious.

Now as I write – four years later – his inner clock knows the state of the tide perfectly well. As it starts to drop, he'll rouse himself from his current hideaway, stretch and commence a thorough and unhurried toilet. This complete, he'll let himself out through the cat door and pause on the doorstep to survey the weather. *Should it be the beach by the harbour or one of the beaches on the far side of the wood...?* Off he'll go for several hours of interest – and refreshment – on the shore. Who fancies dried cat food when there are shrimps and other tasty morsels in the rock pools, there for the taking?

Leo had discovered a rabbit warren. About three hundred yards from the house, across one of the fields, there is a small spinney. As the day advances, the rabbits emerge from the undergrowth and start their evening 'silflay'. The lane out to the main road borders this field and there is bracken, gorse and blackthorn between the lane and the field. Leo sits in the bracken – with eyes like saucers – watching the display. If a plump bunny comes too close, his whiskers will twitch and he'll mutter to it under his breath. He never seems to catch them – it would be too much trouble. It was pure entertainment and he never tires of it.

Lucky, the neutered ram, was becoming a pain. He had a rooted objection to wheelbarrows, prams, motorbikes and any similar objects. It was infuriating to have loaded the wheelbarrow with firewood and then have Lucky turn it over while your back was turned. He also disliked washing on the clothes line and would launch himself at anything long enough to reach. Sheets and bath towels were his speciality. I found it very pleasing to see a line of laundry blowing dry at the top of the garden. This would turn to infuriation, however, as out of a window I would catch sight of Lucky, in charging position, ready to bring down whatever he had realised was within reach. Invariably, before I could get my wellies on and run up the steep incline to the line, he would have torn some of my clean white washing to the ground and be stamping all over it. It was like something from a bullfight except that this bull had it all his own way and was clearly enjoying himself.

On one occasion, a frayed edge of bath towel got entwined with his one horn and he set off down the lane at a gallop with the towel flapping along behind him. I was pleased to see that he didn't appear to find this quite so enjoyable.

It was also annoying when a lassie from the village walked over to show us her new baby. She left the pram in the yard with all the new baby paraphernalia tucked inside. When she came to leave, we found the pram tipped on its side and all the lovely handmade shawls and rugs spread around it – trodden into the mud by Lucky's stamping feet.

So he has had to be confined to a paddock, where he now devotes his spare time to demolishing the gate or the fence. He also thoroughly enjoys a good push and shove session with any visitor who can be persuaded to go and spend a few minutes indulging his whims.

The game consists of seizing his one horn and trying to push him backwards. He will have his legs braced, his head lowered, and all his twelve stone pushing forwards as hard as it can. Just as stalemate is reached and neither contestant can push the other anywhere, he will shift the angle of his attack and, as often as not, watch his human adversary fall flat on his face.

This is pleasure of no common order to Lucky and he'll endeavour to encourage you to another bout, time and time again – snorting and pawing the ground in the most fearsome way.

We'd been worried about Fred, Mama's little dog, for some time. Although she adored him, there was no denying that he'd had a hard time. She'd spend hours dressing him up and petting him. Then she'd shout at him for some imaginary offence. He was a bundle of nerves but clung to her in spite of the treatment she meted out to him.

Since they'd come to live with us, we had fed him and overseen his welfare as far as possible. We'd also intervened if Mama was being particularly troublesome with him, and we'd made sure he had some fun at least once a day, but as he meant so much to Mama, he had to spend most of his time with her. I dreaded his ultimate demise – she'd be distraught.

For a month or two, he had been reluctant to eat, and latterly, he seemed to spend an inordinate amount of time squatting on his haunches trying to go to the loo.

Brian took Mama for a drive one day and I took Fred to see the local vet. The outlook was not promising. He needed an operation, but at twelve, the vet thought his chances of a complete recovery were rather poor. Furthermore, Mama would not have understood and would undoubtedly have interfered with his dressings, not remembering that he was ill.

I explained this to the vet and as he did not consider that the little dog was in any real pain, he suggested we leave matters as they were until Fred was either in obvious pain, or so unwell that euthanasia was the only alternative.

So, with a heavy heart, I brought him home and he continued to spend a lot of time trying to vacate his back end. Initially he was better as the vet had cleared the blockage and he could manage to go to the loo again, but this didn't last. We took him to the vet twice more, and again his blocked bowel was cleared. But it lasted fewer and fewer days until Fred was spending all day and half the night straining to vacate his bowel, and obviously feeling extremely uncomfortable, even if he was not in real pain.

After a particularly horrendous scene when I delivered Mama's tea one morning, we felt the time had come to take action. Brian took Mama out in the car and I took Fred on his final journey to the vet. In the event, it upset me more than it did Mama.

We stood back waiting for the onslaught from Mama, but strangely enough, she didn't seem to miss him. Her hot-water bottle or a rolled-up towel became Fred, and she would love and nurse the current Fred with just as much devotion as she had the original Fred. This included pinning brooches into the velvet cover of her hot-water bottle, and sometimes the pins went right through the rubber as well!

We debated the advisability of getting her another dog, but decided against it. Mama was deteriorating mentally – she was very wild and aggressive at times so a dog that wasn't familiar with her ways could have been a great hazard.

She had become particularly annoying with the lock on the caravan door. During the day while we were all up and about, the caravan was kept unlocked, although she could lock it from the inside if she wished to. The only way we could then get into the van was to find the spare key, kept in the kitchen drawer, and go back over the yard to unlock the door.

If it was raining, or cold, and we were eating our main meal in the van, we'd have to negotiate the mud and puddles in the yard, as often as not trying to hold a brolly up over the tray of food with perhaps a high wind into the bargain. I would struggle up the steps to the caravan door carrying my load, only to find that the door was locked. (It always seemed to be me that got caught out in this way as I always prepared the meals.) Hammering on the door produced no effect at all, so it was back to the house for the key, then back to the van, where I'd find that Mama was holding the door handle in the up position on the inside, and the key on the outside didn't give me enough leverage to force the handle downwards and thus open the door.

Waving and grimacing at Mama through the window merely produced a self-satisfied smirk. It got to the point where, if she saw us coming, she'd get out of her chair, and purposely lock the door. This forced us to rely on various stratagems that were as ludicrous as they were funny. Brian would stand outside the caravan door barking like a dog. Mama would be intrigued and would open the door. The variations were endless and the mirth they induced did much to avert the infuriation. Mama would be in fits of laughter at the sight of her son acting in this strange way, and we too would be convulsed.

But there were times when the tension mounted to alarming levels. I remember one occasion when Mama opened her door and threw almost the entire contents of the caravan out into the mud. It was a grey damp day and Mama had been left in the caravan while Brian renewed a section of sewage pipe. I had been in and out of the caravan all morning but at one point in Brian's activities, I was required to help hold one end of the new pipe while he jiggled the other end in to fit the existing unbroken lengths.

Less than half an hour later, I walked back up to the yard – only some eighty feet from where we were working – and found this heap of clothes, ornaments and bedding clustered around the caravan door. I could have wept. The laundry facilities were difficult and it was so depressing to have wet washing hanging around the Rayburn all the time. This was well before the days of a local launderette.

Perhaps we should not have left her alone, but there were times when it was impossible not to, and this had been one of those occasions. A comprehensive and reliable sense of humour was vital. But a tramp around the farm with a brief stop to inspect some point of interest soon helped to introduce a happier frame of mind.

The bird life was a tremendous joy, but also a great consumer of time. I would be hanging out the laundry on the line at the top of the garden and would notice some activity down on the mudflat by the harbour. After stopping at the house to clutch up the binoculars, I'd slip down to the back of the cowshed and peer through the ivy to get a better view of the scene.

Maybe it was a pair of red-breasted mergansers or perhaps a heron with an eel that it couldn't really manage.

Then I would notice something skulking in a reed bed further along the beach.

When that had been investigated, I would see something interesting that had been washed up just a little bit further along the tideline, and would *have* to walk on to inspect it. And so it went on.

After what seemed ten minutes later, I would return to the house and find that I'd been out for over an hour and was in trouble as Brian had been waiting to go off to clear out that ditch by the gate.

With the oystercatchers, I went through agony at the continual loss of their eggs. Indeed, for much of the time, I stood guard over the nest too. It was a modest affair – really just a depression in the stones at the top of one part of the beach. They'd made a token effort at a lining with some dried seaweed and a few sticks, but it was little enough to welcome a youngster into the world.

One pair that nested on the beach by the house have not brought off a chick in any of the first four seasons we have been here, in spite of two or three sittings a year *AND* our joint efforts at guarding the nest. I cannot understand how other oystercatchers are so successful in raising their young – as they are really very common.

For a time I thought it was my, albeit distant, presence that caused the problem, but on reflection, I do not think that this is so as they seem to accept me quite readily – the hen will continue to sit on the nest with the cock bird pecking about in the stones some forty feet from her. Furthermore, the eggs always seem to disappear more quickly if I do not keep an eye on the nest and scare off the gulls and the buzzards that show any interest in it while I happen to be watching.

To someone from the home counties, used to blackbirds, sparrows, starlings, robins and the like, the range of birds here is rich indeed. Many of them I had not seen before – the redstarts nesting in the old stone walls, stonechats and whinchats in the small scrubby trees on the edge of the bog, woodcock rising out of the undergrowth, snipe, redwing, buzzards and so many more. And this is not to mention the seabirds.

In the wood at the back of us, a pair of buzzards have nested each year and have latterly become almost tame. This did not come without time and patience, both of which should have been expended in other directions, but who could refuse the challenge? Mordicus will now sit in a tree some forty feet from me and watch as I throw him a morsel of fat, suet or a dead mouse abandoned by one of the cats. If I stay quite still, he will flop down to clutch the titbit with one clawed foot, rise again and flap off through the trees to consume it in some more private spot.

Mrs Mordicus is less tame. Being larger than her mate, she is perhaps doubtful of a quick take-off in a confined space. I've noticed though that she sometimes flies off after Mordicus when he has obtained a titbit, so maybe she has a share of the prize.

They're untidy-looking birds at close quarters – almost as if their feathers don't fit very well.

In fact, this little trick Mordicus has learned, is becoming something of a problem as he now haunts the compost heap and turns out choice items that were not intended for the light of day again. In general, this consists of grapefruit skins, onion trimmings and similar items that nobody in this establishment can be doing with, and as Mordicus can have no interest in such items either, I can only assume he is after the small red worms that are prolific, or maybe the beetles that have set up shop in one corner.

Much thought and discussion went into the construction of my compost heap and I did everything John Seymour said. He does not mention in his books however that an evil-smelling black gunge seeps out of the bottom of the heap or that the entire confection is home for about eight million bluebottles in summer. These characteristics must therefore apply in my case only and will have to be sorted out, according to Brian, 'before next summer'. Even Mama has started to yell 'Pooooooh' very loudly every time she is obliged to pass the fetid mass.

The local people have been extraordinarily kind and we have made many friends. During those first few months there always seemed to be somebody here to marvel at the newcomers, and indeed we did present an odd picture – two middle-aged ruffians and an ancient mother.

Almost all the indigenous Welsh families in this area speak Welsh as their first language. Many of them have difficulty in expressing themselves in English as they would wish. Some of the newcomers and first-generation Welsh residents speak Welsh too, but this is usually the BBC version, which differs in some ways from the traditional Welsh of mid Wales.

It is a picturesque, language which apparently loses much of its character in the translation. Many of our Welsh friends, struggling to find the equivalent English words to explain something to us, resort to a literal translation and this is often absolutely enchanting. On one occasion, we were entertaining ten rather expensive heifers for a couple of weeks. They were shortly to be served, or put into calf, and the farmer who owned them wanted to change their diet for a few days. So, there they were, flaunting their bovine charms amongst the wild flowers when the common or garden bullock from the adjacent farm caught sight of them. They were clearly just what he had been looking for, and he lost no time in waiting for someone to leave our boundary gate open for a few moments, allowing him access to our meadow and the forbidden fruit.

The owner of the heifers chanced to arrive that same afternoon and found the bullock nudging up to his lovely lassies. Suddenly the air was filled with Celtic and Anglo-Saxon curses – probably Norman as well for all I know – it was plain anyway, that the farmer was very annoyed.

We rang the owner of the bullock, who also arrived on the scene, and a heated discussion in Welsh ensued. We didn't understand a word of it, but at the conclusion, all seemed sweetness and light again. The owner of the bull then explained to us in English that 'the animal was in company with the vet last week.' We took this to mean that the animal had been castrated but it hasn't stopped Brian eyeing the vet rather nervously in subsequent meetings.

Or again, some of the old Welsh stone houses have large stone or slate slabs holding the roof timbers securely down onto the gable-end walls. The placing of these stones would have been one of the last jobs before the homestead was dry and habitable. They are sometimes known as 'Cerrig Diddos', which roughly translates as 'stones for the safety, snugness and blessing of the house'. Isn't that a lovely name for them?

We'd become very friendly with the chap who runs the local butcher's shop. We did all our shopping locally and found that in general we did very well. Initially I had been concerned at the grocery prices since they appeared to be substantially higher than I had been used to. But after a few months I was pleasantly surprised to find that the housekeeping costs were lower than during our days in suburbia. Maybe we were eating a less sophisticated diet – I do not know – but at all events the housekeeping money seemed to go further than before.

This butcher friend rang us up one day and asked if we'd like about twenty chickens – only fifty pence each. I gladly accepted as we all like poultry and even if they had to be casseroled, they were still a cheap meal. The freezer was half empty and I'd plenty of poly bags to wrap them in.

He turned up in his Land Rover, offloaded two large cardboard boxes and hurried away with a quick excuse.

I stood there transfixed as the top of one of the boxes slowly rose an inch and then fell again.

Then a bulge appeared in the cardboard side of the other box. Visualising some of the hens to be not properly dead – and Brian not at hand – I was flummoxed.

I gingerly lifted up the corner of one lid and a beady eye in a very-much-alive black head looked up. I lifted the lid further – and several more very-alive heads appeared. I dropped the lid again quickly – they were *all* alive.

Neither of us could bring ourselves to conduct a mass slaughter, so we hastily concocted a hen run and emptied them into it. They'd laid several eggs while in the boxes, so they were permitted a reprieve and ultimately joined the original hens to freely range all over the farm. Unlike the original hens, however, they strayed much further afield. Often they would be two hundred yards from the farm – but like everything else in this establishment, they put in a regular appearance at mealtimes.

The next crisis was the demise of the pigs. We kept putting off the evil day until they had grown from porkers into bacon pigs. I'd never previously known that pigs for pork are killed at four to five months whereas pigs for bacon can be kept much longer. We had two girls and a boy, and the boy was starting to do things that grown-up boys do. He was also getting quite nasty. He continually bit through our wellies and tried to bite our knees. It certainly wasn't wise to turn your back on Gammon Steak or he'd have other parts as well.

Time went by so quickly and we kept shelving the issue, but after a particularly difficult feeding time, I rang the chap we'd bought them from and explained our dilemma. He agreed to have them back and came and collected them. Several days later these boxes of meat arrived. None of it looked the least bit familiar and we ate it with relish, although it was very fat.

I did feel very concerned that I could eat it when I had not had the courage to order the execution, and this induced a lot of soul-searching and self-analysis into the question of eating meat at all. In the past I'd had several attempts at a vegetarian diet and although I tried to keep strictly to the recommended diet, I always become weak, with a general feeling of lowness after the first two or three weeks.

I've always been extremely sensitive as to animal welfare. With a head-in-the-sand attitude, I could never read those pamphlets turned out by the antivivisection people or newspaper articles about cruelty to animals and I loathed everybody who could handle animals with disrespect.

And yet I had kept the pigs knowing, even if it was unacknowledged, what their end would be. Perhaps it was to find an excuse to pardon myself with, or perhaps a genuine investigation into what I felt must be acceptable for me. For whatever reason, I spent many hours reflecting on the issue – which was now literally in our own backyard – and although I am still not convinced that I have an acceptable answer, I did come to the following conclusions, which helped me to a more comfortable frame of mind.

Firstly, I feel instinctively that meat is a natural food. For many centuries our ancient forefathers killed wild animals to eat – there was, in many cases, little else. Over the period of our evolution, did our bodily make-up become so structured that we need meat to survive? In the past I have discussed the question of eating meat on many occasions with friends, working colleagues and anyone else with whom the subject cropped up. Usually they were thoughtful, caring, gentle people, who shared my horror of the slaughterhouse. Yet invariably, they would agree to an instinctive feeling of need where meat was concerned. They, like me, forced themselves to divorce the fluffy lamb in the meadow from the meat pie on the table, even though they often felt themselves to be despicable for so doing.

Many of them, also like me, had from time to time tried to convert to a vegetarian diet. Several had succeeded but funnily enough it seemed to be the people who were least moved by the justice of the issue that were the most successful in converting to a non-meat diet. In many cases these people had changed to a vegetarian diet for health reasons, in part.

Did this point to a lack of discipline and self-control with those who felt the instinctive need for meat? Or did those people who were successful in changing have some element in their genes that perhaps came to them from some long-term ancient culture that had other sources of food and did not therefore need to kill animals to eat? Or did they, maybe, have no need of meat to balance their chemical compositions for human life? We are said to have a natural desire for the foods that our bodies require, and that we are driven to satisfy imbalances in our body chemicals. So, do carnivorous humans who have tried and failed to convert to a non-meat diet have an elemental need for flesh?

If then our need for meat is derived from our bodily make-up, which evolved over many thousands of years, is it not unfortunate that our mental sensitivities, over the period of our evolution, became more refined, causing us to dwell on the justice of the issue?

Secondly, all animals, including the human animal, suffer the same termination of life. Whatever our religious views may be, there is no denying that the human race is no more exempt from bodily death than any of the other creatures with whom we share this planet.

It seems to me that nature has seen to it that weak, malformed, injured or otherwise vulnerable animals usually die relatively painlessly and quickly – from predators, from an inability to protect themselves or from a natural ability to die at what appears to be choice. We've all seen the cat bring in a dead mouse. As often as not there is no sign of a hurt to that mouse, however carefully it is checked over. It seems to have died because it switched on its self-destruct mechanism.

The human race has improved its science to repair some of the sick, the malformed or the injured, and this gives them a new lease of life, which is marvellous. But the untreatable ones still suffer. Our improved health care, so wonderful in many ways, also fills our care homes and hospital wards with sad, lonely, confused, pain-wracked people, many of whom do wish to die. Even with support from loving families, old age or long-term untreatable illness makes life intolerable for many people – and how many old or permanently sick folk are in fact supported by loving families? Many animals have a more humane end.

So, on the basis that all life has to die at some time, is it so unreasonable to kill and eat an animal when it is on a high note – before the rot sets in? It seems to me to be *vital* for the killing to be carried out as quickly and humanely as possible and with the animal not knowing what is about to happen. It is also vital that, during its life, it is well maintained in good housing with adequate food and has had a chance to have some enjoyment. The human race owes this much to its own self-respect.

Yet a third argument for man's predatory habits must be the continuance of the creatures who live on and off the meat animals. Many of these would have become extinct if their host had not been maintained for man's pleasure.

Having read this through I seem to have knocked up a lot of far-fetched theories in support of the 'eat meat' lobby. In moments of anguish when our lambs are about to be slaughtered, I comfort myself with them. But I am still most unhappy at the whole business. It is a sad and unsatisfactory arrangement that nature has made for us – our disrespect for some of the fellow creatures with whom we share this planet.

Few indeed of us are 'gentlefolk', in the literal sense of the word.

Chapter Seven

Shortly after Christmas, Dai Gwyn had suggested that we feed the ewes with sheep cake. Although the farm was very lightly stocked – the twenty-two ewes had seventy-five acres to cover, shared only with Lucky and the two horses – the pasture was poor, with little nutrient.

So, with my usual unquenchable desire to overfeed everything, I ordered a ton of the little pellets of cereal cake, or sheep nuts. They duly arrived and I set off on a round of the farm – bucket of cake in hand – just longing to give the ewes a really good meal.

But they entirely misunderstood my intentions. Instead of coming up to enjoy the treat, they scuttled off as fast as their broom-rod legs would carry them.

I walked after them, banging the bucket with a stick and calling 'Sheep' in the approved way – and they ran all the harder.

Shortly after our move to Wales, we had met a family who had also eschewed the conventional life and were now running a smallholding and several other enterprises, some six miles from us. Strangely enough, they had lived within ten miles of our Essex home, although we had not met them prior to our separate migrations to Wales. They were keeping goats as well as a few sheep and it was at a Goat Club meeting that we first became acquainted. I had been interested in keeping a goat or two, but my enthusiasm had been somewhat quelled by the threat of divorce proceedings if 'any other responsibilities are introduced on to the farm in the foreseeable future.'

This family had bought a beautiful old house with a very interesting history. The house, which was large, and the outbuildings were in need of considerable repair, but this did not worry our friends in the least. They derived great entertainment from planning the restoration and were not a bit worried by the practical difficulties that, I'm sure, would have driven many of us into an early grave. They were, and still are, a joy to visit. The remains of several earlier meals will be swept from the vast table in the large old kitchen, the wine bottle – probably several bottles – will be produced, with half a dozen assorted glasses, and you will be pressed, and pressed again, to partake of refreshment. Meanwhile, you will be invited to discuss remote political, environmental or philosophical issues, or perhaps the price and whereabouts of old oak for panelling or door frames. Or maybe you would like a chicken sandwich, the hen that provided the filling having been wrested from a fox that had only partially eaten it.

Amongst their stock was a black Jacob ewe called Naomi, and as they didn't keep a ram, they had brought Naomi over to us to be served. The deed had been done and the ewe was shut in a small paddock to await her collection. But time had gone by, and still Naomi was with us.

She was an interesting animal with a mind that dwelt exclusively on her own interests. She very much disliked dogs – or being rounded up – or any activity that required her to exert much energy. She *had* to have a roof over her head at night or somewhere to shelter if it rained *and* any delectable vegetable waste. If these commodities were not supplied, she would roar – and roar – and roar.

Her vocal efforts were amazing. Quite unlike the usual bleating – more like a ship's siren as a liner is about to leave port. She could cram about three of these blasts into one minute, and after half an hour, the most disciplined and hard-line character would give in and provide whatever she was requiring.

Naomi *did* understand about sheep nuts and was vociferous in her demands for a regular and substantial supply. So we let her out to join the Welsh ewes, hoping that she would teach them to come for cake. Naomi did not share our hopes. She wanted *all* the cake for herself and would stuff it down as fast as possible. But the Welsh ewes began to realise that something interesting was happening. One or two would watch as we tipped a bucket of cake into a trough. Bit by bit they came nearer. After Empress Naomi had finished and departed, they would come and sniff the trough. Then one or two of the bolder ones would come and try to join in as Naomi enjoyed her meal.

She would have none of this, and would position her ample rear end to keep them at bay. She could do wonders with that rear end – juggling it from side to side in the most nifty and athletic way – meanwhile keeping her head in the nuts. It would have been such an asset at the Christmas sales in the high-street shops!

We had overcome this problem by providing two or three little piles of nuts and although Naomi would endeavour to cover all of them, the Welsh ewes inevitably began to understand that food could also come out of a bucket.

Eventually Naomi had gone home, and our ewes had their meal on their own. Dai had suggested trying to encourage them up to the yard, as firstly, this would save carrying the cake down to the meadow, and secondly, if they came into regular contact with the human race, they would surely be less nervous. We would be more likely to see if they needed any attention, an abscess to be treated for example, and also stand a better chance of catching them should we find a problem. If they were used to closer contact with us, then this too would stand us in good stead at lambing when Dai would not always be at hand. Poor Dai, he tried so hard to think of ways to enable us to cope. I'm sure no other sheep farmer has to use cunning and subterfuge to catch his ewes.

So off I would go with my bucket of cake and my stick every morning, and I'd bang my drum until I had most of the ewes in tow, when I would return to the yard and feed them.

It worked beautifully. After a few weeks, they would come up to the yard without being called. They would stand about shiftlessly – behind the machinery – wary of any sudden movement – ready to be off at the merest hint of trouble. They would watch the empty buckets go into the barn where the cake is kept. They would move forward as they heard the cereal rattling into the containers. When the buckets were brought out and placed on the ground, they would watch. As we retreated, they would advance on the nuts – and ten minutes later the buckets would be empty.

As the ewes became more confident, they would collect in the yard and baa a reminder for their breakfast as soon as it was light. The days lengthened and the baaing started earlier and earlier. Upstairs in the big bed, muffled curses were uttered into the bedclothes about those ****** sheep and the ****** noise they made.

So, we started to feed them late in the afternoon – only to find that they still collected in a solemn group at daybreak and then spent all day in the yard, filling it with their droppings and churning up the mud, instead of turning their attention to the grazing. There did not seem a way to get it right and eventually we had to return to a morning feed, but it did give the ewes a good meal a day as well as getting them used to us.

Spring was coming. There was an instinctive feeling of the age-old stirring of the sap – the eternal renewal of life. It induced a heartening, hopeful frame of mind, which helped to make light of the problems.

One sunny day at the beginning of March, I was hanging out the laundry on the line at the top of the garden. I could hear a low rumble – almost a humming noise. It was difficult to pinpoint where it was coming from. It sounded rather like a very distant aircraft, but the noise didn't increase or decrease and half an hour later, it could still be heard.

It was always alleged in our family that Grandmama had suffered from 'noises in the head'. She died when I was eight, but my recollections are of a quiet, stately old lady, always dressed in black with a gold cameo brooch pinned into the collar of her high-necked dress. She had a faraway, detached air, and it was easy to believe she was listening to something beyond the range of our ears. In fact, she was probably suffering from tinnitus, but in Grandma's day it was imbued with mysticism and spoken of in hushed tones.

When I first noticed this unusual noise while hanging out the washing, it crossed my mind that perhaps I'd inherited this family weakness. It was quite worrying – all my faculties seemed to be deteriorating – I already needed spectacles for close work and I was forever mislaying the wretched things. My back would protest if I spent too long on the garden or some other energetic task and my memory was frequently letting me down.

But this low rumble could not be heard in the house, nor when I walked about a hundred yards to the north. It could be heard quite clearly however in the garden and on all other sides, and it didn't seem to get louder or softer at any point. It was either there at the same pitch or not there at all.

Brian had gone down to the London factory for a couple of days so I wasn't able to go far from the house, but for several hours I wrestled with the problem of this mysterious noise. The semicircle of garden in front of the house drops away steeply to the foreshore on the one hand, and to the track leading to the other side of the farm, on the other hand. Bordering the track is a stream – well, more of a ditch really – and it seemed that the noise was fractionally louder in that area.

Having checked that Mama was not in trouble for five minutes, I scrambled down a less steep part of the cliff to the track below and was thrilled to see that the water in the ditch was boiling with activity. This ceased abruptly as I approached, but through the water I could see huge clods of toad spawn.

I sat quietly in the grass for a few moments and bit by bit the activity started again. Large brown toads with backs like pork crackling and butter yellow chins were climbing on top of one another in a frenzy of mating. At the slightest movement they dived down into the sedge but reappeared a few moments later if all was quiet. There must have been hundreds of them. A few at a time had their heads out of the water and seemed to be making this strange rumbling noise, which was no louder when close by than up in the garden, some fifty yards away.

The activity continued for about ten days until the ditch seemed to be solid with jelly. Then as the weeks passed the toadlets appeared and by July we were alive with them – they were indoors in the cupboards, swimming in the cats' water bowl, hiding in the wellies – all over the place. It was difficult to walk at night for fear of treading on them. They waddled along in the middle of the roadway, which inevitably meant some casualties however carefully one trod or drove.

It was – and still is – a thrill to have them, but they are something of a mixed blessing in quite such large numbers. Most of them must be common toads as they fit the description exactly, but I cannot find in the reference books any mention of the noise they make. Perhaps our toads are the result of the mixed breeding of two separate types and the noise is peculiar to them. It would be interesting to know.

As the spring advanced, the local farming gossip was all of the lambing. We were affecting a nonchalance we were far from feeling and we both spent a lot of time reading the various handouts we'd been given on the subject. They dealt avidly with all the problems that could occur until we began to think that every birth was complicated in some way, in spite of what Dai had said.

At this stage Dai did not have his working dog, Glen, so with people posted at strategic points and by dint of much shouting and arm-waving, we managed to drive our twenty-two ewes into a meadow by the house. Once there, we took it in turns to go and inspect them every two or three hours. This seemed to go on for ages without any sign of a lamb until we began to think they weren't pregnant. But eventually we too started our lambing and it really was very exciting.

Brian had gone to do the rounds shortly after six o'clock one morning and he came back, puffing like a steam engine, to report that one ewe had a lovely black-faced lamb. I immediately downed tools and we both went to inspect the new arrival. It could only have been two or three hours old, maybe less, but it could already stand. The mother was just finishing the lamb's first wash and brush up, and as it swayed about on its wobbly little legs, she nudged it towards her udder.

We wasted most of the day in relayed trips down to see the baby. We even took Mama to show her our first lamb but sadly she could not understand what was happening.

Later in the day, our butcher friend called and he too was taken down to see the baby. We *were* naive – he must have seen thousands of newborn lambs – but he very kindly shared in our excitement. He caught the little lamb and showed us how to tell its sex. It was a girl and Brian promptly christened it Veronica.

I hated leaving mother and daughter in the cold wet meadow that night, but they are hardy and must remain so if they are to be healthy. The following morning the lamb was very alert and looked much stronger but the midnight inspection that night was not a happy one. One ewe had given birth to twins but both babies were dead. We felt very responsible as we hadn't been at hand at the birth. We couldn't help wondering if they would have survived had we been able to clear their mouths or give some other sundry aid that would have made all the difference.

But lambing continued really very successfully. We walked for hours around the labour meadow in all weathers both day and night but never once caught a ewe in the process of giving birth. It amazed me that the ewes could lamb without the assistance of a midwife, the National Health Service, Child Benefit or any of the other so-called advantages of civilisation, and within an hour or two of the birth, would have bathed the baby, fed it, and would be peaceably grazing near the sleeping little creature.

At the time, we felt we had learned a great deal about lambing – but looking back, we were spoon-fed by having ewes that were fit and well, and had done it all before, at least once, and by having reasonably good weather. Lambing, as we were to find out, did not always go as well.

But it was a happy time. We raised twenty-five lambs from twenty-two ewes and never did lambs have such care and attention. We made more fuss about it than farmers lambing a thousand ewes, but it felt real and after a lifetime of indoor occupations, many of which were artificial and of doubtful moral value, it was extraordinarily refreshing.

Meanwhile the farm was becoming alive with colour. The wildflowers were starting to bloom and never had we seen anything like it. That first spring when we had so few sheep, the daffodils were even more numerous, followed by bluebells and primroses. But it was the unusual plants that gave us the greatest joy – the milkwort ranging from an incandescent royal blue to pale mauve and shocking pink; the lousewort from the palest blushing pink to maroon; the orchids, spotted and plain, in shades from white to a very dark red; the yellow bog asphodel, the small delicate bog rosemary like a lily of the valley; the creamy white candles of pennywort; the yellow cinquefoil; white eyebright – isn't that a lovely name; yellow cow-wheat, and so many more. The walls and fences hung with scented honeysuckle, and the ungrazed corners between the rocky outcrops were filled with different types of heather, from white to a dark petunia. There were acres of yellow water irises – they bordered all the streams and ditches and as the spring advanced, the yellow flags gave way to banks of mauve and white foxgloves.

The birds too were all producing their offspring and I didn't know what to look at first. The ironing and mundane household jobs were forgotten as I wasted so much time out on the farm if Brian was in charge of Mama.

Father Christmas had brought Brian a timber workshop – a rather posh garden shed in reality – and he had set up his heavy machinery and was building his mechanical/electronic concoctions for about half the working day, while the rest was spent on Mama or the farm. But there were stolen half-hours when he launched the boat and went fishing or just drifted about on the clear water, looking down at the jellyfish and enjoying a few moments of peace.

Shortly after we moved to Wales, the company had opened a new factory in Bridgend in South Wales, and some of Brian's machines had been transferred to the new premises. This meant that he had to visit the Bridgend premises as well as the London factory, so he was away from home for two or three days at least once a month. This was important; as lovely as we found our new home, Mama imposed a great strain, and it helped to have a complete break for a day or so.

For some time it had been difficult to get Mama to wash, and it had advanced to the point where it was literally necessary to carry out an assault to remove her clothes and get her in the shower or to wash her hair. Even to wash her face and hands was a task of mammoth proportions which one dreaded for several hours beforehand.

We both felt it was necessary for her to keep as much dignity as possible, and we failed to force the issue on many occasions. This meant that she would remain unwashed for two or three days at a time, and we became concerned that her lack of cleanliness was a health hazard. It was worrying to get the right balance between destroying her self-respect and independence by insisting on the washing, while at the same time maintaining a modicum of hygiene.

Up to this point we'd had no help from the medical authorities apart from prescriptions for the sedatives she took at night and her incontinence supplies for night-time use. But they now offered to have her in the local day hospital for one day a week to give her a bath, a hair wash and sundry medical attention should she need it.

This was absolutely marvellous. It meant that the cleanliness problem was largely resolved and, as we delivered her to the hospital at 9.30 in the morning and picked her up at 3.30, we had about five hours to devote to our own interests once a week. We could go out together on our own – a privilege we had not been able to enjoy for some time.

Another great advantage was that I could rely on the Sister at the day hospital to notice any problem that was brewing. I was never sure that I would recognise a medical problem that may be starting, and Mama was not necessarily able to tell me if she felt ill, or had a pain, or was suffering with any other matter that required attention. I tried not to worry the doctor on the basis that if I went to him with minor things, then he may not react as rapidly to a serious one, but that did not stop me worrying about what I ought to do if, for example, Mama had a rash on her back or some other trifling disorder.

One of Mama's most annoying habits was the physical battery she could muster. Her old fists would clench and she would give you a push or a poke that could send you sprawling. In general, this was only applied when you were in a vulnerable position. I'd be stooping down to tie her shoe laces and she'd push my shoulders so that I fell backwards on my bottom – or she'd bring one of her knees up to catch me a whack under my chin just as I was leaning forward to stand up. You really do need a strong rein on your temper to cope with this sort of thing. I'm afraid I shouted at her quite often – she probably thought her name was 'You Difficult Old Faggot' – she'd long forgotten her real name.

But immediately I would feel guilty and ashamed. Feeling guilty and ashamed at one's lack of tolerance is almost the greatest burden of all. Heigh-ho – she was in her own home with all her personal bits and pieces about her, and in her own way, I think, felt safe and supported. The bouts of crying had largely gone and there were times when she was happy and quite obviously enjoying herself. These tended to be the times when we were *not* enjoying life.

Partly to ride the stress induced by coping with Mama, and partly because I wanted to get some summer vegetables planted, I resumed the preparation of the deep beds in the kitchen garden at the foot of the hill. Dai, with an exaggerated opinion of my gardening prowess and energy, had fenced off about an acre of the field where I had originally started digging, and thus the inside was free of sheep and chickens. Unless I live to be one hundred and fifty, I doubt if I will ever cultivate all of it, but it is useful to have it fenced.

It was extremely exposed to the prevailing west wind so I planted 300 hawthorn cuttings around the perimeter on the inside of the fence and on the inside of the hawthorn,

I planted a row of Leylandii on the windward side. The early potatoes I had planted in March were doing well, and in the new beds, I planted peas, runner beans, lettuces, sprouts and spinach. It didn't look like something from the gardening magazines, but it was coming on.

Due to the sheep nuts, the ewes hung about the farmhouse with their lambs. It was inadvisable to leave a door open as they'd walk indoors too.

We had stopped feeding sheep cake when the grass began to grow, but, by then, they were hooked on the wretched nuts, and from having been very wild and nervous, they became embarrassingly tame. Over a month after cereal feeding officially ceased, they'd still appear in the yard and range about looking hopeful.

One particular ewe was very tame. Blooey, as she came to be known (after the blue tag in her ear), would push open the back door and conduct her ram lamb over to the vegetable rack by the sink, where, between them, they would consume whatever comestible took their fancy. On one occasion this was a cauliflower, which had cost fifty pence and was intended as the main constituent of a cauliflower cheese for Brian's supper.

If the sitting room door was open, she'd also take her lamb from the kitchen into the sitting room, where they would taste the apples in the fruit bowl on the coffee table. As she was unaware of the sanitary arrangements that prevailed in a human habitation, it wasn't just the loss of the fruit and vegetables that concerned me.

But, in general, the sheep were proving interesting and helped to give another dimension to life. I was acutely aware that we were sharing each day with other creatures who were passing their lives at the same time as us, and this gave us a companionship, a relationship, a joint battle against the elements or whatever the forces of nature threw at us. Indeed, as we began to have closer dealings with the sheep, we began to learn a lot about the weather and how it affected the land and the creatures and plants living on the soil. We also learned about relationships. A flock of sheep contains as many different characters as a group of people. It was, and still is, a book of life that provides endless interest. Those early days at the farm were a particularly happy time of learning how to live our new life, seasoned with the promise of even better things to come.

At the end of each evening, we would take Mama back to the caravan and make sure she was safe and comfortable for the night. The various alarms were set or checked – Mama was tucked into bed with her latest Fred – and we would walk back to the house. It nearly always seemed to be a lovely blue-black time of night – absolute quiet except for the faint fizzing of the waterfall a mile away, or the swish of the wavelets tumbling mechanically onto the beach; maybe a drift of air rustling the tops of the old trees behind the house, and the owls trying to out-hoot the oystercatchers.

Against advice from almost everybody, I'd go and get a small bucket of sheep nuts from the inner sanctum of the barn. The ewes, comfortably settled about the farmyard with their lambs, would heave themselves to their feet and crowd around the feeders. The lambs would blink in the torchlight and momentarily look apprehensive – but within a moment or so the sheep cake would be gone and the ewes were ambling back to their babies. Soon, all would be quietly sleeping the sleep of the just – including the occupants of the big bed upstairs.

Chapter Eight

When the council refused our planning application, they did indicate their acceptance of the house extension 'in principle', so at least we knew we could build something to increase the living accommodation.

We had been given a list of the various points where they felt our plans did not conform to their rules, and with the architect, we went through this list in an effort to meet their requirements and to plan something we felt was acceptable to us.

The major problem centred on the patio doors in the proposed new sitting room. The room was to face south with beautiful views of the sea and mountains and it seemed so obvious to have as much of that view as possible from all parts of the room. So we wanted sliding glass doors, twenty feet wide by seven feet high.

The council would only permit two windows on that elevation, with maximum dimensions of three feet by two feet each – a very substantial modification of what was acceptable to us.

We had given way on a number of points on the list, but we did feel strongly about those patio doors.

The architect had suggested a meeting with the senior planning officer, prior to the submission of the revised plans. We were anxious to have the matter resolved quickly so that the construction could start very soon as we didn't want Mama to have to spend another winter in the caravan. And the hope was that we'd tacitly agree the various amendments with the big man at the council, so that when the plans were resubmitted, they would be accepted without further ado.

So off went the architect to prepare yet a further set of plans. When they were completed, he was to make an appointment for us all to meet at the planning department and it was agreed that he'd ring to tell us when this meeting was to take place. In the meantime, there was little we could do on the building front.

When we started keeping the pigs, I had approached a local greengrocer and arranged to buy all his scrap and unsold produce, and to collect it three times a week. This works very well indeed provided you are not worried about your image. To be seen lugging paper sacks and boxes of damaged fruit and vegetables, not to mention cauliflower trimmings and other such delicacies, out from the back of the shop to the car does nothing for your charisma, but it did the pigs, the hens, the sheep and sometimes even us, very well.

In fact, the output from the shop amazed me. As a race, we waste far too much. Many of the things were perfect but they just hadn't sold before the next delivery arrived from the wholesalers. This particular shop supplied fruit and vegetables to the local hotels and restaurants so they stock all sorts of unusual and exotic things.

When I arrived home with the swag, the hens knew very well what was coming. They'd cackle and crow – crowding around the back of the car and hopping up into the boot if I took my eyes off it.

Those who had been down in the fields, hearing the excitement, would scramble through hedges, ditches and fences, up to the lane – then set off up the hill to the yard in a pelter of flapping wings and peddling legs. They'd take the corner at the top of the lane like motorbikes at a TT event and arrive in the yard in a scramble of dishevelled feathers.

In general, we cooked only the root crops for the pigs, but they also had all the greens they could eat plus a few apples and tomatoes. The rest of the haul was given to the chickens, who did very well indeed. They still do. Within weeks, the chickens became very experienced at coping with these additions to their diet. Different hens have different preferences but they all know not to touch chillis, although the seeds look attractive, and that lemons, limes, rhubarb, and ginger are not to their taste. They also dislike mushrooms, radishes, spring onions and those scrunchy iceberg lettuces that are such a regular feature on our own table. This is slightly worrying as they love the ordinary lettuces.

Then, as now, grapes were the favourite, and as their shelf life is short, they nearly always featured in the waste bags. The hens very soon learned how to unzip a banana, to extract the seeds from a cucumber, to deal with an orange or an avocado, and most welcome of all, the huge red watermelons, full of juice and seeds. Fights broke out amongst the usually peace-loving residents of the hen house for a ringside position around a melon. If I was a good woman, I would cut the melon into small pieces so that it was more equally shared, but it amused me to watch the stratagems and hostilities that ensued when a melon was produced. Sometimes they continued long after the melon had gone.

We'd inherited a cockerel, and that first spring, before we started a family planning programme, we were inundated with chicks.

We were enchanted when the first hen walked out of the wood with a line of fluffy babies behind her. The enchantment declined however after six or seven similar events and was non-existent by the tenth. No sense of responsibility have our hens.

We had to put each family into a run for the first few weeks as the babies were very vulnerable to predators. So Brian built a chick complex. This was like an extended bungalow apartment block, and the quarters were allocated on the basis of how many chicks each hen had. Those with thirteen babies were given the larger apartments and those with only three or four were given more modest premises.

It is sad to have to admit it, but there is corruption everywhere. As Brian pointed out, two hens with quite modest families were given superior quarters, and although I tended to deny it at the time, it was because they had some particular quality that amused or entertained me.

Leo, the Siamese cat, spent hours looking through the wire at the babies. They grew quite confident and were not afraid of him, but I wondered what would happen when they were released to freely range. He was used to hens but partly grown chicks were another matter. But in the event, he took very little notice of them. I recall one or two misunderstandings on the matter, but the vast majority of those chicks survived and the girls went on to become middle-aged biddies who laid us many breakfast eggs.

We had heard nothing from the architect for some weeks, so we rang him.

He was not available.

We rang a week later and a week after that – still without success.

By now it was early June and we were getting desperate. We talked of bringing in another architect, but it meant starting all over again. Brian suggested talking to the council directly to see if we could reach some sort of agreement on the outstanding points, so to that end, we rang them early one Monday morning to try and arrange an interview.

Lo and behold – we were amazed to hear that our architect and builder were to have a meeting with the planning department, regarding our plans, that very morning. Since there was only half an hour before the meeting was due to start and Mama was still in bed, it was impossible for us to attend, but the council official concerned promised to phone us afterwards to tell us what had happened.

An hour later he rang us to say that the architect had phoned to cancel the morning meeting and it was now to be held at two o'clock that afternoon. This was much better. We had a deal stored up to say to that architect. So, we got Mama ready and in the car, and off we went.

It was only an hour's journey and we arrived a little early, so we sat in the car outside the council offices and waited for the establishment to return from lunch. It was just before the 1983 general election and the party bandwagons were out on the streets. The cars were decorated with balloons and ribbons, and loudhailers were flinging the Oxbridge tones around the grey stone streets.

The Conservative Party convoy stopped just by us, and all the posh city suits got out of their cars and disappeared into the public loo – one of the grottiest in Wales as I happened to know – and which sported a graffiti notice that read 'The English need Welsh Water – please give generously'. For some reason this amused me very much indeed.

Just before two o'clock, we clutched up our papers, locked Mama in the car, and entered the hallowed portals of the council offices to start the onslaught. The architect and builder hadn't arrived, so we sat in the waiting area, popping out every few minutes to see Mama.

Half an hour later and still A and B hadn't arrived. Here we were, paying them to support us through the minefield of planning regulations, and once again, they had let us down.

Three quarters of an hour – and still we're sitting there – Mama too by this time. She was restless in the car and had collected a small party of passers-by, who were extremely indignant that we had left this poor old soul on her own to 'shout' for us.

At five minutes to three, the planning officers suggested we start the meeting on our own. We shuffled our papers and tried to look confident – when into the room walked the architect and builder.

Even to my relatively inexperienced eye, they weren't behaving quite normally. The room was filled with noise and bonhomie and I formed the opinion that some of that bonhomie was out of a bottle – probably a series of bottles.

'Now what's all this damn rubbish about these plans?' demanded the architect – a chap in his early thirties pushing his florid countenance up into the astonished face of the senior planning officer, who was sixty, if a day.

'Are you a qualified, man? Because I can tell you, I am.'

Sixty-if-a-day looked at him thoughtfully for a moment before querying what he was qualified for.

It was soon almost a brawl – the council people dropping their reserve and the verbal arrows being discharged from both sides. Brian delivered several very telling broadside swipes and Mama, who was enjoying it very much, crowed and shouted encouragement.

It was like something from a twisted dream – almost unbelievable and extremely worrying although the humour of the situation could not but be apparent.

Suffice it to say, we did eventually reach agreement with the council and they were kind enough to let us have our patio doors, although we had to inset them by six feet, thus forming the patio on which we now spend so much time. I think they felt sorry for us – they cannot have had many such meetings. It was an immense relief to have it settled.

So now we turned our guns on to the builder and began to agitate for a starting date. Things were hotting up at last.

The first big summer job on the farm was the sheep shearing. This is quite a pleasurable business as although the ewes dislike being collected up, they *are* pleased to be rid of their hot tangled fleeces. For a while they look quite trim and clean.

It was a warm, hazy summer morning with diamonds of dew hanging from the tips of the grass stems. The farm echoed with birdsong, including the cuckoos who seemed far more numerous than in any of our previous homes. Dai arrived early so we could gather the sheep before the heat of the day. They were put into the lambing meadow and a few at a time were herded into the bakehouse yard.

Our treatment pen, as the vet rather grandiosely called it, is an old bakehouse, complete with oven and chimney. It has a lean-to shelter on one side, so we have two indoor pens with a small fenced yard serving both of them.

Dai was shearing in the lean-to and Brian was collecting up the ewes to be sheared and handing them, one at a time, to Dai as he finished the last one. I was folding the fleeces in the special way required by the Wool Marketing Board – with the creamy white wool that has been next to the ewe's skin on the outside. This enables the wool graders to assess its quality easily. Mama sat in the car watching. A blank look of incomprehension on her face.

All the lambs stood in a baaing crowd around the gate waiting for their mamas to be let out. As the gate opened, the baaing would redouble in volume and then die back again as that particular ewe found her lamb and sauntered off with it.

Brian and I both had a go at shearing, but it is an art acquired with difficulty and much practice, and as the price of the fleece depends, to some extent, on how well the shearer did his work, we soon gave up.

Most of the professional shearers seem to have learned to be ambidextrous, as it helps if the clippers can be used by either hand without moving the sheep too many times. Needless to say, the ewes struggle to be free unless they are held in the tight grip of the shearer's knees, so the fewer times he has to relax his grasp, thus giving them a chance to escape, the better.

The sheep are sometimes caught by the clippers and this worried me a lot at first. I fussed among them with a bottle of antiseptic, dabbing at the little wounds, but in fact this was quite unnecessary as they heal very quickly on their own and do not seem to cause any problems. But most shearers dislike an audience for this reason.

Earlier in the year we had received a form through the post asking if we were intending to produce wool this summer. This had sounded very grand and we had replied to say that we were indeed hoping to produce wool. After all, we wool producers must stick together – we had all of twenty-two fleeces to help swell the range of Marks and Sparks cardies.

But when the time came for the wool to be collected, we were missed out, and as time went by and our crop wasn't picked up, we rang the depot. They suggested that we deliver it to them, so we spent a morning trying to pack it into the car. Has anyone else tried to get twenty-two fleeces and three people into a Renault 5? It was a comfortable ride, if nothing else.

The wool depot is a high stone building about a hundred yards long and it was absolutely stuffed with bales of wool from floor to ceiling. Several men seemed to be working in a little hole between the bales. Further up the huge building, in another hole, there was a tiny office and a big weighing machine.

One of the men came out to help. He could see we were as green as grass and he was very kind. He called over two other men and we watched as they weighed and graded our wool. There are many different grades and our Welsh ewes do not produce a very high-quality fleece, but it was thought to be quite good for the breed.

It was a very satisfying outing although the car smelled of lanolin from the fleeces for nearly a year.

Amongst the friends we had made was a farmer from up in the mountains. He had been in the services for much of his early working life and on leaving the Army had returned with his wife to the land of her birth. Together they had rebuilt an old farmhouse to make a beautiful, interesting home, with stupendous views. It was a real eyrie – a different world altogether from the homesteads down on the coast or in the valleys. Winter began for them much earlier and lasted much longer. He was in snow for much of the winter while it was apparently rare on our farm down in the valley. In fact, the house was little more than a mile from us but 700 feet of that were vertical. It was immediately next to heaven in more ways than one.

It had been painstakingly and lovingly restored and was surrounded by miles of open mountain, which in summer was carpeted with wild flowers – the haunt of the wild things of nature. In winter there must have been many occasions when they were cut off from the rest of the world – when the winds shook the old walls and the snow was hurled against their windows – but they must have been warm and snug inside. The wife was beginning to suffer with arthritis, so they planned to move back to England to be nearer their family. For this reason the farmer had sold his sheep and the house was on the market.

He rang us up one day – could we do with a sheepdog?

Brian and I talked about it. We were quite useless even at driving the ewes on our own, and apart from help with the sheep, a farm dog had other uses.

We rang him back and agreed to go and see the dog. He explained that it was only a year old and had not really worked but it came from good sheepdog stock and we'd probably make something of it. In fact, he'd got two working dogs, but he didn't feel he could offer us the second one as it was already twelve and really past its useful working life. So one limpid, rose-pink evening, we drove up into the mountains and were introduced to Ben, the young black and white collie. He was excited and eager to please, wagged his tail and cowed his head on the ground. He tentatively took a biscuit I'd brought and ran off a little way to enjoy it privately. He seemed an obedient, gentle creature and we agreed to have him.

Then we were introduced to Spot, the twelve-year-old collie. He had a comical Basil Brush look – eyes and ears alert, waiting for a command – one front leg bent and distorted from arthritis and almost a grin on his funny old face. He had been born in a cave on the mountain and his mother had come to the farm for scraps each day. One day, our friend had followed her back to her litter and found her with two pups – one recently dead and Spot, who was weak but alive. He'd taken mother and pup back to the farm and kept them as working dogs ever since. Sadly, the mother dog had died a few months previously.

The farmer was to be away for the next fortnight and it was intended that Spot was to be shut up in his kennel for this period, with a distant neighbour driving over to feed him each day. This sounded rather hard on the old dog, so we offered to have him for the fortnight. This saved his incarceration in his kennel and would help Ben to overcome the shock of his change of home.

By the end of the fortnight, however, we had grown so attached to Spot that we begged to be allowed to keep him permanently.

They got used to us very quickly. We kept them on leads for the first day or two and then they were left to run loose as we did our jobs about the farm. They always stayed close at hand and were a constant source of amusement. If we were indoors, they sat together on the doorstep.

At first, Ben was a problem with visitors. He wasn't used to strangers and he'd run up to our visitors, wagging his tail and trying to jump up to lick their faces. It was annoying, but we managed to break him of this habit quite quickly.

They were outdoor dogs, as are almost all working dogs, and they did not come into the house at all. They had a large wooden box apiece filled with straw in one of the stables and this is where they ate and slept. Each evening they were paid off for their day's work – the pay consisting of two old frying pans filled with meaty goodies conned from our butcher pal, plus a couple of handfuls of cereal. Early in the morning, their stable door was opened, and even now, some years later, it is still pleasurable to start the day with such a greeting. Ben bounces up and down in an ecstasy of excitement, while Spot waddles out to nuzzle my hand for confirmation that all is well with the world. Life certainly wouldn't be the same without them, although as working dogs, they leave a great deal to be desired.

The cats adapted to the change very well – they had ceased to be very much surprised at anything. Leo dreamed up one or two new swear words, but by and large, we all settled down very comfortably together.

Chapter Nine

As the summer advanced, the campers started to arrive. Many of them had been coming here for years. Some families had spent their annual holiday on this farm for four generations. The great-grandparents had camped here in the thirties with only bicycles, or at best, a motorbike, for transport. Now the grandchildren came, often with luxury caravans, bringing with them the great-grandchildren.

When we bought the farm, we hadn't given much thought to the campsite. We knew, rather vaguely, that we didn't want a repeat of the crowds we'd found on our brief visit here shortly before we moved in, and I think we felt it would be a simple matter to reduce the numbers to more acceptable proportions. This is *MUCH* easier said than done, however.

Over that first winter, small collections of campers from the Outward Bound Centre had stayed on the site, and we'd had Venture Scouts and similar groups. In general, this had been a pleasure – they were usually very nice people who had respected both our privacy and our property. At

Whitsun we'd had a Girl Guide camp and several small family groups, which again was nice – but as the weather started to improve, the holidaymakers started ringing up and turning up in droves.

It is very difficult to turn people away when they have been coming here for years and knew more of the history of the farm than we did ourselves. So, we did our best, but inevitably we were obliged to turn many people away and this frequently earned much abuse and hassle. Those who were already installed were cheering us on, and those who were being turned away were loud in their condemnation of these upstart newcomers who fancied themselves as country landowners. There was no pleasing everybody.

In an effort to help the milkman, who runs his round almost at a loss during the winter months, I offered to take milk for the campers, little realising that they would turn up for it at 6.30am, when I was in a refreshing sleep, having been up several times in the night to deal with Mama. Or they'd complain that it was creamy, and they didn't want today's order, but could they have some tomorrow. As I'd paid the full price for what we already had, this left me at a substantial loss.

Then they'd come and complain that the people in the next tent were making too much noise late at night – had left their rubbish scattered about – had set fire to the bracken – were shooting the birds with a catapult – were breaking milk bottles on the beach – were letting the dog wee up against their tent – and with a thousand other problems.

They'd come up to the house with a broken gas fitting. Did we happen to have a spare? If not, where was the nearest stockist and could they use the phone? Or, the car/ boat battery was flat and could we charge it up? Or they'd got one wheel of the car over the cliff and could we come down with the tractor and pull the car to safety? Or they'd dropped the anchor over the side of their dinghy without first tying it to a cleat and could they borrow a rake to fish for it?

The variations were endless. Some were very funny indeed and it was difficult not to laugh. One couple had tied their tent to the car. The wind had increased one evening and as they were short of tent pegs, it really was quite sensible to put two stays out from the tent to each side of the back of the car.

It was not sensible however to drive off in the car the following morning without untying the stays. The whole equipage had gone off down the campsite meadow at several miles an hour. The tent had collapsed on top of the contents and all was chaos. I happened to get involved as a partly used tin of condensed milk had tipped upside down and was generously spread amongst the clothes and the sleeping bags. They brought the lot up to the farm to be washed, and it took me ages to get that sticky goo off the front of the washing machine and the floor – we seemed to have trodden it everywhere.

Then the phone would ring and the caller would insist that I tell the Crawfords that Tim would not after all be joining them on Sunday or that Tom was coming tomorrow and could he please be picked up from the station? Or I would be directed to the Hunters with a message that their deep freeze had died – that the cat had been taken ill – that

Jill and John had a new baby daughter – that Grandma had broken her false teeth, and where were the spare ones – and umpteen other things.

We had the police here at 3.30am, and the fire brigade at 5.30am.

We had couples trying to get pregnant and others trying *not* to get pregnant. Also some who did get pregnant, whether or not they were trying. They are all on holiday and have time to talk, so I became the recipient of numerous secrets.

Inevitably there were small accidents, or people who were unwell and needed either sundry medical attention, a listening ear in times of a family dispute, or merely sympathy for a patch of bad luck. It was all quite a responsibility and, from time to time, exceedingly tiresome.

On the other hand, we have met many interesting, amusing and caring people, whose friendship we value. Sometimes they came with baskets of plums or strawberries for us – bottles of homemade wine, jam or pickles – tomatoes or plants from their gardens – pictures they've painted – photos they've taken on the farm and many other things. I've had my face beautified by a budding beautician and we've all had our hair cut by a visiting hairdresser.

We've had 18th birthday parties, engagement parties and innumerable bunfights and barbecues.

We've had to play cricket with the Scouts against the rest of the campers and rounders with the rest against the Guides. We've had chair lifts, barn dances and joined in Nigerian Guiding songs. Over the years it has become one big extended family for us, but that first year, it was overwhelming – like a great big uncontrollable animal.

Practical jokes were, and still are, very popular. One group had their toilet stolen from their toilet tent in the middle of the night. Very inconvenient it was too, for them.

The following night the toilet was replaced but the tent removed. There it stood in glorious isolation, decorated with streamers of loo roll. You could see it for miles.

But in spite of the fun, there were many occasions when we were infuriated at the constant interruptions. The ordinary domestic chores took twice as long as usual, and each day sped past with very little advancement on the home front.

But there were bound to be some disadvantages to living in this super place. In a sense it was a privilege to feel that the visitors enjoyed coming to stay. I was mindful of my past when, as an ardent seven-year-old and a regular member of the church Sunday school, I prayed that 'I would be able to make other people well and happy'. I was not to know how literally my prayers were to be answered in later years.

In June we had a notice through the post reminding us of our obligation to dip our sheep and giving us the dates between which this must be done. It is a requirement of the law that all sheep have to be dipped in a special chemical at least once a year. Sometimes it has to be done twice a year. This is to eradicate sheep scab and other major diseases. The local Ministry of Agriculture have to be advised of the time and place of the dipping so that, if they choose, they can come and check the strength of the dipping solution and ensure that the sheep are kept in the bath for the requisite sixty seconds. It is an expensive and time-consuming business, so a few farmers try to cut corners by not adding a sufficient amount of the chemical, or by allowing the sheep to emerge from the dip before it has really soaked through the fleece into their skin.

We had been told that the men from the Ministry do not always attend the dipping but covered a random number of farms, so we didn't know if they were coming to us or not. We sincerely hoped they wouldn't come, as in the past, we had never been called upon to drop a relatively large animal into a big bath and push its head under the water three times before assisting it to emerge, and we felt that even with help from Dai Gwyn, we may well make a hash of it. I was also worried in case we fell into the dip water by mistake – apparently this is not unusual. The dipping bath is a hole in the ground, six feet or so deep, the sides and bottom of which have been lined with brickwork so that it holds water. You need to stand on the very edge of the dip with a struggling, lunging animal in your arms, trying to hold it over the water before you let it go, so for some seconds, with each ewe, you are in a rather vulnerable position. To make matters worse we had recently bought in a lot more sheep. Our farmer mentor/ friend had suggested that we increase the flock as the land needed to be grazed more closely. So we had over a hundred ewes to deal with.

The day of our dipping dawned golden with the promise of the heat to come. We sat on the old wooden seat in the garden, scrunching toast and listening to the birds.

The gulls were squabbling over something they had found on the beach – their raucous shrieks seemed to echo back from the mountains to mix with the gentle liquid 'wheeet' of the redstarts.

Dai arrived just before seven o'clock and was keen to start gathering the sheep before the heat of the day increased. They have to be allowed to cool off before the immersion commences so the earlier they are rounded, the better. Friend Audrey from the village had arrived and was in charge of Mama so we were ready for the off.

We now had six legs apiece to do the collecting, as Brian had Ben and I had Spot. We all set off in different directions to the far corners of the farm and, in our separate ways, tried out our dog-handling skills. I seemed to be doing quite well on my patch. I'd walked over to the southern limits of the farm where Spot had picked up the ewes we could see and we'd got them into a small group that seemed quite content to be driven slowly in front of us.

For nearly half a mile this worked very well. In the distance I could see Brian on the campsite with a similar little group he had collected, and Spotty and I slowly made our way towards him, hoping to meet up with him where the campsite meadow joined the rest of the farm.

As Brian got to the campsite gate, however, his ewes found themselves with a violent disinclination to go through that gate. They stopped – looked at Ben as if to assess his capabilities – and scattered in all directions.

Brian was extremely annoyed – and that's putting it very mildly indeed. In the shouting and the general melee, my ewes decided to panic too. They set off in a gallop, at right angles to Spot and me – then turned to the right again – back to where we had started from.

Spotty tore after them – but the poor old dog couldn't run as fast as they did. He was absolutely flat out and still they were gaining on him. All this on a hot morning when the sheep weren't supposed to be allowed to get heated.

Poor Spot came back full of misery and embarrassment. He looked at me out of the corner of his eyes, expecting a scold. He knew we'd made a mull of it – his anguish was acute and entirely understandable. I knew exactly how he felt. All I could do was to hurl abuse at those ewes, now peaceably grazing, and walk back to where we had started from.

But the ewes all knew what was coming and made it plain they had no intention of being herded in a direction they really had no wish to go. Spot and I did everything we could think of – we ran – I shouted – I waved my arms – and Spotty barked – until we were both exhausted and it was clear that, for the moment at least, the ewes had won.

While I was battling in one corner of the farm, Dai had got his ewes into the meadow by the dipping pen and had gone back to help Brian with his sheep. He'd taken over from Brian, got the ewes through the campsite gate, and was driving them the last 200 yards into the pen.

Brian, with Ben at heel, walked over to where I was having such difficulty. He was still fuming from his little fracas by the campsite gate and was in no mood to tolerate any further nonsense.

The ewes looked at him suspiciously. They separated into several small groups and made off in different directions.

Brian peremptorily ordered Ben off after one group. But Ben had had enough – he sat on the ground panting, his tongue lolling out of his mouth, and made it clear that if Brian wanted the ewes chased, then he'd have to chase them himself.

This reduced my ever-loving to a rage of unprecedented proportions. Flaying the air with his crook and roaring like a bull elephant, he gave Ben a potted history of his past and probable future. It was an eloquent and comprehensive address that reduced both Ben and Spot to shivering heaps of canine fur and reduced me to helpless mirth.

As the tirade reached its crescendo, Ben decided to absent himself from the scene and set off home as fast as his legs would carry him.

Brian turned an even richer shade of puce at the sight of Ben scurrying homewards, deaf to all demands, and if it hadn't been that Dai Gwyn arrived shortly afterwards to help us, I think we would still be out there. I began to wonder if we were cut out for sheep farming – none of the other farmers seemed to have these problems. But Dai has a very calming way with the sheep. Within minutes all was under control and the ewes were moving slowly across the land to the track leading to the dipping pen. They moved easily now, without stress, and were shut into the meadow with their pals to await their bath. All it needed was a bit of experience, tinged with patience.

We retired to the kitchen for a much-needed cup of tea and to relieve the friend who had been sitting with Mother.

All the activity had not gone unnoticed on the campsite – several people had asked what was happening and when we returned to the dipping pen, we found a small crowd of onlookers – some of whom had brought their deckchairs to watch the fun.

I hated it. It reminded me of the women who sat and knitted as they watched the tumbrils roll up to the guillotine at the time of the French Revolution. The ewes were frightened – they choked and spluttered in the evil-smelling solution, then dragged themselves up the steps out of the dip, their fleeces, although short after shearing, still heavy with the liquid. They'd become separated from their lambs and they just wanted to get away from the human race.

The following day, however, it was a different scene. The ewes had found their lambs and all were boasting clean white fluffy fleeces. They still smelled of disinfectant, but we knew they were safe from fly strike for a week or two at least. This is a particularly unpleasant problem that sheep suffer from. Blowflies lay their eggs, usually on the rear end of a sheep, where there may be droppings on the fleece. The maggots hatch out and literally eat their way into the flesh. Sometimes they will eat through the flesh on the tail to the bone. Or they will work forwards, up to the back and the shoulders, if the infestation is not treated in time. Prior to shearing, this bit of villainy goes on under three or four inches of fleece, so it is very difficult to detect. Even after shearing it is necessary to be very vigilant, especially in hot, humid weather. Sometimes a ewe can rid herself of a small patch of maggot by rubbing against a post or a tree but generally they need help. This is given by cutting all the wool off the infected area and douching the flesh with a special oil. This kills the maggots, all of which are eating their way into the flesh head on, so that only their rear ends are visible – much like a honeycomb – so there are thousands in a small area. It is quite revolting and a strong stomach is a great asset when you are called upon to deal with it. But the oil heals the flesh within a few days and the ewes do not appear to suffer unduly if they are treated in time.

So our first dipping was conducted successfully. Neither of us had fallen into the dip, and our ham-fisted efforts had not been witnessed by the men from the Ministry. As usual, Dai Gwyn had done us proud.

Then Mama went missing one day. The first time since we'd moved to Wales. For several weeks prior to our move from Essex, she'd had trouble with her right leg. The doctor thought it was a mild attack of rheumatism and although I was sorry it caused her pain, there was no denying that it restricted her wanderings and therefore made her easier to keep an eye on. She was also very disinclined to get up in the mornings. We always took her tea over to the caravan as soon as we were up, but whereas she had in the past got herself up at a leisurely pace and started the day with most of her clothes on – albeit perhaps in the wrong order – she now stayed in bed.

We allowed her to remain there until our mid-morning coffee break, when we met for a snack and a chat about the day's doings. But when this was over, we set about the business of getting her up.

In a way these late mornings were a bonus for us as we could go out on the farm together if there was a job that required four hands. Usually we were only a matter of a hundred yards or so from the house and the yard where the caravan stood, but these stolen morning hours were very pleasant. Once or twice we got too far from the caravan, and a sudden panic made us down tools and tear back home. But she never was in any difficulty.

Other than the few precious hours we had lately started to enjoy when Mama was in the day hospital, we had not been able to go out on our own together because of the need to be with her. Local babysitters were none too keen to keep us on their books, largely because, in our case, the 'baby' could quite well hurl a shoe or any other missile she could lay hands on at the poor sitters, of which there *had* to be two at a time.

On this particular occasion, I'd been called down to the campsite to settle a dispute and Brian had gone indoors to answer the phone, leaving Mama sitting comfortably in a chair in the yard.

When Brian went back out to the yard some five minutes later the chair was empty.

He called and searched the immediate area but there was no sign of her. I came back and joined in the search and a party of Guides from the campsite also helped. Some of them were really frightened of her, as the previous day, when they had come up to the house to collect their milk, she had shouted at them and told them to 'clear off'. She was always telling people to clear off and throwing anything she could lay hands on at them. It is fortunate that her aim was poor, and it says a lot for the Guides that they could bother to spend their holiday looking for her when she had been so awful to them. Interestingly, I never remembered Mama using this phrase during her coherent life.

After an hour, and there still being no sign of her, we rang the police. We could only assume that someone from the campsite had offered her a lift. Anyone seeing an elderly person walking with a limp could have offered to give her a lift into the village – she could still sound quite plausible in a halting way, from time to time.

Just as the policemen arrived, one of the Guides came to tell us she could hear noises from a patch of stinging nettles and bracken some way up the steep path at the back of the house. The undergrowth is six feet high and very thick in this secluded wooded spot. I had passed it several times in the search, but as it had looked to be untrodden for many years, I had not for one moment imagined that Mama could be hiding there.

We waded into it and there sat Mama on the ground, having removed her skirt and her pants, presumably with the intention of spending a penny. Our relief was terrific. Poor soul – she had sat in some stinging nettles and was badly stung but was clearly glad to see us. It was a brief moment of great joy.

But as the policemen waded into the undergrowth she seemed to become aware of the stinging sensation on her bottom and she started to berate them soundly – for some reason it was their fault that she was in this state. They must have thought it was an unusual menage, as indeed it was.

She seemed to be deteriorating physically as well as mentally. Her speech was often quite poor, but she ate and slept well and seemed content enough. She was replacing more and more words with her humming, wailing noise. On her bad days it could be very wearing indeed, but on her good days she could still at this stage hold a somewhat disjointed conversation that could be understood. We were desperately anxious to get on with the new building and to get her indoors.

The builders had apparently got all the parts made, and as soon as the building regulations department of the local council was satisfied that the job was in accordance with their rules, it could all start.

It was to be a timber-framed affair. It is very exposed here and it seemed sensible to look at the colder, wetter countries and follow their building methods. Invariably, they have timber-framed structures, which are extremely well insulated and stand up to the rigours of extreme weather very well. Another advantage is that the inner skin and the roof are erected in a matter of days, so the interior is watertight before the outside brick walls are built.

So, there we were – poised for action – and after applying the boot to the backside via the telephone on a number of occasions, it was agreed that the fifteenth of August was to be the day of the great start.

We looked forward to it with great excitement – but it came and went without any sign of action. So, we roared and bellowed down the telephone until it was agreed that the twenty-fourth was to be the starting date.

That too came and went without any sign of a builder or his gear. The telephone wires must have been red hot as, late that afternoon, Brian gave vent to his feelings in a very acrimonious conversation with the building firm.

Two more definite dates were given – and passed – in the blissful quiet of a warm September calm, and still we were waiting.

Chapter Ten

On the afternoon of 13th September 1983, two days before the first anniversary of our arrival here, I drove home from work to find three strange men in the access lane, with a load of heavy machinery. They were actually about to start making the base for the new building. I could hardly believe it.

Within two hours they had built a ramp from the yard up to the site, and they promised to be back early next day.

Sure enough, soon after eight on the morrow – and they'd driven fifty miles – they cranked up their machines and all was activity.

Initially we had planned to make the foundations for the new building without professional help, but as it is vital that the base must fit the building accurately, we'd decided, on second thoughts, to have this additional work carried out by the people who were supplying the building. With hindsight it was most fortunate that we came to this decision, although at the time it was something of a worry as we were not able to pin the company down to a fixed price for this extra job. Their argument, which we fully understood, was based on the premise that although most of the site was solid bedrock already exposed from the blasting, the remaining quarter was an unknown quantity. The soil might be only a few inches deep in places and in others it may be several feet deep. However deep it was, it would be necessary to excavate it down to bedrock and then to build proper foundations back up to floor level. So, the price for the job would depend on how long it took to dig trenches down to bedrock, and then how much concrete and how many breeze blocks would be required to fill them back up again.

After weeks of warm, dry weather, the heavens opened and the yard was quickly reduced to a mud slick. We all paddled about in it and I ceased trying to maintain any proper standards of hygiene. Mud and water dripped into the tea and still we drank it – without any adverse effects as far as I know. The men were marvellous. In spite of the weather they went on working, so we did too.

As we might have guessed, difficulties were soon with us. Firstly, the soil to be excavated was a very soft sandy peat. As each scoopful was removed, the sides of the trench caved in, instead of leaving a nice vertical wall. After a couple of hours the excavations threatened to assume the proportions of a major archaeological dig. This meant that far more soil had to be excavated than would normally be the case – and yes, we had to pay a man with a large lorry to come and take the excess earth away.

Secondly, as the soil was removed, it became clear that the bedrock dropped away steeply, just beyond the part of the site that was cleared at the time of the blasting. Where we had hoped to extend the new building into what had been the cottage garden, there was a pocket of peat or a depression in the bedrock, and if we wanted to build out over that area, then we would have to remove all the soil in the hole down to the bedrock.

Many centuries ago, the sea had covered the hillock on which the house stands. It was one large rocky outcrop – the crevices and crannies of which became filled up with sand. As the sea receded, it left the sandy deposits in the creases. A plant would have gained a foothold, perhaps seeding its locality, making composts in which even more plants grew, and thus over the years, most of depressions on the knoll became covered with plant growth. We were clearly trying to build over what had been an ancient rock pool and the men were gloomy in their predictions of how deep this pool might have been. As Brian comfortingly pointed out, the sea pool off the campsite beach is over twelve feet deep in the middle *now* – probably more if the sandy bottom was scooped out, so our problem could assume quite mammoth proportions. What a Job's Comforter.

After a couple of days, they had dug to a depth of six feet and still they were bringing out the soft peat. We didn't have a sleepless night about it – we were too tired – but I did tend to keep worrying with our financial records as I could see that the base would cost substantially| more than the amount we had provisionally allowed for, and we would therefore need to find some additional funds from somewhere.

At the end of the third day, the trench was nine feet deep, and John the digger driver was convinced we were near to the bedrock. He didn't seem to have anything definite to base this on, so after he'd gone home, I got down into the trench with the garden spade, and had a dig of my own, prompted by sheer desperation. I spent some time down that hole and nothing I found led me to believe that the bedrock was within close reach. It is extraordinarily difficult to get soil out of a hole when you are nine feet down in it and have only the garden spade to hurl with. Several lots I tried to throw out came straight back on top of me – and Brian, who took the full force of one spadeful when he came to see what I was doing, suggested I leave it to the professionals. He didn't put it quite like that, but that was what he meant.

But, true enough, the following day, the bucket on the digger struck the rock in the bottom of the hole – over ten feet down. It was a marvellous feeling of relief. Having spent so much capital and endured so many problems with the blasting on the northern end of the site, to find that the southern end could not be developed would have been heartbreaking. I suppose we could have had a smaller extension, but it would have made life difficult. Even with the proposed full-size development, we would only have three quite modest bedrooms in total.

The next step was to clear away all the soil in the bottom of the trench to leave the rock exposed so that the council buildings inspector could give his approval to proceed. Then we had to fill the trench with concrete until there was a level platform on which to build two walls, a foot apart, back up to ground level. The middle of the walls was then to be filled with concrete.

The trenches were much wider than they should have been due to the soil from the sides having fallen in, and thus we had to order extra deliveries of the wet readymade concrete. This comes in those lorries with a snail-shaped container on the back and, when loaded, the vehicle is very heavy. We also had to order an additional load of breeze blocks.

It was exciting when the first delivery of cement arrived – the first step in the construction of the new wing. Until now, all had been destruction. The driver stopped at the bottom of the hill and walked up to look at the roadway. The final fifty yards from the bottom of the hill up into the yard is narrow, steep and with a vicious bend at the top. He did not like it. He did not like it at all. So having looked at the other options, he decided to take the farm track which runs around the base of the hill for 200 yards, and then take a wide grassy path which doubles back in a straight line, and at a lesser slope, into the yard.

We watched from the top of the hill as he drove the lorry slowly along the rutted farm road and then turned into the grass track. It seemed to be doing quite well for the first fifty yards – but the luck was not with us. Fifty yards from the site, one wheel of the lorry sank gently into one of the soft peaty holes and the entire equipage ground to a halt.

Even with assistance from the digger *and* our ancient tractor that wretched lorry of concrete would not budge. So, what did it do? It pumped its load out on to the grass and some of it is still there to this very day. John, the digger driver, was scooping up as much as he could in the bucket of the JCB, and ferrying it up to the trenches, but much of it was lost. It was not a good start.

There was no sign of a break in the weather and thus the grass track route to the site was unusable, so we had to come up with some other solution to get all the heavy deliveries up to where they were required.

At the back of us – some 150 yards away up through the woods – there is another house, originally a barn belonging to the farm. Several years previously, it had been sold, and the new owners had converted it into a separate home.

To reach it by road, our neighbours take the farm track which runs around the base of the hill, turning off the track to climb up a very steep narrow driveway that passes in front of their house. The path then deteriorates into a very bumpy tree-hung path that winds back down the hill to our farmyard. Very kindly, our neighbours agreed to let us use their part of this route, if the heavy vehicles found it to be passable.

The advantages with this path were that it was virtually straight and it had a good solid base that would withstand heavy vehicles. The disadvantages were that it was extremely steep in parts, and extremely narrow and overhung with very large trees in others. In one place there was a huge boulder sticking up through the surface, forcing vehicles up to a precarious angle, and large oaks, birch and pine trees crowded to overhang the worn stones.

It didn't seem possible that these huge lorries could pass through it – but the drivers sportingly decided to have a go. We spent several hours exposing the sides of the track, trimming back the overhanging trees and filling in the biggest holes in the surface, until it began to look hopeful. Ultimately the house itself would come on a lorry and would need to get as close to the site as possible so it was worth spending a few hours exploring the possibilities of this back entrance.

We rang the firm supplying the concrete to tell them we were ready to restart the deliveries. The first load arrived and we held our breath. The big JCB was used to help the lorry up the steep part of the hill, and then it took a rear position to steady the lorry as it crept down the old stone track into the farmyard. I stood in the yard as this huge grey vehicle slowly advanced through the trees, like an elephant emerging from the bush. It looked quite menacing – something to do with a horror movie maybe.

But it had arrived safely in the yard and a few moments of manoeuvring up the ramp and on to the site left it in a position to discharge its load directly into the trenches. It was a great moment.

After eight such deliveries, the novelty had worn off, however, and I was reverting to frantic sorties with the financial records and similar papers. Concrete is expensive as well as heavy.

Mama was enjoying the building project enormously. She sat in a comfortable armchair in front of her fire and watched through her window as we struggled in the mud and rain. Since moving to the farm we had spent a great deal of time with her, but there were inevitably occasions when she was on her own, while we worked in the vicinity, but out of her sight. But with all this visible activity going on, she had a constant source of entertainment. Periodically she would come out of the caravan and chat briefly to the workmen. She was always 'on her way to the shops' or 'going to the hairdresser'. Invariably she would be carrying her shopping bag, which would contain a miscellany of domestic items – perhaps her clock, two flower vases, several cups and a dinner plate. Off she would go down the hill at a brisk hobble. About thirty yards from home she would stop and sit on the low wall for a few moments. Then she would womble back up the hill, have another brief chat with the workmen, before climbing back into the caravan.

She couldn't sustain anything more than the briefest of exchanges without getting into difficulties, so she kept her remarks short and the wailing additions to a minimum. It was interesting that she could sound so normal and hide her condition so readily. It seemed to me that she was almost learning to cope with her mental shortcomings. It was only when she was relaxed and not on her guard that her conversation deteriorated and the wailing became more pronounced.

We had explained Mama's problems to the workmen and they knew to warn us if she left the yard area without us knowing. They were nice family men and they each seemed to have a relative, or knew of someone, with a similar illness so they promised to keep an eye on her. However, when she emerged from the caravan fetchingly attired in a fur hat, a thick woolly cardigan, a pair of National Health net incontinence pants, odd shoes and nothing else, they all found themselves an urgent job in the shed.

I came back a moment or so later to find the caravan door open and no Mama. We pounded off down the hill and found her sitting on the wall – quite happy and unconcerned. She couldn't understand what the fuss was about – and indeed, what did it matter? She was safe and contented enough – only the bystanders felt any embarrassment.

What a strange race we are. Mama was the person with the illness, but she appeared to have little conception of it – whereas we were fit and well but suffered for her.

She seemed to be entering a period when her clothes worried her. She constantly changed her clothing, often to get the new lot on in the wrong order – or in the wrong places. Cardigans were often put on the lower half with a leg in each arm and the fronts tied in a bundle at her waist. But mostly the clothes on her lower half were removed, either entirely, or down to her underclothes.

On the advice of the Sister at the day hospital, we contacted a lady from social services and she came to review the situation. She pointed out that the mirror in the bedroom of the caravan was small and only reflected an image from the waist upwards, and thus Mama, looking at herself in the mirror, didn't notice that her bottom half wasn't as it should be. So we put in a mirror that reflected a full-length image, but it didn't have the required effect.

Likewise, any handy container – a flower vase, the sugar basin, a plant pot, a vegetable dish or similar vessel – was used as a loo, and according to our friend from social services, this was because Mama could not always find her loo. So, we took the door off the wretched small apartment… and then she wouldn't use the loo at all.

For some time she had ceased to use the handle to flush the loo, so thinking that she may not recognise the toilet for what it was, we hung a length of chain with a handle on the end of it over the loo so that it more closely resembled the toilet she had used in her own home for most of her life.

But neither of these amendments made any difference. She continued with her wayward fashions and her uninhibited toilet arrangements, and we all had to make the best of it.

At last the foundations for the new wing were finished and the actual house was due to arrive. It was a moment of great hope. It was all to come packed on a low-loader lorry and as I wanted to record the arrival of my new home as it entered the village, I drove along the main road to the lay-by halfway up the hill and waited with the camera poised for action.

It was pouring with rain, and after sitting in the car for half an hour, I got bored, so when the truck hailed into view, I very nearly missed it. The lorry driver, suddenly aware that someone in the lay-by was pointing a camera at him, thought he must be committing some traffic offence, so he rammed the brakes on, and my precious house very nearly carried on down the hill without the truck. I was aware of the startled face in the cab as the whole lot slid sideways past me on the steep, wet road.

My face must have been equally as startled, as for a brief moment, I visualised the home of my dreams reduced to matchwood in the road.

But it all survived and I followed it on down the road to our turning.

It all looked very precarious as it edged its way along the farm road, but it arrived safely at the bottom of our hillock and almost everybody came down to marvel at the sight. The driver got out and eyed me rather peevishly, muttering some comment about people who cause a distraction on the roads.

After some refreshment, he was taken to see the steep back route to the site. He nearly had an apoplectic fit. He walked backwards and forwards, declaring that it was an impossibility and that he'd have to take the whole lot back to the depot.

This amused the other workmen no end. They'd been laying bets as to his probable reaction. He was a pessimistic, grumbling character, but he was marvellous with that truck. He eventually negotiated that huge vehicle up the very steep hill – slowly and with the greatest precision – and then down through the trees into the yard.

Where the huge boulder on one side of the path had forced the concrete lorries up to a frightening angle, he had the JCB driver dump several loads of shale on the other side of the path so that the truck, with the house perched on top of it, stayed roughly vertical as it bumped over the obstruction. It was a stupendous moment when it arrived in the yard. It had taken over three hours to get 200 yards.

The men lost no time in unloading the parts. It all had to be laid out in a certain order. Brian and I tried to help but we were obviously in the way as we didn't know which bits had to be laid where. The science of the loading now became apparent. Not only had they balanced the load evenly on the truck but they had packed it in such a way that when it was unpacked, it could be piled in the order in which it would be required.

Several times that evening, we went out in the dark with a torch to gloat over the piles of bits – it hardly seemed believable that it had actually arrived and would be erected in less than a week.

It rained that night and I had hideous visions of the wood warping as it lay on the wet ground, but the following morning gave us a fresh, duck-egg blue sky and clear, rain-washed air.

The men set to work and it was amazing just how quickly it developed. It was like a life-size version of Lego. The walls and roof trusses were up in three days – and the roof, felted and battened, in another three. It looked huge inside with no interior walls. Like a big barn.

From that time, every little job that was finished became a thrill. The weather remained fine and Dai Gwyn was able to start on the exterior breeze-block walls. The walls of timber-framed houses have a number of different layers and this is why they are so much warmer than conventional brick buildings. Starting from the inside, our new wing has a wall of plasterboard with a foil backing, then a six-inch-thick layer of fibreglass wool; behind that there are plywood sheets – half an inch thick, made for outdoor use and with a thick bituminised felt backing. Then there is a two-and-a-half-inch air gap. On the outside of that there is a wall of concrete blocks, followed by two separate coats of plaster and finally two coats of weatherproof paint. Each section of wall is on a different level – the lowest on the outside, rising to the highest on the inside, so there is no possibility of water penetration.

We had agreed with the builders that they would erect the shell of the house, finish the roof, put in the windows and hang the exterior doors. After that we were to be on our own.

We were sorry to see the men go. During the three weeks they had worked on the house, we had developed a good relationship with them. They were a jolly nice crowd and gave us lots of technical hints and advice. We seemed to have gone through quite a lot together but I suppose they have this feeling on every job.

It was marvellous to have the building up and watertight. Just before we went to bed on the night the workmen finally left, Brian and I sat on old boxes in front of the non-existent fireplace in the new sitting room, drinking our cocoa and trying to visualise what it would look like when it was finished.

It had seemed to me that when the workmen left, the bulk of the job was over – but as Brian outlined the working programme for the next few months, I could suddenly see that we'd barely started.

The weather had been lovely for a week or more – lovely crisp bright days fading into still cool evenings, but with no hint of frost. Brian was anxious to finish building the breeze-block walls on the outside of the wooden shell, so that the exterior could be completed before the onset of the winter weather. The breeze blocks had been delivered to a site at the bottom of the hill, and while Dai continued with the wall, Brian and I loaded the blocks on to the small trailer and drove them up the hill to the new house.

After a while, Brian joined Dai on the blocking and I was loading and unloading the blocks on my own. There seemed a great many of them, but I was comforted by the thought that I must be losing several unwanted pounds of midriff. However, when I heaved my aching body onto the scales that evening, I found that I had put on at least one pound. I cannot understand this phenomenon, which was to dog me throughout the entire development project.

Every evening, after Dai had gone home, Brian installed the interior electrics. This had to be done in two stages – the first part, *before* the walls were plastered, and the final part *after* they were plastered.

After the progress we had made in the previous few weeks, the blocking and the electrics seemed tedious, time-consuming tasks. But it all went on quite satisfactorily so that the blocking was almost finished before the weather broke, a week or two later.

As the rain lashed down, they made a start on the interior walls of Mama's bedsitting room. It seemed strange to be able to move the walls at will – to adjust the size of the room. We moved them backwards and forwards several times before agreeing the exact position. We were even able to measure the furniture that was to go into this room and thus plan the walls to get the maximum use of the available space. It was really very useful.

I had a glorious day in Aberystwyth choosing the bathroom suites and the tiles for our bathroom and Mama's cloakroom. It was very exciting. Our water supply tends to be dark and peaty from time to time – often the bathwater looks like weak tea – so pale-coloured sanitary ware seemed inadvisable. After many changes of mind, I finally chose a plum-coloured suite for Mama and beige for us – and felt very modern and sophisticated. For months afterwards, the post brought brochures for the latest bathrooms and all the gleaming suites were white or in very pale pastel colours.

We also bought a second-hand Jotul wood-burning stove with a large back boiler. This was to have pride of place in the new sitting room, and would provide the domestic hot water *and* run four radiators.

Brian was an electrician one minute, plumber or chippy the next, and as a diversion, did a bit of farming or engineering. There was never a dull moment.

We were still living in the old cottage but spending more and more time in the new wing. We'd had a problem with the patio doors in the new sitting room since the four doors were three-quarters of an inch bigger than the frame that came with them – so the seals wouldn't meet when they were closed.

We rang the firm that had supplied them, and a little man came out to look. He just could not believe it. He spent all day trying the glass panels in every possible combination – but still those blessed doors were too big for the frame they were supposed to fit into. Somehow or other, he seemed to think it was my fault – and I found myself apologising that he'd had such trouble.

By four o'clock in the afternoon it was finally clear to him that the Chinese jigsaw puzzle could not be solved without amendment to either the doors, or to the frame –

so he decided to take one door away. We solemnly carried it out to his van and off he went with it, leaving us with a hole some four feet wide – through which the winter winds howled.

This was extremely inconvenient as we had taken to bringing Mama into the new wing as soon as she was up and sitting her in an old armchair, almost buried in coats and blankets and with two hot-water bottles to cuddle. There was no heating at all in the new house as yet – and with the hole, four feet by eight feet, in one wall, it was draughty as well.

The new wing, or extension, is in fact a separate rectangular building some fifty-six feet by twenty-four feet, and it lies about eight feet from the west wall of the old cottage. For the first winter we planned to keep the buildings separate, but in the spring, a link block was to be built, joining the two parts of the house together.

We had glass doors in the new wing ready to lead into the proposed link block, but they were interior doors not intended for protection against the weather, and thus the wind whistled through them with gay abandon too.

We were far too busy to feel much of the cold, but Mama was another matter. To make matters worse, she would keep getting out of her chair, dropping the blankets and hot-water bottles, and standing about by us as we worked.

We couldn't tie her to the chair, so we spent a lot of time getting her comfortable and then picking up the threads of what we had been doing – and getting her comfortable and picking up the threads of what we had been doing – and getting her comfortable...

It was at this time that Ben, the younger sheepdog, first developed his love for motorbikes. We'd bought a small 50cc bike to use about the farm and he was fascinated by it. He spent ages propped up against the wheels, and he was beside himself with excitement whenever Brian went out on it. He'd encircle the convoy (Brian on the bike followed by Spot, and several sheep who thought that perhaps they were going to be fed) at top speed, many times, barking wildly, and was deaf to all demands for 'Quiet!' Any visiting motorbike was subjected to a close scrutiny and was clearly of great interest. Perhaps it was the noise they made or their ability to race along the paths. It was certainly a powerful addiction and Ben was well hooked.

Lucky, the neutered ram, liked motorcycles too – but only when he had pushed them over, snorted and stamped all over them, the oil was running out and they were finally vanquished.

Ben was absolutely distraught if they were tipped over – as indeed was Brian or any other unhappy owner – and he arrived at a point where he would stand and defend his beloved bikes against Lucky's machinations, in spite of being quite frightened of Lucky, who could pack one heck of a punch with his hard, misshapen old head.

I was really very glad that Ben was an eighteen-month-old sheepdog and not an eighteen-year-old son. This degree of enthusiasm for motorbikes would have left us bereft of a moment's peace in the case of a son, and even caused us some anxiety in Ben's case.

Spotty too had developed an all-consuming passion – for me – and I soon grew to return it. We idolised each other. He would spend hours gazing up at me with such love in his eyes. If I scolded him for a wrongdoing, he was in miserable despair. If I went out, he moped in great unhappiness. His entire existence seemed devoted to me and it became a great responsibility.

I certainly had enormous pleasure from our relationship, tinged with great sadness that he was already twelve and unlikely to survive for more than another year or so.

But this is the way of farming – you build up a relationship with an animal and then it dies or has to be slaughtered. If you cannot bring yourself to cope with this sort of unvarnished life, then you really are better off with an office job.

I suppose to some extent the sensitivities do get blunted, as births and deaths happen quite frequently in the farming calendar, and as with all things, familiarity, with death or anything else, does tend to soften the blow.

So, while I dread the thought of losing Spotty, I will let him go when his time comes and bless him for all the love and companionship he has given me. Although I will never forget him, I will accept his demise as a natural and inevitable event, and I will start again with another dog.

Chapter Eleven

While all this was going on, we hadn't neglected the farm work. On Dai's advice, the lambs had been weaned, late in August. This was rather upsetting as all the lambs bleated pitifully for their mothers in one meadow, and all the ewes bleated pitifully for their lambs in another meadow.

The first day was particularly noisy and painful, but as the days passed, the noise lessened until after a week, it ceased altogether. They were kept apart for another few days until Dai was satisfied that the ewes were no longer producing milk, and then they were reunited. About half did not resume their close companionship – perhaps they didn't recognise each other.

The weaning is necessary so that the ewes have time to establish their hormone pattern, enabling them to come into season again for tupping, or serving, in October.

We also bought two very elegant Welsh Mountain rams. They were lovely creatures with thick fluffy wool fleeces and each with a complacent grin on his face – as well he might, since we had spent a lot of cash in providing them with a harem of desirable ewes apiece. We called them Bill and Ben but recollecting rather late in the day that they were Welsh rams, they were renamed Llewellyn and Glyndwr. They continued to answer to Bill and Ben, however, throughout their time with us.

As the autumn advanced, we found many of the ewes developed foot rot. Much of the land is soft and damp – an ideal breeding ground for this problem. Almost overnight, the farm seemed filled with these sad, limping, creatures – some with two, or even three legs affected.

We spoke to the vet who suggested injecting them with a vaccine followed by a second injection in December, and then an annual dose every August. It worked wonders. In a matter of days there was not a rotten foot in sight, discounting Brian's socks, and with the annual jab, we have managed to keep it that way.

Sometimes ewes lunge and struggle as they are being injected – and it is very easy to inject yourself by mistake. It all sounds rather unlikely but several of the local farmers have given themselves shots of sheep vaccine from time to time. I've never heard of anyone being ill afterwards though. I wonder if the wellies would last any longer if they were each given a foot-rot injection.

Among the people we had come to know was the local village elder. I suppose almost every village has one. They're always something to do with the council and have a hand in all the parish pies – usually village born and bred with a knowledge of all that has happened locally, since Methuselah. They influence village life and, in general, determine what is, and what is not, permitted in village society.

Our representative of this august body had been a great help with our planning application and we felt his advice had been instrumental in the successful conclusion of the business. So, I took him a bottle of sherry and a dozen new-laid eggs with a little card of thanks, and left them on his doorstep, since he was not at home when I called. He subsequently rang to thank us, and thinking this a duty done, I promptly forgot about it.

Six weeks later, I was appalled to find that almost the entire village was in fits about it. The said village elder was apparently well known to be of a strictly temperance persuasion, and, so I was told. Not only did he not drink alcohol himself, but he had a poor opinion of those who did participate. What had been intended as a little thank you for his time and advice had in fact been a gross insult. This is typical of what happens when I try to be socially responsible.

A week passed after the little man had disappeared with one of the patio doors, and we'd heard nothing from him, so we rang the firm to enquire when it would be replaced.

'Any day now,' came the reply.

That was also the reply when we rang at the end of the following week – and the week after that.

Brian had temporarily boarded up the hole with a sheet of plywood, but it was still draughty and inconvenient.

The breeze-block wall on the outside of the new wing had been finished with the window sills in place and the fire stops inserted. The council had made great play of the fire stops, and without knowing in the least what they were, I knew they were important. I kept enquiring about them and was assured that they'd not been forgotten.

The kit for the house had been delivered as a whole package, and as the work on the building progressed, the pile of parts still to go up got smaller and smaller.

Amongst the bits that were left, there didn't seem anything that looked as if it could be a fire stop. I think I imagined a metal screen or something of that sort. In fact, they are simply vertical strips of wood covered in damp-proof felt, and they are tacked to the outside of the inner wall of the house, so they fill up the gap between the two skins. If a fire breaks out between the inner and the outer skins, then the draught will not drive the fire further along the skin and into the next section. So now you know.

Personally, I cannot understand how wood covered in tar felt can possibly be any sort of impediment to a fire, but no doubt the building fraternity know what they are doing.

On fine days, Dai was plastering the first coat on the outside walls and Brian was labouring for him. On wet days, they were erecting the interior walls and screeding the floors.

After Dai went home each evening, Brian was assembling and installing the wood-burner and its chimney. We were looking forward to our first fireside evening in the new wing. And, indeed, it was lovely. We unearthed some chairs from the barn and sat amongst the piles of wood and building materials on the bare concrete floor, toasting our toes in the firelight. I found a couple of half-used candles, left from Christmas, and we ate casserole from pudding plates on our laps. It was truly memorable.

When the blasting was in progress, we had hoped to be able to remove enough rock to make the new single-storey

Mama aged 58 on holiday in Wales.

Mama aged 74 in her enterprising days as confusion took hold.

Mama aged 76 in full wail with Leo on her lap.

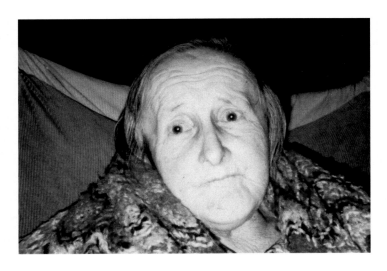

Mama aged 79 at Christmas 1986.

The farmhouse when we first saw it.

The farmhouse while blasting was in progress.

Digging out soil to build foundations for the new wing.

Building foundations for the new wing.

The oversite ready for the new building.

The arrival of the kit in the farmyard.

The kit laid out ready for construction.

Construction begins.

Construction continues.

The roof watertight at last.

Only needs a roof on the link block now.

The roof on the link block and the building finished.

wing on the same level as the ground floor of the original cottage. But this had not been economically possible, so the new wing was three feet higher than the ground floor of the old cottage and five feet lower than the upper storey of the old cottage.

The back door of the old cottage, the door we generally used, was on the east side of the old building, opening on to the farm lane. The lane then dropped away steeply to the yard on the north side for a distance of some thirty feet. So, emerging from the back door in the kitchen, it was necessary to walk down the few feet to the yard – then avoiding the piles of building materials, scramble up the muddy bank – some five feet high – to the door on the north side of the new building. That muddy bank could be lethal. Although I was still fairly active and a climb of five feet would not present any problem, it was quite a different matter to negotiate it with a tray containing our meal, or something large, hot, awkward, or all three, in the rain, or wind, or both. The supper and I came to grief on that bank several times.

Mama always seemed to find this terrifically funny if she happened to be watching the spectacle through the caravan window during day time. I was still cooking on the Rayburn in the old kitchen and one wild November night, a frying pan full of curry intended for our evening meal came to a sad end in the struggle up that muddy bank. Next morning the chickens enjoyed the spillage. Nothing is wasted in this establishment.

The yard was a sea of mud and Mama had to be helped to and from the caravan each day. We were desperate to have her installed in the new wing and as the weather worsened, Brian and Dai concentrated on her bed-sitting room and cloakroom, to the exclusion of everything else.

Poor old girl – she was becoming a little unsteady on her feet and disinclined to let herself in and out of the caravan on her own. To some extent this was a help, as it lessened the chances of her getting lost, although I was sad that she was losing her mobility.

When she was in the caravan on her own, she muddled about – packing and unpacking her cupboards and wardrobes and changing her clothes. Sometimes in the middle of the day, she would undress and get into bed. Sometimes she would get into bed without undressing. Sometimes she would take her dress and cardigan off, put her hat and coat on – and then get into bed.

The human race can be very adaptable. We got to the point where it didn't seem unusual to find her in this state. It ceased to be a matter for comment. It clearly amused and entertained her, so on what grounds could we say her nay? It was infinitely less distressing for us than the periods of crying and depression, when we had seemed unable to reach her or to improve her lot in any but the most basic of ways.

It was at this time that she first became incontinent during the day. Brian was very cross about it – but all the talking and explaining in the world didn't stop the problem. I found it quite difficult to cope with, but understandable, and as it upset Brian so much, I tried to play it down. If possible, I didn't mention it, and many pairs of pants dried unobserved in the greenhouse, which is my particular preserve. There was even some small sense of satisfaction that this was a problem that was within my coping capabilities.

Her increasing dependence pulled me much closer to Mama. We had never enjoyed a good relationship in spite of efforts on both sides. We did share many common interests and we had enjoyed the odd shopping spree together, but I often felt we had not been able to reach what could have been a very worthwhile friendship, which would have supported us both.

Part of the problem was that she'd known me as a child – a grubby but hopeful little girl who used to play with her son. It was easy to admonish or dismiss me then, and I'm sure she found it difficult to break the habit of years, as Brian and I grew up and became more serious friends.

Brian had always found it difficult to keep friendships as a child. His mother had stepped in to break up whatever she felt were connections that took him away from under her wing.

Her own childhood had been difficult as her parents were in their mid-forties when she was born – their only child. Her father had been a blacksmith – indeed one of the blacksmiths mentioned in George Stuart's book, *The Wheelwright's Shop*. This book, illustrating artisan life in the early 1900s in the Surrey town of Farnham, is something of a classic. Before the book had been published, Mama had read a draft copy to her father, only shortly before he died, and he had offered criticisms and corrections to the text, since he had worked for the firm for most of his life.

Her mother ran a local tobacco and confectionery business and the family lived in the accommodation over the shop so Mama was not subjected to the poverty and deprivation experienced by so many children born during the early part of this century.

Indeed, she had not been permitted to go to the local state primary school but was sent, as a Protestant, to a Catholic School for Girls, where as one of a handful of Protestants amongst over a hundred Catholics, she learned to stand up for herself. This period obviously had a great effect on her. All her life she was aggressively outspoken so that she had great difficulty in keeping a friend. Many of her birthdays and Christmases saw her with cards from only my parents and from us. Isn't that sad.

When she left school, she joined her mother in the shop and continued to live and work at home, until her father died when she was twenty-one, and her mother when she was twenty-two.

She sold the business premises and with a part of the proceeds, bought herself a house on the outskirts of town. Shortly afterwards she married Father-in-law and three years later, Brian was born.

Father-in-law had spent many years in hospital prior to their marriage and suffered with ill health for the rest of his life. Their relationship was often stormy, partly through Father's ill health, and partly through Mama's inability to cope with their finances.

We always felt that she had been indulged as a child and left in comfortable financial circumstances on her parents' deaths, so had never become used to practising economies.

In spite of considerable ambition, Father's poor health made it difficult for him to pursue a career – and to maintain Mama in the manner to which she had become accustomed – and thus financial troubles were frequent. They did silly things too. They sent Brian to a fee-paying school for the first few years and they ran a car – two great expensive luxuries at that time.

Looked at from years later, however, we could both understand that Mama's resources were concentrated almost exclusively to Brian. Her husband was ill and unable to fund her – but her son was to be the restorer of the family fortunes, if only she could keep him away from the rabble.

Since I was in the front line of the rabble, it cannot be wondered why Mama and I had such a problem with our relationship.

For several weeks Dai had been pressing us to sell the ram lambs and as the winter advanced and the grass became sparser, we could see it was inevitable. We had ten of them, all semi-tame with fluffy, hopeful faces. It seemed such a breach of trust to sell them.

Some time previously, we had bought a road trailer to transport some of Brian's mechanical devices from home to the factory. Many of his 'brainchildren' had arms or legs or bases in awkward places, making them unsuitable for transport in the car. Over the years the trailer had been useful in many different ways. We'd moved house with it twice and now Brian built a top for it and a wire window, and it became a stock trailer. While not looking particularly humorous, it had a jaunty, nautical line and it was the subject of some comment and leg-pulling. But it was a handsome equipage for the conveyance of the lambs to market.·

Mama was at the day hospital on the morning when the lambs finally went off, so I was able to go and watch the sale. It was very sad, but at the same time, I felt amused and proud to see Brian – as the vendor of the stock – standing in the pen with the lambs as they were being sold, knowing that they were as good as anything else in the market.

I felt very choked as the bidding started – very inclined to join in and buy the whole lot back again – but this would have been silly. So I let them go and hoped that life would not be too hard on the little ramlets.

Back at home, it was all hands on deck to get Mama installed in her new quarters by Christmas. The walls had been plastered, and her loo, basin and shower installed and connected. The electric power was also laid on, but as yet there was no central heating.

She was to have the whole of one end of the new wing, with her own little hall and front door. From the hall there was a door leading to her bed-sitting room on the right and a door leading to her cloakroom on the left.

We had decided against wallpaper as it was becoming important to be able to wipe down the walls. Mama would pick up a cup of tea, or a potted plant, or some similar container and then lurch into the wall, smashing whatever she was carrying, the contents of which then dripped dejectedly down to the floor. So a surface that could be sponged clean was vital.

In her sitting room she had two lovely big windows through which the sun lit up the pale apricot walls, making the room look like the inside of a cosy, warm cocoon.

Unfortunately, when choosing the apricot paint, we forgot that Mama's old sitting-room curtains were blue, and her old dining-room carpet was maroon and black – and that both items were to be used in the new room. The finished effect was therefore colourful, rather than coordinated, but she seemed very happy with it.

After some deliberation, we had decided to install all her old bits and pieces in her new quarters rather than buy new things. She had lived with her sideboard, her dressing table, her wardrobe, her cupboards and her chairs for forty years, and although collectively they looked like candidates for a seedy auction sale, they were a part of her past and she recognised them.

So we sorted it all out in the barn, lugged it indoors, washed, ironed, sponged, mended and hoovered in an effort to make a silk purse out of the ear of a rather bedraggled, pre-war sow until, in the week before Christmas, it was finished.

It was also very damp. The windows streamed with condensation and although it was warm, it was difficult to make it dry and aired. As the plaster walls were filled with water, the paint was water-based, the screeding on the floor was full of water and all the goods and chattels in the room had been out in the barn for over a year, it could hardly be wondered at. Mama could not move into it yet.

The rest of the new wing was still in the process of construction. The kitchen and bathroom walls were up, the floors screeded and most of the bathroom fittings in place, even if not connected. There sat my posh new bath and loo and I was unable to use them.

The kitchen had been the subject of a bit of marital disharmony. The popular Sunday supplements were full of adverts for that new kitchen and I must have filled in half a dozen coupons, asking for literature. For weeks the post sported these colourful brochures showing all the different models, surfaces and makes, and people kept phoning up, and turning up, to show us their wares and give us quotations.

Brian had wanted to build the cupboards himself but I felt this would take too long, and as he already had so much to do, it would be easier to have the kitchen fitted out professionally. And for once, my view prevailed.

We had agreed on solid mid oak cupboards with heavy-duty work surfaces, and we gave the order to a little local man who was not only cheaper than the big boys, but was available to be contacted if we subsequently had problems with it.

The little local man was delighted and spent two hours explaining how superior his kitchen would be, compared to those of his rivals.

He came along the following day and spent two hours telling us that it was all ordered, and he turned up the day after that, just to see how we were getting on.

We began to dread the actual arrival of the parts, and sure enough, he made a meal of it. His face beamed with pleasure as he unloaded the boxes and parcels from his van. He reverently carried it all into the embryo kitchen and unpacked it. We watched in awe as he lovingly ran a coat sleeve over the doors and held them up for us to admire the colour of the grain. He *did* enjoy himself.

At this point Brian and Dai were working outside on what was to be the new front door, finishing the manhole and sundry other pipework for the sewage disposal. Every few moments, a head would appear in the doorway and would ask which way this particular cupboard door was to hang – how far apart were the shelves to be in that cupboard – how much room had to be left for the gas or electric fittings – and a great many other questions.

It all got quite tense and the little man and I came in for a lot of stick. He, because he was the instigator of the interruptions, and me because I had employed him to do the job.

I'd already had a bit of trouble over the sinks.

We'd chosen a metal sink unit with two sinks. The little man however always referred to them as 'bowls'. So we had a unit with two 'bowls' and a drainer. The trouble arose because he made the word sound like 'bowels' – the intestinal sort.

Brian and Dai had coped with this at the planning stage with only modest schoolboy merriment, but as the units were put together, this wretched word kept cropping up again and again and I was on tenterhooks that their ill-suppressed amusement may cause offence. A number of times, I hurried into the conversation with some twerpish remark in an effort to keep the peace. Needless to say, our sinks are now invariably known as 'bowels'.

Fortunately, my little man did make a good job of the kitchen, so the pain of the installation was worth the outcome.

One evening towards the middle of December, Brian unearthed all the Christmas decorations from the barn and installed a Christmas tree on the bare floor of the new sitting room. Mama's new bedroom was at last dry and aired and it was hoped that she could be installed in it on Christmas Eve.

There was a huge stack of plasterboard sheets on one side of the new sitting room and a pile of pine planks, ultimately intended for the ceiling, on the other. Covered with Christmas paper these made makeshift tables for the Christmas cards and the Christmas fare.

The man came back with the replacement patio door, still marvelling that the original one hadn't fitted. Brian generously refrained from pointing out that the new one only fitted because it was three quarters of an inch smaller than the other three – and by Christmas Eve – it really started to look like home.

We'd had a constant stream of people calling during the day and by nine o'clock, Mama was very tired. For the first time in all her adult years, she seemed to have no understanding that it was Christmas. We tucked her into bed in her new bedroom with her current Fred and then piled driftwood logs on the sitting room fire so that it crackled and flamed – burning with a blue light and smelling of the salt sea.

Christmas Eve always seems the best part of the festival. We've always tried to go out, however briefly, to look at the night sky – to try and capture some of the magic of the Christmas story.

This year, having seen Mama safely asleep with the listening intercom working, we walked down to the little harbour to look out at the Christmas sea. The moon briefly drifted through the clouds to cast a blue, almost fluorescent, light on the slate roofs of the stable and the old bakehouse as we passed.

We stood on the beach for a moment and looked up the coast to a village some four miles away.

The gentle ripple turned the lights into a zigzag pattern in the water. It was so still, and quiet, and peaceful. Even the birds of the night were silent, the high tide covering the mudflats.

In our village, across the inlet, we could see the lights of a party of villagers making their way along the road with flaring torches, and then a faint sound of carols as they rounded the bend in the road and were lost to view.

On the way back up the hill we stopped at the bakehouse where a sick ewe blinked doubtfully at us in the torchlight. She had been hit by a car in the lane earlier in the day, but looked to be only bruised and winded. We gave her more hay and left her snuggled up in the straw, going on to give the dogs a biscuit each – their festive treat – before returning to our fire and our own recording of the service of Nine Lessons and Carols from King's.

Countless reflections of the fire danced on the uncurtained windows, on the tinsel and the silver baubles on the tree.

We drank a glass of sherry, watching the fire through the pale liquid in the glass until all the world seemed charged with warmth and comfort. Would that everyone had it so.

It was a simple, spartan Christmas, but one of the best we have had.

Chapter Twelve

After weeks of intensive work on the new building – often for sixteen hours a day – we were tired. Over the Christmas period, we tried to relax, and as a break from the chores, we went out. If we stayed at home, we would inevitably get involved with some job that was crying out to be finished. It was impossible to sit and look at the work – so with Mama tucked into the back seat, surrounded by rugs and hot-water bottles, we did a little modest exploring.

This part of Wales is so beautiful and interesting that we tended to stop almost before we'd started, but there was one drive that we'd always enjoyed when on holiday here with the parents back in the sixties, and we wanted to see it in its winter glory. This was the road from Dinas Mawddwy over the mountains to Lake Vyrnwy and then on over the second mountain range to Bala.

On a grey, still day at the end of December, we set off. It was bleak and desolate as we climbed eastwards over the high pass from Dolgellau, and then dropped down the steep open road into the beautiful valley of the Cerist. A mile or so further on, we turned off the main road and slipped down into the village of Dinas Mawddwy. The village street was deserted, almost unreal, like a scene from a film set.

As we wended our way along the valley towards Llanymawddwy, drifts of low cloud obscured the lower slopes of the mountains on the far side of river – but the tops rose out of the mist, gaunt and silent.

Further on, we struggled up the pass – the road is narrow, with a steep drop on one side and a steep rise of sheer rock on the other. At the top of the pass where the metalled track of the civilised world has pierced the mountain range, we paused to enjoy the view. There was absolute and total silence. The land was empty except for the sheep and the creatures of the high moors.

The cloud in the valley drifted apart, briefly disclosing the tiny village of Llanymawddwy many feet below. It looked like a toy town – too small to be real.

Away to the left, the almost sheer slopes of Gallt Ceiniogau towered above us. Here and there, creases in the steep mountainside showed cascades of white water sliding down the bare rock face, the colour of burnt toast, to disappear into the donkey-grey scree and then to reappear further down in time to join the streamlet before it grew into the foaming torrent at Aber Rhiwlech.

We resumed our journey but stopped again within a mile. This time the silence was broken by a million miniature rivulets weeping from the moors into the roadway. On turning a full circle, there was nothing I could detect in the landscape that could not have been there a thousand years ago – probably longer. Even the sheep had forsaken this part of the mountains. There was a feeling of primeval isolation – being back at the roots of the world, before the human race started to destroy it. We climbed back into the car and continued to pick our way along the narrow lane. The leaden sank into a drizzle. Soon we were enveloped in misty rain. Brief glimpses of distant hills drifted into vision and out again. We were isolated in a grey, empty world.

The rain increased to a heavy downpour as we started the descent down to Vyrnwy. Small ribbons of silver water bubbled out of the banks at the side of the road, forming fairy-tale waterfalls.

At the bottom, by the lake, we stopped again. The water looked deep and chill. Water oozed up from the sodden land and we seemed to be totally alone in the wet, wet landscape.

Mama sat in the back of the car – staring uncomprehendingly out – sucking a fruit pastille.

We drove on towards Bala, over the second pass, through dense, dripping woodlands. It seemed incongruous to breast the hill at Rhos y Gwaliau and look down on the grey stone town of Bala, its street lights already ablaze. As we slowly drove through the town, glimpses through uncurtained windows showed us warm, cosy front rooms with Christmas trees and decorations. The white glow from the television lit up children lying on their tummies on the floor, their faces propped up on weary arms, as they watched the Christmas panto or a cartoon film while Grandpa, in his new Christmas cardigan, slept in a fireside chair.

A few brave souls were scurrying home along the shining streets and we too turned the car towards home to enjoy an evening all together, by the fire.

My diary does not tell me if it was that night, or a subsequent night, but there was one occasion over that Christmas period when I suffered a fright.

I had been knitting a sweater for Brian, and for some reason that appeared to defy explanation, one arm was longer than the other. The number of rows in each arm was identical – as were the pattern repeats – and I had sat over this imponderable puzzle until quite late at night. The room was dimly lit except for the angle lamp beamed onto the work on my lap. There was a spooky film on the television and I was half watching this as I fretted with the knitting. The fire had burned low – it was well past the witching hour and Brian had dozed off in his chair.

I was sitting with my back to the uncurtained windows and I suddenly felt a violent chill of fear. Something was moving in the darkness behind my chair.

I glanced behind me and came face to face with a pair of fearful, flaming eyes, framed by a pair of wicked horns, looking at me through the window.

Another pair of eyes and horns joined the first set.

My nervous system, already tense from the ghost story on the television, jangled convulsively. I really felt quite ill for a few seconds – until I saw that the two fearful faces had wool on them and in fact belonged to Bill and Ben, the two rams. Their tupping duties over, they had joined forces and had come to see where the humans lived.

They often did this afterwards, but never with such dramatic effect. Technically, they were supposed to have been separated from the ewes when tupping was over, but at that early stage, we were unaware that the divorces were necessary and we had left them all to mix together as they wished.

Another of our Christmas trips took us to Llanelltyd, a small village just to the north west of Dolgellau.

It doesn't look particularly interesting when you drive through it now on the new bypass, but in 1960 when we were in Wales for a few stolen days with a tent and our first old car, we'd had an enforced stay in the vicinity, and we'd come to know it quite well.

I cannot remember if it was the gearbox or the exhaust. Suffice it to say, the car of the day, an ancient banger, had ground to a halt about half a mile south of the village.

Brian had tinkered with the trouble for some time without success and since it looked as if it was going to be a long job, I had offered to walk into the village to review the possibilities.

At that stage the bypass was still a pipedream, but the old road was not busy and I was able to explore the village in some detail.

After looking around the church with its curiously round churchyard, I wandered back to hear the latest report on the mechanical problem.

All was gloom and despair. A spare part was required and we were miles from anywhere.

A local farmer helped us push our offending vehicle into one of his fields and we set up camp there for a day and a half. As Brian struggled with our recalcitrant motor, I could only explore the immediate locality and it proved to be very interesting indeed. Within a stone's throw were the remains of Cymer Abbey and over those few hours, a seed was sown that has blossomed to give me endless pleasure.

We had a couple of guide books in the car and I read what they offered on the question of the abbey and its environs. I crawled all over it and viewed it from every angle. I walked back up to the church in the village to see if there was any literature on the history of the abbey, and there I was fortunate enough to meet a lady who was able to tell me the story of Llanelltyd in such a way that it was suddenly touched with magic.

She must have been in her sixties – very Welsh and with a sense of humour that does not call for laughter but for inward quiet amusement. She also had an outstanding ability to paint a picture with her words. I think she was renewing the flowers or carrying out some other such service – I remember she had lots of small booklets and she was writing in each one. She certainly had a thorough knowledge of the village, its history, and especially of the abbey. I sat in a pew as she worked and talked. She really made it all come to life – the gift of so many of the Celtic storytellers. I could actually *see* the abbey as it was when it was a working, living home.

It had apparently dominated the area from the time of its development during the early part of the 13th century up until the dissolution of the monasteries. During that time the local people had been succoured, educated and inspired by the inhabitants of the abbey.

It was said to have had a curiously enlightened attitude to those who dwelt outside its walls in that it did not just teach of Christian matters but also of iron smelting, tool making, architecture, medicine, crop management and improved methods of farming. It was no doubt of great assistance to the neighbourhood, bringing comfort, relief and an improved way of life for many.

On that lovely June morning, after I left the lady in the church who had illuminated the scene for me so vividly, I wandered back to sit on the solid old stone bridge just below the ruins of the abbey, and with her words ringing in my ears, I could see the scene as it must have looked five or six hundred years before.

The river has carved a steep, meandering valley through the open hills and where it emerges from amongst the rocky heights, there is a secluded green sward of land at the foot of the mountains, sheltered from all but the south winds and the narrow valley through which the river flows. In the distant south, the Cader mountain range rises triumphantly into the sky. In the foreground, the river tumbles down its rocky course to become a more subdued affair as it starts to thread its way through estuarine water meadows, which, in turn, reach out to touch the wooded slopes that rise steeply up to encircle the estuary.

On this awesomely beautiful site, the abbey had been built. The river is wide at this point, with a deep salmon pool below the bridge, the clear, pure, mountain water eddying and scurrying on its way towards the sea, now only five miles away.

From my new friend's words, I could imagine the monks purposefully going about their business in simple white hooded gowns of coarse cloth. They had apparently lived lives of great simplicity on a diet of bread and water, relieved by a small amount of fish. Their order at Cymer was one of strict Christian disciplines and, so I was told, in all 300 years of its working life, no breath of scandal was ever attached to its name.

I could almost see some of the monks tending the gardens, others in the fields – they would be shearing the sheep at this time of year. Much of the wool was apparently stored for their own use but any surplus was dispatched by boat from a quay they had built just below the bridge. I wondered what they did with their ram lambs – were they perhaps kept for their wool?

In the abbey precincts, some of the men would have been working – baking the bread, spinning the fleeces, and weaving the wool into cloth. Others would have been cleaning the vestments, writing, making medicines and, of course, singing and praying. Outside, there would have been monks attending to the pack animals and others setting off with rush baskets, or perhaps leather bags, containing medicines, or tools, to some outlying area.

There would have been a tranquillity, unbroken by the roar of the petrol engine and in which faulty gearboxes could have had no part.

But, according to my friend in the church, even more interest attached to the abbey. When the threat of the dissolution of the monasteries became known in the middle of the sixteenth century, the monks must have been very concerned as to the future of their abbey home. Nothing is apparently known of the precise action that was taken when Cymer was closed – but closed it was.

Most of the abbots of the time were apparently pensioned off and many of the monks became secular clergy, but it must have been a great sadness for them to lose their spiritual and physical home. It must also have been a great loss for the local community.

In February 1890, over 300 years after Cymer was closed, two men working for a local gold mine were up on the mountains not far from the ruins of the abbey. During their prospecting, they came upon two small metallic objects – a small plate and what appeared to be a drinking vessel. They took them home and cleaned them, to find that they were made of silver, with beautiful and skilful decoration. They proved to be the silver chalice and paten that had belonged to Cymer Abbey.

The area of the find was diligently searched but no further objects came to light. Even so, there may well be other treasures lying hidden somewhere in the hills. It is an exciting prospect and there may well be a sequel as the centuries pass.

For me, the interesting question is how and why those two relics, which would have been of great sacred, as well as economic, value, came to be on the open hillside, only partially buried. Did the abbot of the time, fearing confiscation of the vestments, order them to be hidden – perhaps in the hope that the Abbey would one day reopen? Or did some of the monks take matters into their own hands as perhaps news of the arrival of the King's agent became known?

Or were they stolen?

How and why did they come to be in that hiding place on the hillside? Had they been moved twice, or had the elements, over the years, eroded their original hiding place, causing them to slip down the hillside?

It is an intriguing story.

As I again sat on the bridge, this time on a bleak grey January day, I let my mind wander over what could well have happened at Cymer in the mid sixteenth century. I could visualise a small party of monks with the vestments wrapped in wool in a leather bag. The King's agent was expected within the hour – the advance party may well have arrived already. In silence, the monks enter their church and with prayers, they lovingly wrap up their precious objects. They fleetingly depart for the hills. Maybe the King's men follow.

The monks are hurrying along searching for a suitable hiding place. Maybe they are about to be overtaken – the King's servants would have had good horses. They quickly remove their treasure from the bag to bury it in the shallow soil of the mountainside, then they hurry on to draw the scent away from the hiding place.

What happened to those monks – what happened to the abbot if it was he who made the arrangements? He would certainly have lost his pension – if not worse.

Or were the vestments stolen at some time before the dissolution of the monasteries? Did some chance traveller stay at the abbey, perhaps on his way to Harlech, and make off with the treasure to bury it, hoping to recover it at a later date?

I wonder what did happen. If only the paten and chalice could tell us of their adventure.

After a somewhat chequered history over the last one hundred years, the vestments are now in the National Museum of Wales in Cardiff.

Standing on that bridge, now a cul-de-sac, I looked up the river, in full spate, through the trees that now rather spoil the view of the steep wooded crease through the mountains. A place of fairies, elves, and things that are sadly only real in childhood.

The nearer hills were a charcoal velvet. Each more distant slope was a paler shade of grey until the outline of the far bluff was only just discernible from the pale sky.

Then I looked westwards – towards the sea – where banks of black and grey cloud allowed bands of bright orange light to suffuse the sky as the setting sun struggled to see our lovely land. How well the monks had chosen the site for their monastery. How much easier it is to attain spiritual growth and contentment when living in such surroundings.

Chapter Thirteen

Mama was eventually fully installed in her new quarters on 2nd January 1984, with all her goods and chattels about her. Since Christmas Eve she had virtually camped out in her new quarters but she now had all her personal bits and pieces to sort and arrange to her liking. Her rooms were at last her permanent home, all trace of dampness having been overcome.

My own mother had always nurtured a fetish concerning 'the damp'. When I was a child, it had always seemed that 'the damp' was a bogeyman, or a fiend, who would catch me if I went out in the November fog and played in the wet leaves, or made my clothes sodden in some other hooligan activity.

I had forgotten this until my mother came to live with us after my father died. During those difficult months, Mother's fad was a constant source of amazement. Did you know that corsets have to be aired for three whole days even though when they come out of the tumble dryer the little metal parts are almost red-hot? Mother conducted her life with the maxim that if you looked after your body, it looked after you – and airing her clothes came into this category.

True enough, she never suffered with rheumatism or arthritis. In fact, in spite of the cancer operation when she was in her early seventies, and the hair-raising year that followed, she remained extremely spry until the stroke that caused her death. At the party we held to celebrate her eightieth birthday, she had danced the valeta at three o'clock in the morning attired in a gold lurex dress, which I still possess. Her partner had been Brian's old friend who had originally introduced us to Wales and with whom we had maintained a lasting friendship.

Some five months later, she had spent several hours on a cold November day standing in the shopping precinct of her home town, selling poppies for the Remembrance Day appeal. She had found this quite enjoyable at the time, but suffered a severe reverse a week later when the local paper sported a photo of her in her hour of glory, with a caption that read, 'Octogenarian Braves the Weather to Help the Poppy Day Appeal'. For years she had been passing herself off as 'early sixties'.

Be that as it may, we officially opened Mama's part of the new wing and she was ensconced in her armchair with an assortment of boxes and cases at her feet on that momentous day early in 1984. Brian and I staggered to and from the caravan with her ornaments, her crockery, her brooms, brushes and sundry other bits and pieces. We had thought it would give her pleasure to sort it all out and pack it in the wardrobe and cupboards, but in fact she was not able to understand what was happening. She sat in state among the debris, which, in some strange way, seemed to be multiplying. Every time we popped in to see how she was getting on, there seemed more of it.

It was sad to have to accept that this was another landmark in mama's illness. For months she had enjoyed turning out her cupboards and repacking them, sometimes twice a day. Now she was totally lost amid the furniture, the goods, and the chattels she had lived with for much of her life. Perhaps it was the sheer scale of the operation – and that it had been arranged for her, rather than started at her own instigation.

It was all rather depressing. We packed it away and sat down to the celebration supper, but it was not a really happy evening.

It was lovely to have her indoors, however. She was the sole occupant of the new wing at night, so we still had to cross the mud, negotiate the slippery bank and avoid the building materials and the boulders, if we fancied we heard an inexplicable noise on the intercom in the small hours. But at least we didn't have to bring her across the yard each day, and the business of her locking the caravan door when she saw you coming was over.

She still spent most of her day with us in our end of the new wing, which we were still working on, but on the occasions that she was left on her own in her flatlet, she spent the time ambling about, moving the ornaments and looking in the drawers and cupboards. Her prize possessions suddenly lost favour and an old cracked sugar bowl was placed in state on the mat on the sideboard, instead of the antique clock which had stood in that position for donkeys' years. Two ferns that I'd nurtured and cherished for months, and which had looked very nice on the sideboard, were severely trimmed and put into the bottom of her wardrobe. The toilet roll in her cloakroom was removed and placed over the candlestick on her dressing table, and there were many more adjustments to the décor.

The Battle of the Bed first started shortly after Mama moved into the new extension.

For some time we had allowed her to remain in bed for an extra hour or two in the mornings. There was no reason to get her up earlier – she was warm and cosy in bed and provided her incontinence things were changed and she was washed, however sketchily, early in the morning, she was really better off in bed.

It had slowly become more difficult to get her up – she would grumble and protest, she would push and shout, and now there were some mornings when it was a real battle. To start off with we would try to choose a suitable moment when she was off her guard. If she knew what was coming, her old fingers would grip the bedclothes and she'd roar with rage. Her reactions were quite slow so the technique was to wait outside her bedroom door until she was relaxed and unprepared for action, then rush in and seize the bedclothes before she could get a grip on them.

Having got the bedclothes off, one was treated to a vision of arms and legs lashing out in all directions.

Here again, the technique was to wait until she paused for a moment and then seize a hand – both hands if possible – and somehow pull until she was sitting upright on the bed. It is jolly difficult to kick in this position, so briefly, her legs would be still.

With one deft movement, her legs could then be swung over the side of the bed. If you were lucky, you could also get her slippers on before she regained her breath and started to belabour your head or kick your shins.

All this latter bit was accompanied by ear-splitting yells.

If you relaxed for an instant, she would be back on the bed and trying to cover herself up.

Inch by inch, you would get her to the toilet, where she sat in state on the seat while you tried to wash her face and hands. Then on to a stool in the shower while you tried to attend to her bottom half. Then back to her room, where you would try and get her day clothes on and install her in her chair.

As often as not, she would then sit with a disarming grin on her face as she downed her tea and cereal. I think there were times when she really enjoyed being difficult. It gave her great amusement and a lot of power. And indeed, why shouldn't it? She didn't have many pleasures.

It is all very well for the uninitiated to purse their lips and look disapproving. Faced with the daily reality – sometimes single-handed – all the textbook recommendations for helping an elderly patient to rise and maintain life in a dignified manner went out of the window. Or perhaps we never had the textbook that applied to us.

I am not saying that we reached this stage immediately after Mama moved into her new quarters. It all happened quite slowly. We'd have a bad morning followed by several easy ones. Gradually, the bad mornings got closer together until they were nearly all bad.

They still are. Now as I write in 1986, she is less strong physically, but her fighting spirit is unimpaired.

It was quite difficult to deal with her without causing her some injury. If you took her arms and legs in too tight a grasp, you would be rewarded by lurid bruises in a day or so. She seemed to bruise exceptionally easily.

Her incontinence pads were obviously uncomfortable, so she constantly pulled at them. Little bits of wadding littered the bed, and some found their way into her mouth.

Her hands were always very suspect so we tended to try and lift her either from under her arms or, if a frontal attack looked likely, by her wrists. But in either case, it was difficult to deal with her without causing a bruise.

The Battle of the Bed did not stop there.

After she was made comfortable in her chair and had finished her breakfast, I would make the bed and tidy the room. She would watch this and we'd probably exchange a comment or two. Most of her conversation did not make sense. Many words were not real words at all and they were often partly, or entirely, replaced by a wail.

Sometimes she *could* say something relevant – or at least I could understand it quite well.

Sometimes it seemed that she was *trying* to say something relevant but could not get the words out.

At other times she was clearly pretending to have a proper conversation but with make-believe words.

But we talked to her as if it was a normal exchange of conversation.

When her bedroom was tidy and safe, I would leave her, and go on my sheep rounds, which usually took about an hour. Brian would remain within earshot of the intercom and either pop in to see Mama every so often, or perhaps glance through the window if he was working outside.

I would leave the room in a state of orderliness and warmth. When I returned, I would find that the bed had been stripped, with the bedclothes on the floor, and the windows were wide open. So, I would make the bed again, close the windows, turn up the heating and depart.

Half an hour later, I'd pop back again and find that the bed was stripped, the windows were wide open and the contents of one drawer of the dressing table were strewn all over the floor.

So I'd make the bed yet again, tidy up, and half an hour later… and so it went on.

There were days, mercifully few, when the working programme meant that she was confined to her own quarters for a protracted period albeit with frequent checks. On those occasions, the disruption could happen so continually that I would give up restoring her room to order and it would remain in chaos until she joined us for the evening meal.

Sometimes she would go for several days without any disruption at all.

But there were compensations – sometimes rather funny. If there had been a faux pas or perhaps a degree of parsimony with the catering arrangements, Mama had not the least recollection that she'd eaten turkey for four days in a row.

Likewise, when I tipped far too much blue colouring into the icing sugar for Brian's birthday cake – and was forced to tip in more and more icing sugar to dilute the colour from navy to pale blue – I was left with a bowl of blue icing sugar that I'm sure most people would have thrown away. Not me, however. Guess who had pale blue rice pudding and their chocolate drink served up with a bluish tinge for the next few days.

But the main problem with Mama at this stage was the disruption she could cause, coupled with the fact that if she was left on her own, she tended to wobble about her room, banging against the furniture and giving herself colourful bruises, in addition to those we'd given her. Strangely enough, they never seemed to hurt. If you touched them, even quite firmly, she would never flinch or give any indication that they were painful. So we did what we could to remove every possible obstacle and we let her womble about on her own. I hated the thought of her indefinite confinement to a chair. I wanted her to retain the small degree of independence she still had for as long as possible.

But I was reduced to the absolute depths however by the Sister at the day hospital, when she commented that, 'Your mother-in-law is often covered in bruises'. This lady had given me endless support and encouragement. I had come to respect her and knew her to be fair and honest, so her words struck home in a very lethal way.

Furthermore, intentionally or not, the comments were made in a manner that gave the impression that we were not caring for Mama properly, and it made a deep and lasting hurt.

I went over it in my mind endlessly. Did she think we weren't caring for Mama? Were we indeed *not* caring for Mama properly? Did she think we manhandled the poor old lass? Perhaps we did – with our rough and ready ways of getting her up. But how else were we to cope? Did she think we didn't care? *What* did she think?

It didn't seem to worry Brian too badly; he could not see any alternative, but it preyed on my mind for months.

Thinking back to that time, I suppose it was right that the Sister should mention it. Had we been manhandling Mama in any aggressive or temperamental manner, then at least it would have shown us that someone else had noticed, and it may have served to stop the rot.

But at the time it seemed an unjust and almost insurmountable blow. When you take on the responsibility for someone like Mama, no one warns you that this sort of bomb is likely to be dropped on your head from a source you have come to respect. It has to be accepted and understood that this is one of the pitfalls of the circumstances.

As the winter advanced and the weather worsened, the grass became scarcer. The older ewes we'd bought in during the previous summer started to succumb. Most of them were in lamb and I suppose they didn't have the resources to cope with pregnancy and the winter weather. I was frantic as one after another, they went down.

We bought in sheep nuts by the ton – but the new ewes were unused to processed food and would run with their last ounce of strength rather than face a bucket, or trough, of sheep cake.

Our surviving original ewes all looked very well, and they did teach some of the new ones to take cake, which helped a lot, but all in all it was not a happy time on the farming front. I would spend hours coddling a sick ewe in the bakehouse, only to have her die while my back was turned. Every day I scoured the land for signs of a white body lying on the ground and several times I carried a sick one, often nearly half a mile, back to the yard where she could be given shelter, a calcium or vitamin injection, or whatever else she seemed to need.

No end of times I called the vet until he got quite tired of me. The farmers do not generally seem to ask for veterinary help with a ewe unless it is a particularly valuable animal. Over lambing they will perhaps take a ewe with a prolapse, a breech birth or some other lambing problem, but by and large they seem to treat the sheep themselves.

Brian and Dai got awfully fed up with my constant panics, but I couldn't seem to help myself. Every morning after Mama was attended to, I would set off on my rounds and invariably I'd find some catastrophe.

It was very difficult to accept at the time but it did teach us a great deal. I said some hard words, under my breath, of the farmer friend who had sold us the older, cheaper, extra sheep, but I did come to acknowledge that he was right.

Firstly, we began to acquire a knowledge – albeit doubtful at first – of the type of the illness, whether it was a calcium deficiency, viral pneumonia, a cyst or any one of a number of other diseases common to sheep.

With Dai's help, we did rectify some of the problems and the ewes recovered, but we did lose many of them.

Secondly, we learned a lot about the habits of sheep.

In general the Welsh Mountain ewes tend to colonise one particular area. They will scratch out a little hollow to sleep in and will usually be found in that locality. They get to know the terrain very well indeed. They know just how wide the ditches are, and where to jump over, where the watering places are, and where to make for in the event of danger.

We began to realise that if they weren't in their own home territory, then there was a reason for it, and if you looked for that reason, you could often nip trouble in the bud.

Stray dogs sometimes made them leave their home patch, but more often it was walkers with children or dogs. Like the human race, sheep suffer with stress, but whereas stress rarely kills us, it kills sheep very readily. As often as not, a nervous ewe will die of the stress induced by the treatment you are giving her, rather than the ailment you are treating her for. If they are chased, or made to run unduly, particularly if they are in lamb, they will become stressed and will just drop dead. This may not happen for several hours after the stress has occurred, but it is important to avoid as much harassment as possible.

Funnily enough they seem to know the difference between a visiting dog and the working dogs who are under control, and they can cope with even the manhandling at shearing and dipping time. Perhaps because it is happening to them collectively, whereas visiting dogs and children will chase a single ewe or a small group of sheep at a time.

I've had a number of differences with ramblers, and even some of our own campers, who have allowed their dogs to chase the sheep. Almost always, their argument is that the dog won't hurt the sheep – he never bites, he just wants to play. They just don't seem to realise that it is the chasing bit that often causes the problem and will even lead a pregnant ewe to abort her lamb in some cases.

When they are unwell they will also sometimes leave their home territory. Like many animals, sheep will often go and hide if they feel ill. If you can find them quickly, you are more likely to be able to treat them successfully, so getting to know who lives where is quite important.

We came to know many of the ewes personally. There was one with a very mournful expression – a large ewe who hung her head, and always managed to look as if she'd just been to a funeral. But that enormous egg-shaped body and those sturdy legs could bundle along at a very impressive speed if you produced a bucket of sheep cereal. She was a true glutton and used her head as a battering ram to barge her way into the line of white woolly bunties that were lined up each side of the feeding troughs. Her technique was subtle. She would eat, at top speed, all the nuts in her particular part of the feeder, then back out and barge her way in further up the trough, where perhaps there was still a quantity to be consumed.

Some of the ewes ate delicately – one nut at a time, savouring the flavour of the cereal – but Face, as she came to be known, almost inhaled them. Great mouthfuls were scooped up and swallowed, and she didn't stop until the troughs were empty.

Her gluttony finally caused her demise. The following autumn, the greengrocery bags had featured about fifty pounds of Victoria plums – some had soft patches of bruising but they were otherwise very nice indeed. On the day they arrived, there was also a big box of grapes, and the chickens, who normally love plums, were stuffed to capacity with those sweet little seedless grapes, so that the plums weren't given as much attention as would normally have been the case.

Face, who always appeared in the yard each day, even in summer, in the hope that there might be sheep nuts, carrots or something else with which she could stuff her bulbous interior, came upon the plums, which she found delicious. According to a small child who was staying here at the time, she ate *all* of them. The following day she was scouring and the day after that she died.

What a death. It also taught me that the animal foods must be kept covered and only available to whatever it was supposed to be fed to. We were, in many cases, learning the hard way.

We were again trying to discourage the ewes from coming up into the yard as they made such a noise in the mornings, their hooves churned up the mud, and their droppings added to the mire between the barn and the house. Over the winter feeding season, Brian and Dai had imposed a ban on the feeding of sheep nuts in the yard, or the vicinity of the house.

The theory was that if the sheep were not used to being fed in the yard, then they would go and eat grass for most of the day – only turning up at the feeding troughs down on the campsite when the nuts were taken down to them.

So, every afternoon, I would trundle a wheelbarrow containing a 25kg sack of nuts down the grass path and round the farm track to the campsite. Once there, I would empty the nuts into the troughs – small metal containers, about twelve feet long by nine inches wide – before pushing the wheelbarrow home.

Sounds easy, doesn't it?

But it wasn't. The sheep become totally addicted to sheep nuts. They are as powerful as any of the drugs that the human race abuse themselves with.

Hardly before I started from the yard, there was a group of ewes that had been grazing nearby waiting for the off. They rushed from all directions – down the banks – through the trees – jumping over rocks – and baaing their pleasure at the start of the nut run.

After fifty yards, there would be a procession of twenty or thirty following. One or two of the bolder ones would try to mount the barrow – or bunt at it with their heads – trying to turn it over. You needed strong wrists to keep it under control.

By the time I arrived at the campsite gate, there were fifty or sixty following and I would be beginning to feel like the Pied Piper of Hamelin.

Negotiating the campsite gate was fraught with peril, as you had to control the barrow with one hand while opening the gate with the other. The barrow was stationary and the ewes could have a good sniff through the paper sack. They crowded around – a sea of heaving, white woolly backs. I came to grief at this point on a number of occasions and once the barrow was over and the nuts, although still in the bag, on the ground, it was almost impossible to pick them up again. I could roar and wave my arms, but the sheep pushed and shoved around the bag in a solid block of white wool, totally oblivious to everything but that bag of nuts, now within reach.

Even when you did get to the troughs safely, it was extremely difficult to get the nuts into the feeders. No end of times I had the bag open and in tipping position only to be taken off my feet and almost carried along on a sea of woolly backs, so that the nuts went all over the place.

We developed a slightly better system as time went on, but in those first years, we must have wasted almost as much as the ewes ate.

Bill and Ben, the two rams, were always in the forefront of this daily performance and did very well owing to their extra weight and the candelabra on their heads. Their horns enabled them to force an entry into any line of noshing ewes, however closely the botties were jammed together.

The ewes had waited all day for their treat, and it was over in just a few moments. I would return to the house with the empty barrow, looking as if I had just survived several rounds with Henry Cooper.

All this jaunting about the farm looking for sick sheep, and feeding those that had survived, was not without some compensations. The land looked bleak and untamed. Few walkers were tempted on to it and the wildlife was undisturbed except for my daily round and the afternoon nut run. I was therefore privileged to see many things of interest, and as often as not, my tale of woe when I got home was alleviated by a tale of some interesting sighting.

Woodcock are common here – the dogs are always putting them up. Snipe too are often seen, and among the grazing sheep, big flocks of curlew step delicately across the mossy ground, pecking the soft soil with their long curved beaks.

A flash of white, red and black would be a woodpecker making for the group of silver birches by the blackthorn spinney. Why does it seem odd to see wild birds with bright colours?

Occasionally, a kite would be drifting high above the trees, in an effortless flight – its forked tail and its thinner wings with 'elbows' marking its difference from the buzzards that are so common.

Foxes were a frequent sight – often on the beach – turning over the wrack at the top of the tide line. The old story that they only take live food seemed inaccurate, as I have often watched a grey-muzzled old Reynard eating dead birds, fish and even the carcass of a dead lamb washed up by the tide.

I once saw a buzzard attack a jackdaw for the titbit it was carrying. The buzzard appeared to drop out of the sky onto the smaller bird. Its clawed feet seized the jackdaw's shoulders, and as it started to rise, the jackdaw dropped its catch. The buzzard released the jackdaw and dropped down to retrieve the prize. I didn't see what it was as, at that instant, I fell flat on my face, one foot having sunk into a hole.

I saw a peregrine falcon take a sick rabbit. In fact I saw the rabbit first, and had stopped within the cover of a tree to watch it (and if possible catch and treat it), when I heard the rush of air as this large brown–grey bird with yellow legs hurtled out of the sky to clutch up the rabbit in one clawed foot, before struggling off into the air.

It seemed to have trouble with the weight of the rabbit and landed again about 200 yards away on the bog. I left the cover of the trees and made off after it, hunching myself up to look as inconspicuous as possible. As I got to within a hundred yards, it took off again with the rabbit. I followed on to where it had stopped and a bloody stain and lots of fur on the grass told its own story. I suppose this is nature's way of treating sick animals justly.

We had a pair of red-breasted mergansers that worked their way up one particular rill as the tide rose. I always seemed to lose sight of them and never knew where they spent the rest of their time, but they'd be back again in the usual place as the tide started to rise.

One of my biggest problems was that of identification. I've always been interested in birds, beasties and plants but it was not until we moved here that I realised how very little I knew. It was a joy to learn of the creatures with whom we share this world, and it still is. I would rush back from my perambulations around the farm and find a reference book to identify what I had just seen. Life was very full and most of it was interesting and enjoyable.

Driftwood for the Rayburn and the wood-burner in the sitting room was another useful bonus from the morning sheep round. The campsite beaches are more exposed than the beach by the house and the yield was therefore higher. At high tide there was little to be found. As often as not the sea would be crashing against the rocks, shooting the spray high into the air. But once the tide dropped to below the rocks so that the sandy beaches started to be exposed, the pickings were often rich.

It was curiously satisfying. I suppose to gather something for nothing appealed to my frugal nature, and to be able to tidy up, and then use, something that would otherwise have been wasted, appealed to me even more. The dogs and I would have a happy few moments on the beach. The fresh morning air, often keen and searching, would drive the dry sand along in small blasts over the lonely shoreline, filling the creases in my jeans so that it tipped into my wellies at each step.

Spotty the old sheepdog always stayed close by, trying to understand what we were doing. He'd look at me doubtfully from time to time and sniff at the pile of wood we had already collected. Sometimes, down on the tideline, I'd give him a piece to carry in his mouth. This worked quite well except that he didn't want to give it back when we got to the main pile at the top of the beach, above the tideline.

Ben, the young collie, also tried to help. He'd seize one end of the branch I was dragging, and with the mistaken impression that we were having a tug of war, he'd pull and tug it back down the beach, bracing his legs, rolling his eyes and growling fiercely. The louder I shouted at him, the louder he growled and the more excited we both got. The wood was mainly dead branches from trees, and it had odd bits sticking out at angles, so it was difficult to drag it along even without an impediment. With a large collie dog hanging on to the other end and pulling as hard as he could in the opposite direction, it often became impossible, and I frequently gave up the struggle and let him win.

We would all three return to the house looking much the worse for wear. The dogs would be heavy with sand and seaweed. It would hang from their muzzles, their tummies and their legs. My face would be the colour of a Belisha beacon and I'd be liberally covered with a mixture of mud and sand, especially if I'd had to heave a ewe out of a ditch, or maybe unhook it from brambles, as was quite often the case. I'd wash my face and hands, make a steaming mug of coffee, and feel absolutely marvellous.

Every week or so, Brian would take the tractor and trailer down to pick up my hoard of wood, and after a couple of weeks in the barn, it burned readily, giving us more or less free heating and cooking facilities. This suited my parsimonious temperament very well indeed.

Chapter Fourteen

After the Christmas break, work had resumed on our part of the new wing. The bathroom did not need to be plastered as the bottom half of each wall was to be tiled, and the top half would be planked with pine boarding. The ceiling was to be curved and also covered with the pine cladding. I was looking forward to a good soak in the bath. We had the little bathroom upstairs in the old cottage, but it was immediately behind the wall that had suffered so much damage during the blasting, and we were reluctant to use it in case the floor supports were not strong enough to withstand the weight of the bath full of water, plus the body in it. I felt disinclined to lower my portly pink person into the bath in case I found myself descending to the ground floor, bath, water and all. Coupled with that, the pipework had been disconnected, so any water discharged from the bath was temporarily draining into the yard, reducing the mud and manure soufflé through which we were constantly paddling to the consistency of a consommé, which was even more difficult to navigate.

Most of the wall was to be rebuilt when the link block was erected, so the upstairs bathroom would be reinstated in due course, but for the moment, a scrub-down with a bucket of warm water had to suffice.

One day at the end of January, Brian was installing the central heating. Dai was laying brick pavers around the fireplace in the sitting room, and I was cleaning out the hen house – a smelly, unpleasant job that I'd put off for too long. The hens enjoyed it though. They pecked out small insects and squabbled over a beetle as the rich droppings were disturbed.

Brian was grovelling under the bath in the new bathroom, muttering to himself. The central heating installation had been devised and drawn up by a professional firm, and they had ordered all the component parts, which had then been delivered as a kit. We had adopted this scheme when installing central heating in our Surrey home and it had worked very well indeed. However, the service seemed to have deteriorated, as with the present kit, we seemed to have too many of some things and not enough of others and clearly this was a day when the missing parts predominated.

After the lunch break, I continued my onslaught in the hen house and Brian got back under the bath.

The afternoon tea break came – and went – and still Brian was battling away under the bath. Dai and I were both given short shrift when we offered to help and it was obvious that the business was becoming desperate.

Brian eventually emerged – face like thunder – and announced his intention of driving into town for a special fitting – the one provided with the kit was apparently useless.

Off he went at the double – treble or quadruple would be more accurate – to reach the shop before it closed, and Dai and I resumed our separate tasks (both of us praying that he *would* get to the shops in time).

By the end of the afternoon, the hen house was immaculate – or as immaculate as it is ever likely to be – and a heady aroma of essence of dung heap clung to my person. But it was pleasing that the job was done and the woodwork and perches sprayed with an insecticide. I had a scrub in the sink in the old kitchen but I still felt itchy and smelly. Chicken droppings have a fragrance that is difficult to eradicate.

Brian returned, triumphantly clutching the part he needed, and immediately crawled back under the bath. Dai departed home and I went back into the old kitchen to make a start on the supper.

Half an hour later I returned to the new wing to hazard the present position with the central heating job. I paused in the doorway to remove my boots and to try and detect the mood of the moment. Would it still be fraught, or had some measure of success been achieved? I could hear water running in the new bathroom. I crept down the hall and peeped around the door. Brian stood with a grin from ear to ear, as lots of lovely hot water gushed into the bath. There in the soap rack was a gift pack of expensive soap and bath salts. A most welcome bit of foresight on the part of my old man and it turned the day into something special.

It was heavenly to immerse my aching body in the soft, sweet-smelling water, after months of trying to soak each bit of me in turn in a plastic bucket. The sense of well-being suffered a slight relapse however, when later in the evening, my ever-loving, also cleaner than he had been for ages, disclosed that he'd made a major effort to get the bathroom functional before nightfall, as he didn't fancy sharing our marriage bed with such a strong smell of chicken house. Was the gift pack supposed to be telling me something, I wonder?

Within a couple of weeks the bathroom had been tiled, the pine stripping pinned up, the shower installed and the electrics finished. I wished I could bring myself to buy a new carpet. We had bought one for the new bathroom in the Essex house shortly before we moved, and as the people who'd taken on the Essex house didn't need that carpet, we'd brought it with us. It seemed such an extravagance to buy yet another, so we found all the original offcuts, sewed it all back together again and then cut it to fit the new bathroom. It didn't look quite as good as a brand new carpet but it would do for a time.

It was the first of the rooms in our part of the new wing to be finished, and in moments of stress, I was apt to go in there and gloat over it.

The new kitchen was coming along too. The hob unit and the new oven had been fitted and the business of cooking our food in one house but serving it in the other should have been over. Unfortunately, my curmudgeonly nature forced me to use the oven of the Rayburn in the old kitchen, since it was always hot, rather than heat the new oven. Negotiating that muddy bank between the two parts of the house, with a very hot roasting dish containing the joint and its satellite roast tatties, could be fraught. On windy nights, I occasionally lost a potato or two, but one of the advantages here was that whatever was spilt was bound to be consumed by somebody – usually the ravening horde from the chicken house.

The dogs were useful in this respect too. Normally they were not allowed into the house, but if I dropped an egg, spilled some milk or had an accident with anything remotely edible, I called them in and they cleared up the bulk of the mess before I got down on hands and knees with a floor cloth. It was really very useful, especially with Mama, who tended to drop quite a high proportion of each meal in a circle of confetti around her chair.

The Rayburn in the old kitchen was a tremendous blessing. It pumped out heat, it dried and aired the clothes, it cooked and it provided all the hot water for the old part of the house. It must be one of the original versions. I'm sure Noah would have recognised it. It wasn't very good with cakes, but it cooked a casserole to a turn. It was also very good with wet wellies, anoraks and anything else that needs a long, slow baking. It was not unusual to have a casserole, a rice pud and the dog's meat in the top oven and a pair of wellies, a slipper and two pairs of over-trousers in the bottom oven, with Leo the Siamese cat lounging against the open oven door. Perhaps some soup would be simmering on the hob beside the kettle, and festoons of washing would be hanging over the top. Life without that Rayburn would have been intolerable.

We tended to eat a lot of soups and stews – we still do. They simmer and bubble to themselves on the top of the stove for hours at a time without any attention. We would have several servings and then I'd top the pot up with leftover meat, bones, or something from the garden. If we were short of vegetables, I would add pearl barley or other cereal and at lunchtimes it made a warming, satisfying meal, sopped up with chunks of homemade bread. Not haute cuisine but honest-to-goodness nourishment, not over-dramatised by elaborate preparation or presentation. Man, the ordinary human animal, has lived very successfully on this sort of thing for centuries – many cultures still do, and I am all for it. It always seems rather immoral to me that top chefs spend so much time and money on the preparation and ostentatious presentation of their food, while many people in the Third World are hungry. If those starving ones were standing outside these posh-nosh establishments in the big cities of the West, there would be a rush of people trying to feed and clothe them, but because they are a nice long way away, most of us manage to overlook that they exist for much of the time.

Soon after we'd bought the farm, the Nature Conservancy Council had written to ask if we would let them rent the forty acres of peat bog, or raised mire, as it is technically termed. It's an interesting place – wild and desolate with small peaty pools of black water on which ducks roost, and frogs and toads leave their spawn in spring. Grass snakes and adders slide through the undergrowth and ditches, leaving their shed, wrinkled skins as evidence of their occupation of this untamed place. Lichens grow on sodden hulks of long dead trees – preserved by the acidity of the peat – and in places, cushions of greeny-yellow sphagnum moss cover the soil, like a luxuriant swansdown duvet.

There are several trenches or workings showing where, for centuries, peat has been dug for the fires in the homesteads. In one of the barns we found a strangely shaped spade, which, on enquiry, has proved to be the implement with which the peat was cut. It has a sickle-shaped blade set on a stout wooden shaft with handlebars at the top, rather than the usual spade handle. The blade is set so that when the spade stands upright, it sits on one point of the sickle. When it was used, the left foot must have been put on the flattened-off end of the upper part of the blade, driving the pointed end into the soft peat. The handlebars must then have been pushed sideways until the left hand almost touched the ground, making the blade slice through the soil. The blade was then pulled upright again, lifted almost out of the peat, and slid some twenty inches sideways, before the next cut could be made. Thus, at one thrust into the soil, a cut of over twenty inches could be made by a small, relatively lightweight blade. The old boys who designed this tool were obviously quite ingenious.

These spades were used all along this coast to cut the bricks of peat – like rich fruit cake – which, when dried, burned with a smoky tobacco smell, warming the cottages and cooking the meals.

It was also sold to supplement the meagre income of the farming community. Indeed, local stories tell of a Welsh woman who herself dug the peat, carried it from the bog to our small harbour, presumably with help from a donkey or pony, and loaded it onto a small hired boat. She then boarded the boat and sailed up the coast to the nearest settlement where the peat was sold. The woman then used the proceeds to buy essentials for her family, loaded them on to the boat and sailed back home with the goodies.

As she neared home, I wonder if her mind ran on the domestic chores awaiting her, as mine did when I turned off the road into the farm lane on my way home from work. Did she, like me, have a mother or father, perhaps sitting propped up by the range in the inglenook, waiting for her attention, as many families did? Did she, like me, have a drink made from the kettle of simmering water on the hob, before she unpacked and sorted out her purchases? Unlike me, however, she would not have had a jar of instant coffee granules or cocoa powder with which to make the drink.

During that first summer, the purple moor grass and the myrtle had grown to a height of two or three feet, swamping the orchids, the bog rosemary, the asphodels and many of the smaller, more delicate plants. This was apparently because we hadn't any cows to graze the grasses off. What had seemed an innocuous part of farm conservation had proved to be otherwise and although we were both interested in natural history and wanted to preserve what we had acquired, we felt unqualified to cope with it adequately. To find yourself in possession of something of this sort is a responsibility. The bog had remained unchanged for centuries. Successive farmers had raised their cattle on it and had lived their lives in tune with it. We felt we were merely short-term stewards of something rather precious that must be properly and caringly maintained. But what to do with it?

The Nature Conservancy Council seem rather unpopular with the local farming community and it was for this reason that we'd not rushed into a lease with them. But after being overwhelmed with all the excess growth and becoming aware that to do nothing was almost as bad as taking the wrong action, we rang one of the wardens and asked for advice. He came over to see the site and was most helpful. We subsequently came to meet one or two of the more senior members of the council and were persuaded that a lease was a sensible move. So, we entered into a management agreement with them and they now manage the bog for us. We've learned a lot from the warden and it is good to know it is being maintained in a suitable manner.

First of all, the NCC suggested that the bog should be fenced off from the rest of the farm and ten or twelve cows kept on it. It was hoped that they would eat off the commoner growth in order to let the smaller plants have a chance to expand. I found this quite worrying as cows are heavy animals with large feet and they walk about for most of the day. Surely the smaller plants would stand a better chance in competition with a bog myrtle bush than with a ton of cow? But I was assured that this was not so and sure enough, that first year after the fence was erected and ten bovine ladies took up residence on the bog, there was a goodly showing of *Andromeda polifolia* and other, previously smothered, plants, so the experts were clearly right.

In the early spring of 1984 the NCC warden suggested burning off the old dead growth on the bog, and with it the few seedling rhododendrons that had established themselves and would no doubt take over if given a free rein. Rhododendrons are almost a rude word in NCC circles as they obliterate all forms of life beneath their canopy of shiny, almost plastic leaves. Several NCC people who seem quite sane and well balanced become vehement and bloodthirsty at any attempt to defend the poor rhodos.

It is necessary to obtain a dispensation from The Powers That Be if you wish to burn off land that is listed as a Site of Special Scientific Interest. I'm not sure who these reverend bodies are, but the NCC warden dwelt on the subject for days. It seemed, however, that they were disposed to be gracious in our case and the necessary permission was given. We notified the Fire Service, the neighbouring landowners, waited for the right weather conditions and the conflagration began.

Early one morning at the end of February, the NCC warden arrived in the yard with a van full of NCC estate workers. Another van full of workers followed and, after a cup of tea, the plan of action was explained. The sheep and cows were driven from the bog, the neighbouring farmers and other interested parties notified, and the men walked down to their appointed positions.

It had been a dry winter in general, but this land lies wet, so although there was a brisk breeze, the general consensus of opinion was that the operation would take two days, even though the top growth was tinder-dry. The men spread out in a line with their flares and at the appointed shout, put light to the fire.

Within a minute or so, it was well alight and starting to move southwards at a walking pace.

Within five minutes, the small patches of burning undergrowth had joined up in a line reaching from our boundary fence almost to the sea and the men were following along behind at a business-like walk.

Within ten minutes, huge waves of flame licked high into the sky, sending charred wood and smoke up into the wind. The scorching dry undergrowth crackled and spat as the flames passed over it – and the word quickly went around that the fire was out of control.

The line of the fire was advancing faster than the men could run and within twenty minutes it had cleared our boundary fence and was advancing down the coast in a very determined way.

Within thirty minutes it had cleared much of the next farm and was still going strong. Men were frantically scrambling through hedges and ditches – running over the boggy uneven ground after it, and the noise of the siren from a fire engine added to the general melee.

It eventually burned itself out but not before we had all had a jolly good fright. I had not known that heath fires could become so rapacious so quickly. But it was typical of life here – the unexpected being more likely than the obvious. In fact, the speed at which the fire had passed was a blessing as it only touched the top growth, leaving the smaller plants unharmed. Most importantly, it also allowed the wildlife – the toads, frogs, snakes, small mammals and insects – to hide in the holes and depressions while the flames roared by. I accompanied the wardens over the whole area within an hour of the fire having passed, and I think we only found one casualty, although there would have been others with damage from which they did not recover and for whom I am very sad.

It was also late in February that the ADAS man called. {a Farm Advisory Service}. We'd asked him to come and advise on our course of action for the future. We wanted to improve the land that was not covered by the NCC agreement and, perhaps, to improve the outbuildings.

He suggested that our most pressing need was for more trees – in fact a small wood. This would provide shelter for the sheep, harbour wildlife, make the farm visually more interesting, and most of all, serve to dry the land. Apparently, trees take a great deal of moisture out of the soil. Ultimately it would also provide firewood too, so it all seemed a very good idea.

It was the end of winter and the grass was threadbare. The sheep would eat almost anything so clearly the first step was to fence the area of the intended plantation.

We lost no time in ordering the posts and the wire netting, and Dai was soon at work erecting the whole thing.

We summoned the Forestry Commission for advice on the types of trees we should be planting and we worked out how many of each variety we would need. We had hoped to plant a few broadleaved varieties, but the Forestry people were not enthusiastic in view of the wet, acidic conditions, so we finally settled for Sitka spruce, Corsican pine, lodgepole pine, and just a few trial samples of larch, rowan, willow and alder.

The order was placed with a nursery in the Wye valley, again on the advice of the Forestry people. The salesperson from this nursery was most helpful but regretted they did not run a delivery service. However, he assured me on the telephone that the plantlets would comfortably fit into my

Renault 5. The wife of the proprietor who ran the nursery owned a Renault 5 and she, apparently, often ran local deliveries with far more than 3,500 trees.

As it happened, there was a time lapse of several days between the placing of the order and the collection of the goods. When I arrived on their doorstep with a hopeful smile, they suddenly realised they did not have the Sitka spruce in one-year-old plants, so we would have to buy the two-year-old trees instead. This also applied to over half the lodgepole pine trees ordered.

We were very lucky – so they assured me – as the older trees were more expensive, but they were only charging the rate for the smaller stock.

Very kindly, they had also made up a free bundle of plantlets in case some of the stock did not survive. Then they tried to get them all into my car.

There was – just – room for me. I had all the windows wide open and trees protruded by at least six inches on all sides. They were solid from floor to headlining, except for the tiny space I was crouched in. They were jammed between me and the right-hand door and between me and the gear stick, and I had to drive over ninety miles along dark, narrow country roads – without stopping to get out. It was fortunate that the car had wing mirrors. It was also extremely cold, but I eventually arrived home safely and had a nice comfortable grumble about it over a cup of the inevitable coffee.

It had taken me a very long time to plant the 300 hawthorn cuttings around the perimeter of the vegetable garden, so Dai suggested we ask two forestry workers he knew to come and plant the spinney for us. The two of them planted nearly 4,000 trees over a long weekend and it has given me immense pleasure to watch their progress ever since. I hope future generations will enjoy and benefit from the little wood.

Chapter Fifteen

Four weeks before we were due to start lambing, the ewes were gathered and inspected. Sundry first aid was given where necessary, generally to overgrown hooves which needed trimming or perhaps wool that needed to be cut back from the udder, leaving the teats exposed and readily available to the lambs, which were soon to be born. They were also given their pre-lambing injection and those that looked particularly weak were given a vitamin injection as well. The pre-lambing inoculation protects the ewe from eight of the common sheep diseases, and if given just before lambing, will protect the lamb too for the first few weeks of its life.

Having absorbed the words of the vet, we had dished out all the recommended doses and injections to cover as many eventualities as possible. It helped to compensate for our lack of experience – but it also taught the ewes that the gathering process was followed by some very unpleasant experiences. Either they would be immersed in a bath of evil-smelling sheep dip, or something revolting was going to be forced down their throats with a drench gun, or a hypodermic needle of vaccine was going to be stuck into them – and they were disinclined to suffer any of these indignities.

The ewes were heavy with their lambs and were submissive, but not so Bill and Ben, the rams, who put up quite a spirited resistance. I cherish a heart-warming little picture in my mind of Bill, the big ram, standing on his hind legs, towering over Dai the shepherd, who was reaching up to grasp the ram's front legs in an effort to turn him over onto his bottom so that his feet could be attended to.

Bill must have weighed fifteen stone or more – a big shaggy monster of a creature with wicked horns – and Dai was small, wiry, and little more than ten stone. For a brief, silent moment, it looked as if they were engaged in a courtly and elegant waltz as they swayed and sidestepped, until Dai's superior footwork brought the ram down. His feet were trimmed, his injection given, and he was released to stamp his foot with annoyance in the gateway. He then took himself off in offended silence to watch the rest of the proceedings.

Some of the older surviving ewes looked very dejected. Although we had dished out sheep cake and as much hay as they wanted, they still looked poorly and we were distressed to see them so. Many of them had never been used to sheep cake or hay and had not taken advantage of these daily handouts. In some cases their age was against them too, and we were powerless to help. There was a tremendous difference between the good-quality younger ewes we had bought in 1982 and the mixed older ewes we'd bought in during the summer of 1983.

For the few weeks immediately before her lamb is born, the ewe is subject to great depletion. The lamb is growing bigger and draining more of the mother's nutrients, it's heavier to carry about, the grass is poor and the weather often bleak. We lost several ewes just before lambing started. They seemed to give up the unequal struggle against age and adversity. For two or three weeks we seemed to be digging graves every few days. It was a depressing, thought-provoking time. It didn't seem fair to have put them into lamb when their chances of a successful conclusion were poor. But then, had we not taken them on, they would probably have been stacked up in tins of pet food on Sainsbury's shelves. Was this a lesser fate than a relatively peaceful end in a winter meadow? On balance, I think most of them would prefer the latter.

We were still trundling a wheelbarrow containing a bag of sheep nuts down to the campsite meadow every afternoon. The procession usually started from the yard at about three o'clock, but as the grazing became almost non-existent, the bolder ewes collected in the yard in dribs and drabs from mid morning, and they hung about with watchful eyes in case the barn door was left open for any reason, when what seemed like the whole flock would disappear inside and find the sheep nuts they desired so mightily.

This happened many times and invariably resulted in a post-mortem to establish who had left the door open and in what circumstances. Once or twice I could see this being cited as a reason for divorce. It was *painfully* easy to be sidetracked and forget those blessed doors.

The ewes would slip quietly in and the first intimation of the trouble would be the sound of tearing paper sacks and objects being knocked over, as the sheep pushed and shoved towards the nuts spilling out onto the floor. It was immensely difficult to get rid of them once they had made a successful raid. They were impervious to shouting and arm-waving. Even seizing their woolly botties did no good – you were merely towed around the barn until you fell over something.

This was useful experience, however. We learned to be very careful about doors and gates from that time on. It is vital on a farm and we were lucky that we learned it without greater expense or loss.

I remember one hideous occasion when a party of Jehovah's Witnesses called just as the ewes were enjoying a successful raid. Brian had discovered their transgression and was inside the barn roaring loud and comprehensive blasphemies – quite unaware that we had visitors. I stood in the yard with a bucket of sacrificial nuts and was banging the bucket with a stick to encourage the ewes to come out – and to try and drown the profanities emanating from the barn.

There, in all our mud, stood this small group of elegantly dressed, God-loving disciples, who had given up their afternoon to try and save our souls, listening to Brian's eloquent words and witnessing the bedlam that was our lives. It was difficult to think of something suitable to say.

I read this last bit to Brian and he points out that there are three separate doors into the barn and this is usually the cause of the problem. The difficulty arises when I (notice that) go in through one door, pulling it to behind me. Some minutes later, I (again) go out through another door, forgetting that the first door isn't latched. All the time the ewes can hear me rummaging through the vast pile of assorted boxes and bags in the barn, they make no attempt to carry out their villainy, but once all is quiet, it only takes a bolder ewe to get her nose behind the pulled-to door to push it open.

Furthermore, Brian tells me, I am *constantly* leaving the barn door open, as well as leaving the house doors open in exactly the same circumstances, so that all the hard-won or expensive heat from the Rayburn and the wood-burner evaporates into thin air, and the sheep come and go as they please, and so on and so on.

This coupled with my total inability to grasp even the *basic principles* of the most simple mechanical device, or to tie a knot that does not resemble a bird's nest, would surely be more than adequate grounds for divorce.

I magnanimously overcome a desire to retaliate with facts about dirty socks and pants consistently left by the bedside or on the bathroom floor, together with a number of other domestic aggravations and hasten to agree that it *is* annoying when the sheep steal an extra helping of nuts, as apart from the expense, it is almost always the ewes that are fat and well, and who do not need the extra food. In spite of all our efforts, many of the older, poorer sheep still would not eat the cereal – they didn't even come to the feeders for their share of the daily handout, so the bolder ones had already had a double helping.

We had spent a lot of time trying to get the reluctant ones to take cake. Some farmers shut them up for several days with nothing else to eat so that they are forced to eat the cake and thereby become hooked.

We did this and after three days they *still* wouldn't touch the nuts, so rather than let them starve, we released them, having depleted their resources rather than having helped them.

In the early days of our sheep keeping, I'd been under a great deal of misapprehension about the technical terms of the sheep industry.

Firstly, I thought that drenching was to make them very wet. This seemed entirely rational – the drench water would have insecticide or something similar to keep their fleeces healthy. Not so. Drenching is the dishing out of medicine, given with a drench gun and fired into the backs of their mouths so that some of it at least is swallowed.

Sheep cake was another difficulty. I knew it wasn't like a Victoria sandwich or a gateau, so perhaps it was those large slabs of compressed brown stuff that looks like flapjack or a muesli bar. Again – not so. Sheep cake is another name for sheep nuts or pellets. The slabs of flapjack are mineral blocks which the sheep are supposed to lick but which our sheep chew off in lumps.

Tupping, which sounds as if it might be something to do with a game of tiddlywinks, is in fact mating or serving. The rams are sometimes called tups.

What a nitwit I was in those early days; I still am in some ways. Given another few years, no doubt I will look back to this time and laugh at the stupid things I am doing and saying now. Life, with its unlocked treasuries, is an eternal teacher.

Mama was still attending the day hospital once a week but there had been a few problems. Most of the ladies she met there came for the social occasion, the lunch, and a good natter with their contemporaries, coupled with sundry medical attention or a bath.

It was a happy place. They brought their knitting or crochet, the photos of their families and they had a good day out with people in similar circumstances.

The sitting room was full of plants, magazines and gossip, interspersed with bursts of laughter. The ladies arrived in the day room soon after nine thirty. The week's news was exchanged over coffee and biscuits, after which the Sister and her staff dealt with bandaged legs, necks in collar supports, and many more small medical problems. It was so nice for some of these ladies to be able to have a bath using the special facilities for getting in and out of the water, and to have a nurse standing by to help if necessary. Many of them would not have felt sufficiently confident to get into the bath at their homes, even with a caring family member in attendance. There is something so heart-warming and therapeutic about bathing in hot water, apart from the subsequent feeling of cleanliness, and it must have improved the quality of their lives in no small way. As life advances, it seems to me that small things, like baths, matter a great deal.

The staff could also advise on any medical conditions that may be worrying the patients, many of whom would not have gone to see the doctor until the condition had advanced to perhaps untreatable levels. There was dignity and understanding in that place and it was worthwhile. There should be more such establishments.

At midday they were given an excellent lunch, followed by some handicraft or other activity, and then tea and cakes at three thirty, before being released.

Into this band of contented, mentally able, senior citizens, had come Mama – guns blazing and unprepared to share the attention. In fact, she enjoyed it very much, as they tolerated her mental aberrations with calm and soothing words whereas, try as we might, we were often anything but calm and soothing.

She was a difficult passenger in the car. Even strapped into the back seat, she would lean forward to poke the head of anyone in the front passenger seat. Sometimes she could even manage to poke the head of the person driving the car – it was very distracting. She also wailed and sang in the car and this too was sometimes difficult to cope with.

Having arrived in the hospital car park, she was nearly always disinclined to get out.

It is inordinately difficult to get somebody out of a car when they are determined to stay inside. But inevitably, sometimes with help from the nurses, we carried the point and she was escorted into the warmth and companionableness of the Friday day hospital.

It seemed so unfair to the other ladies who had their day spoiled. We worried about whether we should let Mama go at all, but it was so good to have her bathed properly once a week, to have her hair washed, her nails cut and other attentions provided. It was a marvellous service and we were most grateful for it. So different from our days in Essex when the authorities had given us no assistance at all.

But we *did* understand that Mama was disruptive. Poor old love – she was happier and more confident than I could ever remember her. The periods of crying and depression had gone – she was often in a rage – often grinning happily – and totally ungoverned by any need to restrain whatever she had a mind to do. She had lost all knowledge of normality and saw no need to put a brake on whatever actions took her fancy.

The staff at the hospital kept quiet about most of mama's excesses but we did hear about some of them.

Apparently one nurse wore her white wrap-around hospital skirt with only a Velcro fastening at the waist. One day, carrying a tray loaded with dirty crockery, she chanced to walk past Mama's chair. Mama's arthritic old hand reached out and clamped itself on to the skirt. Before the nurse could stop, her skirt had been peeled off and there she stood in her undies, still carrying the tray.

On another occasion Mama disputed ownership of a hat – in fact *all* the hats. They were *all* hers and she was taking *all* of them home with her. For some reason we could not be sad at many of these stories. They made us laugh – not unkindly – but almost with affection. We were proud that our old girl had so much spirit. With a strange reversal of roles, Mama had become our child and we tended to act like doting parents with a difficult infant.

But it could be unpleasant if you were on the receiving end of her machinations and the problem came when you were perhaps unable to perceive the humour of the situation. On many occasions it would be hours before the comedy of the contretemps would strike you.

Several times the Sister at the day centre had offered to arrange for Mama to stay in the geriatric ward of the hospital for a few days. As geriatric wards go, it is a pleasant place. There are four or five old ladies in residence at a time. It is light, warm and friendly with single bedrooms, or very small wards – very much the cottage hospital with everyone knowing everyone else.

But we were concerned that Mama would feel she had been abandoned. She would be unable to tell us if she hated it. It would be strange – she wouldn't recognise the layout or the furniture. It was tempting, but for the moment, we had decided against it. It was, however, very nice to know that the offer was there if we were really desperate. The knowledge that we had a backstop carried me through many a difficult time. I'm no saint. Thoughts of packing her off to the hospital permanently, whether she liked it or not, comforted me through many a crisis. But within minutes I would know that we had not yet arrived at that stage and probably never would.

It was many months before we did arrive at a point where it seemed sensible to allow her to spend a few days in the geriatric ward. With hindsight, I wished we had taken up the offer earlier as she appeared to enjoy it and it gave us a break, although much time was spent, particularly on that first occasion, in worrying about how she was.

But lambing was almost upon us again. We were entering our second season with more confidence, but it was tinged with concern that some of the stock was below par and there was little we could do about it.

But there was a feeling of optimism. Creatures who had kept their heads down over the winter were beginning to stir and raise themselves to look around. It was time to rejoin the living world – the start of a new cycle.

We'd let our rams out to start their tupping duties during the third week of October, so our first lambs were expected from the 17th March onwards. Dai was to come and collect up the whole flock on the 12th, and those who were to be early with their lambs would be confined in the labour meadow straight away.

Some farmers make their rams wear a harness with a colour block strapped on the front. As the rams serve the ewes, the colour from the block marks the ewe's wool. The colour of the block is changed every few days so that the shepherd knows which ewes will lamb first. We had not done this, and were instead relying on Dai's ability to tell how soon a ewe will bring her lamb.

With our first lambing, we'd confined all twenty-two ewes in the labour meadow from the start, but with our present flock of nearly ninety breeding ewes, it was clearly impractical as firstly they would have been too crowded and secondly they would have eaten all the grass within the first day or so – and it doesn't grow very quickly in March.

One morning early in March, before lambing was officially due to start, I set off on my morning round. It was a bleak, grey day – still, cold and cheerless.

As I reached the campsite gate, I could hear a tiny lamb

bleating somewhere in front of me.

The dogs and I tore along the track and rounded the bend at the double. There on the sodden grass stood a tiny waif, sopping wet, with wobbly legs and a plaintive, persistent cry for its mother.

Beside it lay a twin, clearly beyond help.

I picked up the poor little crying mite and stuffed it inside my anorak to give it warmth as quickly as possible. The ewes nearby were all grazing peaceably. None of them, as far as I could see, showed signs of a recent birth.

I rushed the baby home and we dried it as best we could. Brian found an old wooden box which he filled with hay, and we laid the lamb in it – putting the whole thing in the warming oven of the Rayburn.

It seemed to be surviving so we fed it with a weak solution of the special dried milk powder produced for orphan lambs. We fed it again a little while later and we were hopeful that it would pick up.

But it was tired – too tired and weak to struggle for life – and it died in the oven.

Our first thought was that it must have been a premature birth, but Dai, who was, of course, summoned to debate the issue, felt it would not have been so well developed had it been early. He went down to the meadow to look for the mother and found a very young ewe with signs of a recent birth. It was her first lambing and clearly she had not known what was happening to her. It was our only first-timer and it had to be early and before we were ready.

We know from subsequent events that this does happen quite often and it is very important for the ewe who does not have the maternal instinct delivered with the baby to be bonded with it for several hours after the birth. This just means keeping them together – often in a confined space – so the ewe does not wander off and forget she has a lamb. Often a ewe who is totally disinterested in her offspring when she is first introduced to it becomes a devoted and attentive mother within a few hours – if you can only find them in time, and bond them together, before the lamb dies.

It was a rotten start to lambing and something of a double disaster as this was a young ewe who should not have had problems. Furthermore, had *we* been more attentive we could perhaps have saved the situation. It was a sobering thought that our negligence had caused the loss.

We had a miserable evening. I walked around the farm with the dogs just before we went to bed and I shone the torch on all the white botties I could see. There didn't seem to be any further disasters, but it was all rather depressing. Dai was to come on the following morning and collect up the whole flock in case there were other ewes with an imminent confinement. We didn't want to risk a repeat of this sad little experience.

The following morning, before Dai arrived, I set off on my rounds. All seemed well. The overnight rain had stopped and it was a clear brisk day with intermittent bursts of sun.

One of the timid older ewes was lying down. She looked at me warily as I passed within fifty yards of her. It seemed odd that she didn't get up and move away. I watched her for a moment from a distance.

Several times she glanced down on the ground at a point between her front and back legs. I began to suspect that she too had a problem. So feigning disinterest, I ambled slowly up on to the bank some fifty yards to her right. She watched me with suspicion – and repeatedly looked down at the grass between her legs.

As I climbed higher and higher up the bank, I could see a tiny, tiny, pure white lamb lying within the circle of her body. It looked quite composed and comfortable so I scrambled down the bank onto the path and beetled off home as fast as my poor old legs would carry me.

Dai had arrived and was having a cup of tea. My latest news spilled out and the boys quickly went off to inspect the scene.

Apparently, the ewe was very weak and the baby so undersized that to move them to shelter would have imposed too great a hazard. So, they left them on the cold wet hillside to make what they could of life. The ewe was a pitifully devoted mother and unlikely to leave the lamb.

The remaining ewes were collected up, leaving the new mum in sole possession of the campsite meadow. I walked down to see them several times during the course of that day, to check that they were both surviving. It was so frustrating to be unable to help them. If only I could have got a bucket of sheep cake or even some hay into that ewe.

The weather turned cold and wet again that evening and I had a miserable time followed by a disturbed and anxious night.

I was off down to the campsite at first light the following morning. There was a biting wind with drifts of sleet. The ewe had moved and was lying within the shelter of a stone wall but there was no sign of the lamb.

Again, the ewe eyed me warily and in my efforts to try and see what had happened to the little creature, I took too great a liberty and went too close to her. She struggled to her feet but stood still. I slowly advanced towards her. She moved slightly, and I could see the little soul wedged in a hole in the wall – completely sheltered on three sides and from above.

When the ewe laid herself down again, the lamb was entirely cocooned from the wind and the rain.

The relief was far beyond that warranted by the occasion. I felt good all day – especially as just before nightfall, I was able to watch the little mite struggle up to feed from the ewe's undernourished udder before being nudged back into its shelter.

The mother and lamb continued to cling to life, in spite of several days of hard weather. The lamb became stronger, and the ewe was able to leave it for short periods, to try and scrape a living from the poor pasture. They were both pathetic specimens of life and only the exemplary care of the mother kept them both going.

That happened in the spring of 1984. As I write this in the late spring of 1986, that baby, a little ewe, has just given birth to a lamb of her own – a healthy, full-weight creature who never gives her a moment's peace with his constant demands for sustenance.

Brian and Dai couldn't be doing with all this sentimental stuff and I suppose someone had to keep their feet on the ground. To Dai, a lamb was an immature financial asset. If it lived, we were better off than if it died. I suppose this is the attitude of most of the farming community.

Brian took more of a middle line. He was depressed at our losses and concerned for the well-being of our animals, irrespective of their financial worth, but they had to take their place in the rough and tumble of our home without any excessive amount of additional attention. In his view, we couldn't shelve, even temporarily, all our other responsibilities to cope with this one aspect of our new life.

This is where people who have not been bred to a farming life suffer unduly. I know perfectly well that it is not sensible to allow myself to be upset – that if we are to live, enjoy and learn from our new way of life, then the losses have to be accepted with stoicism. But it is often extremely difficult to maintain this practical approach.

It is easier to bear if the animal is old and has reached the natural conclusion of its life – where perhaps respect for the dignity of the creature makes me glad that it has been spared any further pain and embarrassment. But it is still very difficult to get to grips with. It is one of the only unhappy elements in the way of life here and I do not find that suffering does my soul any good at all. Instead it makes me depressed and fractious.

Chapter Sixteen

We struggled over that lambing meadow every two hours for another nine days before a further lamb was born.

It seemed so odd that two ewes had produced full-term lambs over a week before anybody else. It was reasonable to expect some lambs to be born a day or so early and others a day or so late but to have two early lambs and then nothing for nine days seemed inexplicable.

Then Brian remembered a seemingly small occurrence from the previous autumn, when a ram from a neighbouring farm had been found on our patch, eyeing up some of our girls. This was nearly two weeks before we had intended to start tupping, and Bill and Ben were still confined to their paddock. The intruder had obviously trotted down the lane into our territory when someone had left the gate open.

Fortunately, Audrey, a friend from the village, had noticed the unrest in the rams' meadow as she passed it on her way over to visit us. The two lads had been gnashing their teeth, pawing the ground and raising their heads to sniff the air – obviously distressed about something.

When Audrey arrived at the house, she mentioned it, and Brian had hopped on the motorbike to go and investigate the problem. The intruder had been found and thrown out, but obviously not before he had served two of our ewes. Whoever had declined to get out of their vehicle and shut the gate had cost us two lambs and made a lot of work. Reason enough for many farmers to discourage the visitors.

The next new arrival was a strong, healthy ram lamb, born to one of the original ewes. She was a confident, unworried mother who attended to the washing and drying of her offspring in a methodical, unhurried way. She nudged him towards her udder and let him feed. Then, while he had a nap, she wandered around nearby, to pull a few nibbles of grass, before settling herself down for forty winks beside him. She had been one of the ewes in the forefront of the nut run each day – she was well nourished and in good shape. It was a joy to see them.

The next arrival was also a success. A small ram lamb born to an older ewe but both survived the ordeal quite well and looked to be improving. This particular ewe was one of the few that had actually taken to sheep cake when they were shut in the bakehouse yard for three days. She had subsequently come to the feeders in the campsite meadow each day but as she was timid and retiring, she had not bothered to fight her way into the scrum and thus had probably enjoyed precious little of the cake.

But nemesis was with us again the following morning. Brian returned from the morning round to report a problem. One ewe was contracting regularly and frequently but was unable to give birth as the lamb was back to front.

This news, delivered at 6.15 when I was still battling with a desire to return to sleep, caught me at my most illogical. My 'Why don't you turn the ewe round then?' wasn't very well received. Matters having been explained more fully, I dragged myself up and went down to the bakehouse where the ewe was lying – Brian having carried her from the meadow and installed her on some straw, under cover.

She was weak from the contractions but an otherwise healthy animal. Her rear end showed only a lamb's tail hanging disconsolately against her own tail.

I've read all of James Herriot, and with his stories in mind, I found a pair of rubber gloves, a bucket of warm soapy water, and in the gloom and dampness of the old stone building, I soaped my right hand and tried to ease it into the ewe's bottom.

She groaned with pain – I was fearful of doing more harm than good. I tried again, gently, tentatively searching for the lamb's back legs. But only tight, wet wool met my exploring fingers.

It was just after seven – surely the vet would be up by now? I abandoned the James Herriot bit, rushed back up to the house and rang the surgery. Happily – mercifully – the vet was up, and he suggested driving her over to his home some seven miles away.

We spread lots of newspapers in the back of the little Renault, piled straw on top and carried the ewe to the vehicle.

Brian set off within a few moments, and on the front lawn of the vet's house the lamb was delivered – dead.

Brian arrived home some half an hour later looking tired and dejected – with the ewe looking about the same. But she recovered quite quickly. Within a few hours she was up – and was frantic for a lamb. We'd let her loose in the labour meadow so we would keep her in view and by late afternoon she was running from pillar to post, baaing pitifully – searching – searching – for her lamb. Nothing would pacify her.

We hadn't realised at that stage that dead lambs are usually left with their mothers for the first few hours, and we suffered with the ewe, and mourned with her the loss of her lamb.

That evening we consulted with Dai on the phone and he suggested giving her a foster lamb. An hour later he arrived in the yard with a tiny ewe lamb – a twin, abandoned by its mother. It was a Suffolk lamb, and therefore had a black face and feet, with short matted curls of creamy wool over the rest of its body – whereas most of the Welsh Mountain lambs are pure white, or perhaps have just a collar of beige wool.

We collected the ewe from the meadow, shut her in the bakehouse yard, and showed her the lamb. She sniffed at it suspiciously and turned her back.

We held the lamb and let it feed. It was very hungry and pulled lustily at her teats.

The ewe was not amused.

In the darkness, Dai rummaged at the back of the cowshed and found an old sheep hurdle. We carried it into the barn and wedged it in one corner to make a small triangular pen. He then spread straw on the floor of the pen, hung a hay net at one end and stood a bucket of water on the floor at the other end.

Then he carried the ewe and the lamb, and put them both in the pen. We turned out the light and left mother and foster daughter alone together.

Later that night, just before we went to bed, Brian and I walked down to see how they were doing. The ewe blinked in the sudden light, noticed the lamb and sniffed doubtfully at its rear end. We held her again and let the lamb feed. The ewe hardly struggled and seemed relieved as the tightness went from her udder.

The following morning, the ewe was allowing the lamb to feed quite readily. She continually sniffed at its rear end, as if to assure herself that it was her own milk that was beginning to pass through the lamb.

The baby stood with her long wobbly front legs wide apart, enabling her to get low enough to reach under the ewe's tummy, her own little tail wiggling excitedly as she pulled at her mother's udder.

Within another few hours they were inseparable and Mari lamb grew up to be a confident ewe in her own turn – always in the front of the nut run in subsequent years.

We've fostered many lambs since Mari and it nearly always works very well. Through Dai's good reputation with the local farmers, we have been most fortunate in having access to orphan lambs and indeed lots of other useful items. We've borrowed all sorts of bits and pieces to do jobs about the farm, and, in turn, our concrete mixer was missing for several months while somebody put in a concrete base for a new cowshed.

It is a very nice cooperative spirit and we have been very lucky to be able to join in. The local Welsh farming community have been extremely kind to two inexperienced English immigrants – and Dai has been very helpful. He knows everyone and where unlikely items can be sourced.

The lambs started to arrive more frequently, from one or two a day up to four or five. Some were lovely healthy animals. Bill and Ben had certainly been worth the extra cost. Others were pitiful little things, some of whom died within a few moments of birth. Some struggled on for an hour or two then died, and some went on for a day or so, and then gave up the ghost, after we had spent many hours caring for them. If they survived for two or three days, they were usually safe, but it was only too apparent how vital those first few hours are.

Brian and I walked the lambing meadow like two zombies in all weathers both day and night. We also had to check the campsite meadow where the mothers and lambs were taken after their initial bonding, when it was clear that they were both well. Several pairs who had appeared to be happily bonded proved to be otherwise the moment your back was turned.

This was usually due to the mother ambling along as she grazed until she was out of sight of her lamb. Her baby would wake up, not find her close by, would look around, see another ewe and assume that she was his mum – so he would join her and follow behind as she ambled along.

Then he would try to feed and suddenly realise that it wasn't his mum at all. So he would bleat and run around looking for his real mother.

Sometimes as the lambs grow older and more confident, they will go off and play in a group. These games are a joy to watch. They love to climb on a rock and then jump off – one after the other – and turn and turnabout. Or they will all set off down the meadow in a horde, jumping, leaping and skipping. Their mothers baa a remonstrance, but without the least expectation of being attended to. Then the little hooligans will realise they are hungry and they will bleat back to locate their mothers.

But by now the ewe has laid herself down to chew the cud and she's sleepy and contented – for the moment she has forgotten her lamb. The lamb starts to baa frantically and rush around looking for his mother. But he tires very quickly and will suddenly lie down and have a nap.

Meanwhile, the ewe starts to feel the tightening in her udder, so she remembers the lamb, heaves herself to her feet, and baas a 'Where are you?' The baas getting more and more frantic.

Thus it seems that there is always someone baaing with an urgent note in their voice, and that second lambing, I took it all very seriously.

Several times I rushed around the campsite meadow carrying a bleating lamb, looking for a ewe that didn't seem to have a lamb, or who was baaing from, as it seemed, a long way away across ditches, through hedges and boggy ground.

I would set off carrying the baby and eventually get to the distant ewe, whose lamb was lying a few feet from her, hidden in the grass.

So still carrying the lamb I would struggle back across ditches, through hedges, over fences and through boggy bits to where I started. By then I was almost bleating too.

Invariably the mother would turn out to be the ewe that was nearby in the first place, and the lamb that had been standing by her really belonged to another ewe who was grazing just behind a rock.

The campsite meadow is very undulating with steep rocky banks and lots of trees. There are outcrops of rock everywhere so that it was easy for the ewes and the lambs to lose sight of each other – and indeed for me to be mistaken.

One ewe continually left her lamb down on the beach. This meant that as the tide got to within an hour of high water, I would have to hare off down to the campsite beach to make sure she had brought it to safety.

She always had, and just as surely she took it back down onto the piles of wrack as soon as the tide had dropped sufficiently.

We really made a spirited effort to cover all these potential danger points but it was arduous work and I now know that much of it was unnecessary.

The redeeming feature was the weight loss. I was thrilled to be able to wear a pair of jeans that had stayed unworn at the back of my clothes chest for several years. But sadly it didn't last. As soon as the campers started to arrive with their offerings of chocolates and other goodies, I became a pudding again and the jeans will probably lie in the chest for nine months out of twelve for the next ten years.

Once or twice we were able to help a ewe with the birth of her lamb. It was a heart-warming and satisfying task. The first time this happened, I was doing my two-hourly stint when I saw a ewe that was clearly about to give birth.

They are much happier if left to their own devices, assuming there are no complications, so I left her for an hour, and did some weeding in the vegetable garden while keeping her in view.

After an hour or so, the contractions were very frequent and as she looked to be in trouble, I went to get Brian. This was easier said than done, however, as not only did I get Brian, but also Mama who was restive and could not be left. We bundled the poor old girl into her coat, muffled her up in scarves and got her into the back of the car to drive the fifty yards to where the ewe was lying.

She seemed noticeably weaker, so we carried her from the field into the bakehouse lean-to.

Her rear end showed only one tiny hoof whereas there should have been two. I ran back up to the house and found an old bath towel.

Back at the delivery room, I shredded the towel into strips and looped one of the strips around the little hoof.

The next time the ewe's exhausted body contracted, I heaved on that bit of bath towel, and out came a miniature nose to join the foot.

Every time she contracted, I heaved a bit more until the whole head was born – and I could see that one front leg was bent backwards and lying along the lamb's body.

The birth of the shoulders is always a difficult point in the delivery. They are often wider than the head – and this ewe had a pair of shoulders *and* a leg to deliver at the same time.

Suffice it to say, we all heaved and grunted – including Mama who sat in state in the back of the car, making a brave attempt on a piece that sounded as if it could have been Mahler – until eventually the lamb was born.

The ewe lay still – unable to summon up the energy to even raise her head. We cleared the lamb's mouth, checked that it was breathing and laid it by her face. Her eyes turned towards it and after a few moments, she lifted her head and started to wash her baby – muttering to it all the while.

Within an hour the ewe was sitting up and the baby was on its feet. With help from Brian, the ewe drunkenly dragged herself up – wobbling from side to side – and allowed the lamb to explore among her fleece for her udder. We held our breath – the little mite took so long to find the maternal font – would her strength hold out?

But it did – and the lamb had its first feed of the vital colostrum.

After a few hours the ewe was much stronger and they both turned out to be one of our great successes of the year. It was one of the most enjoyable times in our farming life. I still remember that afternoon and can readily recall the sense of satisfaction and achievement it engendered.

We lurched on from crisis to crisis with Dai's help until all the pregnant ewes had lambed. A total of eighty-nine lambs had been born or fostered here of which twenty-six had died. An extremely depressing proportion.

Some of the failures had been due to mismanagement and inexperience and several to foxes but the majority of the losses had been due to the age and poor state of the ewes we had bought the previous summer. The farmer friend who had steered us into the purchase had been right. They had given us a great deal of experience and it has stood us in good stead ever since. Our first lambing with those original twenty-two young healthy ewes, all of whom knew what they were doing without any help from us, had taught us very little.

Bully for you, John Griffiths – you did us well in spite of the hard words we uttered while it was all happening.

Chapter Seventeen

It was such a relief to have lambing behind us – to see the surviving lambs starting to graze, and thereby gain weight. Some of them were beefy jobs, with fat woolly faces and hefty shoulders. Others were smaller but nonetheless healthy, and would improve. Even the delicate ones started to look happier – as if they might give us a try, rather than give up the struggle. The weather was improving, the grass was growing, and things looked brighter altogether.

We were very anxious to get on with the doorway through the west wall of the old cottage. Since Christmas, when the new wing had been habitable, all foot traffic between the old and new parts of the house had needed to survive the obstacle course between the back door of the old house and Mama's front door on the north side of the new building. I know I've mentioned this several times already but it really was a major hazard. I suppose, too, it is enjoyable to dwell on the difficulties we had at the time and to feel that they have now been overcome.

Over the winter the double doors that would eventually lead from the new sitting room into the link block between the two houses had been temporarily blocked up. They were not exterior doors and they didn't fit very well so the draughts had whistled through them, making the new sitting room very cold. Therefore Brian had made a barricade to protect them from the weather, and to help to keep the sitting room warmer. But the weather was improving now and that barricade could come down.

Mama slept in her posh new quarters in the new wing but we were still using a bedroom in the old cottage, and I still cooked on the Rayburn in the old kitchen. If connubial bliss was to be maintained, Brian was going to have to join up the two parts of the house so that I could leave the old cottage on the west side and walk the few feet to the double doors into the new sitting room in the new wing. OK, I would settle for a non-existent roof over those few feet for the moment, but a doorway through the west wall of the old house must be made urgently.

It was particularly annoying to have to turn out of doors at night, especially if it was wet at 2.15am. I would be in a deep sleep – warm, clean and comfortable – when the intercom would start to chatter.

I would lie in bed listening. Surely it was just a matutinal gossip – perhaps with Hitler, the Pope or the Duke of Windsor. All people who had featured in Mama's conversation for much of her life.

Then I would wonder if she'd thrown the bedclothes off and was cold. *Perhaps she's thirsty – what did we have for supper – was it salty?*

Inevitably, I would heave myself out of the warm, comfortable bed, don a dressing gown – down the stairs, still half asleep – on with the wellies, which feel cold and damp – let myself out of the door into the night, through the mud and up the bank to the door.

I have no key.

Back down the bank – through the mud – find the key – back through the mud – up the bank – find the keyhole in the dark, and let myself in. Mama is lying in bed with a fatuous grin on her face and twinkling eyes – as comfortable as you please.

She doesn't want a drink or a biscuit – her incontinence pad is still dry – I tuck her in more tightly and reverse the procedure back to bed.

Feet are freezing and the bed seems less comfortable than it was. All desire for sleep has gone so I plan the meals for the next few days, dwelling on the possibility that the summer dress, bought last spring but never worn, will fit this summer; or whether the weather will be good enough, early enough, to wear it before the annual spread of the waistline overtakes one.

I review my wardrobe generally and decide on a couple of new nighties. My undies drawer could do with a general sort out. I never, ever will wear that daring black lace bra that must have been in the drawer for at least ten years and a couple of the slips have lost their colour and could go.

The intercom announces in unusually clear tones that the prime minister is coming.

I find myself wondering if Margaret Thatcher wears French knickers and if I would find them comfortable!

At 3.30am, I am debating the likelihood that the Duke of Edinburgh really understands what some of the youngsters go through to win one of his awards – how much harder it is for the slim lassies to carry all that weight over such difficult terrain, often in dreadful weather, compared to the boys with their heftier frames. Why don't they include some activity where the girls would have a natural advantage – nursing a patient with senile dementia, for example?

By 4.30am I have planned the meals for the forthcoming visit of old friend Terry Collins, sadly now parted from his wife, and this is followed, hopefully with no connecting thought process, by a recollection of my annoyance that the local hospital have run out of the long blue incontinence pads, and were only able to supply me with the thick white ones, which will not stay in place.

In my mind I compose an eloquent and comprehensive letter to the local health authorities complaining about this – and another letter to the local paper about their recent article on community care.

At 5.30am, I wonder if it is too early for a cup of tea. My feet are still very cold and I'd be better off up and about, perhaps making a start on that pile of ironing, some of which has been in the cupboard for months.

At 7.30 am I am deep in the land of nod, with a violent disinclination to be dragged from my bed.

So no matter how great the technical problems, a door through that wall must be made with all speed.

Most of the six feet of land between the two buildings was in fact just a large hole where the rock had been excavated back in the days of the blasting. On the north side of the hole, there remained a rocky wedge tucked up against the west wall of the old cottage – the rock that we had not been able to remove. Some of this could perhaps be chipped off with a small hammer. It would be slow, painstaking work but it was only necessary to clear sufficient space to make a pathway from the yard up to the link block door on the north side. Following that final catastrophic charge, sufficient rock had been blasted away to enable the north wall of the link block to be built, leaving the outcrop, or wedge of rock, on the outside of the house. This was something of a bonus as, from first sight, it had appeared that we would have to live with that great lump of rock as part of the decor in the new link block or hallway.

As I've already said, we had originally hoped to be able to remove enough rock so that the new wing could be built on the same level as the ground floor of the old cottage. But quite early on, it had been obvious that any more blasting carried out close to the old cottage would severely damage the gable-end wall, and maybe even the roof. Coupled with that, the extreme expense of removing another three feet of solid rock over a surface area of forty by twenty-five feet would have put the operation beyond economic sense.

So we had abandoned any attempt to join the two buildings up at ground level and had settled for a short flight of stairs from the ground floor of the old cottage to the level of the new wing, and a hall or link block between the two buildings.

The hole where the new hall would eventually be built was in fact quite useful as the drainage and sewage pipes from the new bathroom and Mama's cloakroom had been laid through this space. On instructions from the building team, I had from time to time tipped stones around these pipes to fill the hole. This was generally when I had an odd five minutes to spare to scoop up a couple of buckets of shale and hurl them into the hole. There is something quite satisfying in hurling a bucket of stones into a hole and watching them rattle down into the corners.

But Brian and Dai now set about filling that hole with hardcore and it was soon up to a level just below the intended floor line.

We had rather a difficult afternoon when the top was filled with cement – and it rained – and the sheep trod in it before it could be covered up – and then the dogs managed to tread in it even after it was covered up – and tempers generally were rather uncertain. But eventually we had a flat platform about ten feet by six feet that would become the hall that linked the two buildings.

Even that modest improvement was pleasing. We could at last get into the new wing through the sitting room doors, from which the barricade had been removed, rather than through Mama's front door.

The next stage – the creation of the doorway through the damaged wall of the old cottage – was extremely delicate and fraught with peril. Brian and Dai discussed it at length and I was filled with apprehension that the whole of the gable-end wall would collapse when they started to interfere with the already crumbling stonework. There were *huge* cracks in that wall. From the inside of the cottage, one section between two of the cracks had bulged inwards to a distance of over a foot and I could easily pass my arm through the cracks in some places to the daylight on the outside.

The wall, 3 feet thick, was very old, probably built in 1700 or thereabouts, and constructed of local slate – never a good building medium. It was also built in the dry stone fashion – the irregular lumps of slate being piled on top of one another without any mortar. To make it reasonably solid, it had been built to a thickness of over three feet. But after the blasting, the whole thing was unstable and very dangerous. The thought of even getting near enough to tamper with those huge loose boulders seemed madness.

The men set about it slowly and carefully. They gently loosened one of the large stones where it was intended to form a lintel, and prised it out. This left a space about 15 inches in height by 18 inches in depth so the remaining 18 inches of the 36 inch wide wall was still supported. In the hole that was thus created, they set up a concrete breeze block, bedded in cement.

A second breeze block was set up at right angles to the first, bedded in and backfilled with cement – and thus we had a corner.

Then they left it all to set for two days.

Later that week, the men gently eased out more stones, bedded in more breeze blocks on top of the first two, backfilled the hole, and left it for a few days.

In this way, instalment by instalment, one side of the door frame was constructed.

The other side was gently – carefully – built up in the same way, until we had a doorway about eight feet high. Eighteen inches into the doorway one came face to face with the back of the old wall – still intact – but it was exciting to see how it would all work out.

As this was going on, the wall was supported by a series of props on the inside and in other places where it looked vulnerable. The props were not those generally recognised by the building industry, but old iron bars, gate posts and anything else remotely suitable. It all looked very precarious and all I could do was to pray it would all go smoothly and safely, and in the meantime, keep out of the way.

At the top of the proposed doorway, they built a wooden box spanning the opening and projecting back into the wall to a depth of eighteen inches. They laid iron bars in this box, and filled the lot with cement to make a ferrocrete lintel, eighteen inches deep by about six feet wide.

When that set, the gap between the top of the lintel and the old wall was also filled with cement. When that was set, the box casing was removed, and we had a finished surround to the passageway, and this extended halfway through the wall to a distance of three feet. Then the men set up camp *inside* the old cottage to make the doorway from that side.

Still supporting the upper part of the wall as they went, they worked down to floor level – some three feet below the level they'd started from on the other side of the wall. The boulders at the base of the wall were huge – big foundation stones placed there many centuries ago when the original building on the site was erected. This had probably been an old barn or shelter erected by the Welshmen of the day, from materials they found in the vicinity – some even from the beach. During this work, it became clear that the present cottage had been built in about 1700 from the ruin of this earlier building and some of the foundation stones dated back to the earlier construction.

By degrees, Brian and Dai set up new foundations, built up new door frames and started to remove the stones so that we could actually see through the opening.

It was a moment of much satisfaction – the first step in joining the two parts of the house – a landmark to be enjoyed.

Eventually the doorway was built up to meet the one already made on the outside. A lintel was made to match and meet with the first one. And we had a doorway that could be walked through. Indeed, I walked through it so much during those first few days that 'Here she comes again, happy as can be' was the theme song hummed by the men whenever I appeared through the new portal. It was bliss.

Even though the space between the two buildings was still open to the heavens, it was so much easier to cart the food, the laundry and everything else over a flat, mud-free surface only a few feet wide.

Brian concocted a makeshift staircase out of a pile of breeze blocks and a milk crate so that we could cope with the different levels from the floor of the old cottage up to the floor of the link block, and life immediately became much easier.

The men checked and repaired the rest of the gable-end wall on the inside and built a breeze-block wall to support the outside. The space between the new block wall and the old wall was filled with cement, so it all became safe and solid again. And I stopped praying about it.

Meanwhile the weather was improving, and as we were all working out of doors, Mama had her chair in a sheltered place amongst the rubble, and spent her days beguiling us with a selection from her repertoire. This included her usual chatter, some of it comprehensible, some not, and also singing, wailing and shouting. Some of her performances showed great dramatic flair, rivalling the greatest operatic soloists.

Rather strangely she also started to use the odd rude word. At first I thought she was trying to say something else, and I had merely misheard. But after several repeats – some of them when her speech was quite clear – I had to concede that they were indeed *rude words*. Goodness knows how she came to know these words as I never heard her say them during her earlier life.

We all turned the colour of mahogany and Mama's legs, which had been troubled with scaly and sore patches over the winter, became the envy of many of the campsite teenagers. She sat there in state, amongst the debris, in an old armchair, under a frilly umbrella that my mother must have bought in the twenties, looking as happy as a cricket. The Sister at the hospital had suggested that we leave her legs exposed to the fresh air as much as possible. They really had been a problem. A small scaly patch would appear and Mama would scratch and pick at it until it was really sore. There seemed nothing you could do to stop her fratching with these bad places at night when her stockings or tights didn't cover them up. We'd treated them with various potions and ointments, largely without avail. But the fresh air was making the world of difference. She sat there with a soft cotton T-shirt on the top half, and a shawl draped over her undies on the bottom half, so that as much of her bare legs as could decently be exposed, were exposed.

We found it pleasing to see her so, in the midst of the meagre family she possessed and as comfortable and contented as we could make her, circumstances permitting. But this was made the subject of doubt by several callers, one of whom was outspoken enough to comment on Mama's clothing and wonder why we hadn't bothered to dress her properly.

Having considered the matter, we felt that Mama, in her days of normality, would not have cared about her clothing, and as her legs, which had been quite a problem, were now so much better, we allowed her to remain in her off-beat garb, but I did tend to rush out with a bath towel to make a better job of the covering up if we heard somebody arriving.

For some time she had trotted out a 'What are you doing?' every time we passed her chair. This had deteriorated into 'whayerdoin?' and then 'wardoooooooooinnnnnn?', and it could be repeated two or three times a minute for *hours*.

It is extraordinary how tiring that became. I tried so hard to reply civilly but there were many occasions when I am sorry to say I marched past without making any answer at all, and I once heard Dai, who was struggling in a heroic fashion with a wheelbarrow full of wet concrete up a steep bank on a blazing hot day, mutter something about 'not tying knots in my hanky' as he passed Mama's chair and the usual phrase was wailed from under the umbrella.

So there we were. We had a super doorway – but no door. So at night sheep could come and stand in the doorway and baa, and one or two actually came down the breeze-block/milk-crate staircase, and stood in the bottom hall to gaze up the old staircase that leads to the two bedrooms in the old cottage.

They would stand there looking thoughtfully up the stairs, I suppose wondering if it was worth climbing up them to see if a cache of sheep nuts was to be found at the top.

They also did things that animals do if they're not house-trained, and jolly annoying it was to stagger out of bed in the morning, down the stairs still half asleep, and put your slippered foot in it.

I suppose we could have put in a makeshift door, but Brian was keen to build up the sides of the new hall, and get a roof on it, so he and Dai got on with the block walls while I carried the blocks up to the site from the pile in the yard.

Here again, you would have thought that all this effort would have had a satisfactory effect on my spare tyre, but not so – I struggled manfully and still stayed as plump as a Christmas pud.

Eventually the walls were up to eight feet, but as they both contained a doorway to the outside world, but no door, I was no better off as far as invasions of sheep and visitors were concerned.

The visitors were turning up in droves – there was no turning them away. 1983 had been a warm, dry summer and everybody seemed to be convinced that 1984 would follow suit.

The campers varied enormously from those who came on a shoestring with a borrowed tent and a very ancient motor, to those who had suddenly found that the peasant classes are now admitted to the Hiltons of the world and, to be different and original, it was vogue to buy the latest technology in touring caravans and go out on safari to see how the savage tribes of outback Britain live.

Among the latter category was a rather elegant middle-aged lady – always beautifully groomed and smelling of something extremely expensive – invariably carrying a small, equally well-groomed, sweet-smelling small dog. I have hideous recollections of her standing amongst the mud and animal droppings in our yard in her high-heeled shoes, the small dog placed in a dryish spot on the ground while she tied a silk scarf over her newly tinted and permed hair. The dog was still attached to her by a piece of pink ribbon, knotted into a floppy bow attached to its collar, with a similar bow tying the other end to a gold bracelet on her arm.

Around the corner of the house came Ben the sheepdog, who was anything but sweet-smelling. He trotted up to the little dog, who was by now yapping furiously. Ben sniffed at it doubtfully, turned sideways and thoughtfully lifted his leg – releasing a drench of Ben's best all over the poor little thing.

It all seemed to happen so quickly – it was over before I could stop it. I felt so sorry – I would have found it annoying, but it must have been infinitely more so to someone who was turned out like a plum duff.

When I related the tragic event to Brian later that afternoon, he uncharitably went into howls of merriment.

Peter and Pip were another couple who came quite frequently. Peter was about thirty-five – a tall, thin academic type – serious, quietly spoken and with a great air of sadness.

Pip was about eight years old – always dressed in dungarees and also very quiet and serious.

They were clearly devoted to each other but we never discovered whether Pip was a boy or a girl, and whether they were father and child or brother and sister.

They were nice people to have around, but being the nosey parker I am, I would love to have known why they were so sad and to have tried to do something about it.

There were, of course, many nice, ordinary folk who come to enjoy the scenery, the fishing, the swimming and the peace and quiet of this lovely place. But many of them had peculiarities. Almost all of them would erect impromptu washing lines almost as soon as they got here and within a few hours these washing lines were loaded with tea towels, swimsuits, undies, and other personal bits and pieces.

Several of the ewes have learned to turn the campers to good account. Blooey, one of the old original ewes, would wander from tent to tent looking as lean and hungry as she could contrive, and it was surprising how many biscuits, apples, jam tarts and similar offerings came her way as a result. She also had the odd cabbage or lettuce somebody had placed in a bowl of water to keep cool, just inside the flysheet of their tent or under their caravan. I often had visions of her consuming somebody's best blouse or bikini from the washing lines, as she was none too fussy about her diet.

She would also haunt the yard with her two lambs looking such a picture of gnawing hunger that even Brian's heart would melt and he'd give her two slices of bread. This would be consumed at express speed, giving no hint of the vast bowl of mashed potatoes she had consumed not two hours previously. She had cultivated a hopeful, woebegone expression – a starving mother with two little ones to feed – and it served her well – as most of the campers didn't notice that both she and the lambs were as fat as butter. They would stand in a group hanging their heads and baaing pitifully, but when the comestible was produced, a metamorphosis took place, and from drooping, wan, unhappy animals, they suddenly changed to aggressive, single-minded, competitive gluttons. I suppose it was less trouble than finding dull old grass all day and made for a more interesting diet.

Summer also brought two new additions to the ménage.

The big old red Peugeot car had served us well but was clearly now in the geriatric class. Bits fell off it now and again and Brian riveted, welded, screwed or stuck them back on, but there was no making a silk purse out of a sow's ear. We really no longer needed a big car as, at most, there were only three of us to transport about.

Brian busied himself with the motoring magazines to get an idea of what would be suitable, and after lengthy deliberations, plumped for a small diesel, as the fuel was cheaper, the insurance costs were lower because of the reduced fire risk, the vehicle would cover more miles to the gallon of fuel, and there would be less maintenance. We were also persuaded to arrange the purchase through an import agent as it saved a substantial sum. So Brian paid the deposit and we started the promised six weeks' wait for delivery. We also paid a small additional charge for a transporter delivery service to the Midlands, thus saving the business of flying off to some European capital to collect the new car.

After the six weeks we rang the agency. 'Has our car arrived?'

'No it hasn't. The car manufacturers have been on strike, but it should be here within two more weeks.'

After eight weeks we rang again. 'Haven't heard anything from you. Has our new car arrived?'

'No it hasn't. The car manufacturers have gone back to work but the steelworkers are on strike – there's no steel to make it with.'

After ten weeks, we rang again. 'Still haven't heard from you. What about our new car?'

'Mr Jones isn't available – nor is Mr Smith or Mr Brown, but I'll get someone to ring you.'

Long silence.

We rang again at thirteen weeks. 'We paid a deposit on a new car promised for delivery seven weeks ago. Any news of it yet?'

'Mr Jones has broken down but should be in the office later today. I'll get him to ring you.'

Long silence.

We rang again at fifteen weeks – sixteen weeks – seventeen weeks – nineteen weeks – twenty-one weeks – and almost daily thereafter.

After twenty-four weeks, Brian was minding his own business in the workshop one morning, when the local policeman arrived in the yard. Funny how it is that one still does a rapid mental résumé of one's recent omissions, indiscretions and transgressions when one finds a member of the constabulary on the doorstep, even though one has reached the age when policemen look barely old enough to be out of school.

None of our sins had caused his call however. He merely wanted to know if we could give a home to a black Labrador puppy – only seven months old, but proving to be too much of a handful for his present owner, who had acquired the pup from his late father.

Meanwhile, the dog looked hopefully at Brian and tentatively wagged his tail. He had the rounded puppy shape, with a lovely clean shiny coat, still not grown on his tummy so that the pink skin showed through. Rolls of baby wrinkles hung down his face as his eyes looked up imploringly.

We already had the two so-called working dogs so a third seemed a silly idea, but who could resist those sad black eyes and the hopefully, doubtfully wagging tail? So yes, he had passed the examination and was in. His name was Flash – an apt if not very attractive name – and he soon had us under his thumb.

For a start, he was hyperactive. He bounced up and down in an ecstasy of excitement *all* the time. Anything remotely edible disappeared in a flash – as did slippers, wellies, washing, and anything left on the doorstep. When all else failed, he would start on the dried sheep droppings.

But to get back to the day he arrived. The two sheepdogs had witnessed his coming and were skirting the yard, watching the proceedings from under or behind the machinery.

As the policeman left, Brian called them to heel and let them meet the newcomer at close quarters. They sniffed him over and he cringed against Brian's legs, his eyes rolling with apprehension.

I arrived home in the yard from work having passed the policeman in the farm road – and very anxious I was to know what had necessitated his visit.

All was soon told, and as we felt that the canine introductions could more easily be made during the progress of a walk, I gave Mama the once-over to check that she was OK, and then set off with the pup on a lead and the two sheepdogs running free, as usual.

Every few yards or so, we stopped to have a communal cuddle, and thus we all got to know each other, and the pup became less nervous.

As we were arriving back in the yard, nearly an hour later, the phone was ringing. I heard Brian take the call, and his half of the ensuing conversation. He was clearly elated and promising to leave immediately.

It was, of course, the arrival of the new car – and would we please pick it up before five o'clock, as otherwise it would have to be left on the forecourt all night, at our risk.

It had gone one o'clock – we'd not eaten – Mama was up but had undressed herself and was sitting in her big chair in her underclothes, with a straw hat on her head. The new car was seventy miles away. Such local transport as there was, would not have got us to the pickup point that *day*, let alone by late afternoon. Furthermore my little Renault was low on fuel, so we would have to stop for petrol.

For half an hour our house resembled one of those old silent films – with all the action speeded up. We tore around, dressing Mama and spooning the contents of a bowl of soup into her reluctant mouth. We made a temporary home for the pup in one of the stables, rang insurance brokers, locked up, and departed in a cloud of dust, with Mama rolling about in the back seat of the car.

Poor old girl. There were so many occasions when living at home with us meant being bundled into things, out of things, and bounced about in the back of the car like a cork in a millstream.

But that was a part of the life she shared with us – perhaps one of the bad bits – although Mama showed no disinclination for this particular jaunt. She shouted and whooped as we roared along, giving every indication that she was enjoying a treat of no mean order.

Fortunately the luck was with us and we arrived just as the agency was about to close. The formalities were completed and Brian sat himself at the wheel of his new baby – a happy moment, which very nearly ended in disaster as, in joining the fast-moving rush-hour traffic in an unfamiliar vehicle, he stalled the engine in the path of an oncoming container lorry. But being a diesel car, it restarted readily and he was able to take evasive action in the nick of time.

We drove home in a convoy at a sedate pace, and started joyous new relationships with our two new possessions – both of which gave great satisfaction and pleasure – perhaps tempered slightly in Flash's case with concern at his various canine misdemeanours.

Chapter Eighteen

One of the only disadvantages in moving to our Welsh arcadia was the loss of close social contact with all our old friends. When informed of our project, many of them had promised to visit us in our new home, and I'd readily acquiesced. During the summer of 1983, several had written or phoned to ask for dates when they could take up our offer. This had induced great panic, and I hastily did an about-turn on the invitations, citing our difficult living conditions as being responsible, as indeed they were.

But we had now almost finished the new wing and any further excuses sounded like prevarication. In fact we were no better endowed with accommodation, since there was only one bedroom in the extension, and this was occupied by Mama. True enough the bedroom that had housed all the soft furniture in the old cottage was now available since the furniture had been moved into the new wing, but I was reluctant to have to ask guests to use the old cottage in view of its condition. It had been in need of major renovation when we arrived here, and after the blasting, when it took such a hammering, its structural state was even worse. Really major jobs needed to be dealt with. The roof needed to be renewed, the exterior walls totally stripped and sealed, a full set of new windows, a new staircase with landing, the bathroom rearranged and the plumbing rerouted. This was not to mention the interior decoration, to make it even modestly clean and savoury. The list seemed endless and very frightening.

Meanwhile, we were still making cosmetic, but necessary, additions to the new wing – concrete paths to surround the building – a flight of steps up to the new front door – a concrete ramp from the yard up to Mama's front door so that she could be transferred from home to car easily – and so many other things that needed to be finished before the onset of the winter weather.

But we were also anxious to see some of our old friends and to introduce them to our new way of life, so Brian hurled a lick of paint on the walls of the two remaining bedrooms in the old cottage, and the first lot arrived. Then the second lot, the third lot, and so on, until we were giddy.

My diary does not tell me who was in residence in my bedroom on this particular day, but suffice it to say, Brian and I were sleeping on the ancient put-you-up sofa in the new sitting room – hard up against the patio doors. This was the sofa that lived on the patio. It was heaved indoors at nightfall and turned into a bed. The next morning it was turned back into a sofa and heaved back through the doors onto the patio, the visitors – and very occasionally Brian or I – lazing about on it during the course of the day.

Soon after six on a bright summer morning, Brian nudged me awake with an imperative elbow.

I raised a weary head and looked through the glass doors. There, not six feet from us, was a fox, sniffing over the remains of the barbecue from the previous evening. We watched as he greedily ate a piece of steak fat somebody had dropped, and picked one or two morsels out of the embers of the fire. He spent some few minutes checking over the remains of our supper, and then ambled unhurriedly back onto the grass.

As his back was turned, Brian slid out of bed and felt for his slippers. Crouching behind the bed and taking advantage of the cover provided by the rest of the furniture in the room, Brian crawled over to the big cupboard where the shotgun was kept.

Here I must stop and let you into one of our domestic secrets. Brian sleeps in the nuddy. Back at the time of our marriage, Mama, like all good mothers, had equipped her son with two pairs of thick winceyette pyjamas with which to start his married life. These, together with some rather racy underpants, which he had bought for himself, constituted his trousseau.

We had both laughed about the pyjamas, since Brian had never worn them in the past, and it seemed funny that Mama had considered them necessary in our marriage bed.

So here we have our hero of the piece, with a shotgun, a pair of carpet slippers and a watch, letting himself out of the back door in the new kitchen, keeping himself hidden from the fox and climbing up to the top of the garden. The fox is just ahead. He stops to sniff at an ancient bone left by the dogs – then ambles off down the ridge over the dew-washed grass towards the farm road.

A ewe in the background prevented a shot.

Brian climbs over the sheep fence – minding his dangly bits on the barbed wire – clutches up the gun again and makes off after Reynard.

Every time a shot was possible, there was either a ewe in the way or some other reason for not firing.

A quarter of a mile later, Brian reaches the footpath. The fox is still in sight, but moving more rapidly.

Brian suddenly realises he hasn't a stitch on, and that there are voices coming from somewhere near at hand. He quickly does an about-turn and makes for home. The fox can live to see another day.

This particular fox had been a great problem. It was a donkey-grey colour and not the least averse to appearing in the yard in broad daylight. We were always seeing him when the shotgun was not handy.

The woods at the back of us, owned by our neighbour, are almost impenetrable. Steep flights of stone steps carved down the rock face, leading into dark narrow alleyways bordered by banks of rhododendrons, through which glimpses are caught of the rocky beach and blue sea below. Holly, oak, birch, pine and rowan press in on each other, and the floor is thick with bracken, underlaid with the soft peat of countless years of autumn leaf fall. It is rocky, with sheer cliffs in places and small caves whose entrances are padded with thick green moss and ferns. In spring it is a misty mauve with wall-to-wall bluebells. Mordicus the buzzard nests there, and it is an altogether enchanted place

– like something from a fairy tale, or a half-remembered childhood dream.

Reynard had wandered into this desirable residential area and had set up home. What more could a fox want? There were any number of dry holes and a diet of rabbit could be alternated with a plump hen from our harem.

With all the new chicks, our poultry stocks had risen dramatically but this had been whittled down by more than a third in a matter of two months. Thus Brian's overwhelming desire to send this particular fox to that woodland in the sky could be understood.

Arthur, the shepherd, fence-builder and fox-catcher, had been over to review the situation several times and had followed the movements of the fox.

But Arthur's visits did not coincide with those of the fox. He knew where it was getting over the wall from the wood into our farm, and of two places where it had burrowed under the wire, in the parts where the wall had been replaced by a fence. But the fox was clearly living and spending most of its time in the wood. It was probably engaged in the artistic decoration of its sitting room with feathers from our hens – and short of getting into the wood, there was little we could do.

We had intended to ask our neighbour if he would allow Arthur to go into the wood, but time goes so quickly. The work on the house, Mama and all the visitors absorbed most of our waking hours – so that we had never actually made the arrangement for Arthur to enter the wood.

One Sunday morning, Brian had taken the boat out into the bay for an hour or two. The mackerel were supposed to be running and I wanted some for the freezer. Part of our economic strategy, when we planned the move here, was that Brian would keep us in fish. However, in spite of many hours out in the boat, and many gallons of fuel for the outboard motor, I have only had one minute mackerel delivered to the kitchen – and this did not provide even a snack for one of us.

Brian loved being out in the boat – and as a break from Mama, the building, and the farm work, it was of great therapeutic value. It was quite important that we both had a break from the pressures at home and to this end I had started to work on a very flexible basis for a local firm of chartered accountants soon after we moved here. Thus I was obliged to don a skirt, heels, tights, make-up and so on, in place of grubby jeans, sweaters and wellies that formed my normal wear.

So there was Himself, bouncing about in Cardigan Bay, and totally out of reach, when Arthur turned up with three equally silent friends and his dogs. They parked their vans in the yard, and before I could say Jack Robinson, were over the wall and into the wood – to disappear in a crashing of twigs.

I tried to ring our neighbour but there was no reply. He was, almost certainly, out on his land, and would probably come face to face with the intruders at any moment.

The next half hour was miserably uncomfortable. I rehearsed lame excuses, expecting the appearance of a justifiably irate neighbour at any moment.

I could hardly deny knowledge of the trespass, as the vans were parked in the yard.

Eventually I heard a shot ring out and within a minute or two the men were climbing back over the wall with the deceased Reynard. It was a moment of great relief.

The fox had been living well. Remains of a number of lambs were found by the entrance to his den, as well as seagulls, which he must have found washed up on the beach or perhaps injured, and lots of dismembered rabbits and hens.

Over a celebratory can of beer, Arthur haltingly explained that they had waited in a nearby layby on the road until they had seen our neighbour pass on his way to church, so they knew they would not be disturbed. Isn't that awful. They might have told me before they set off into the wood. I would have been saved a very difficult half-hour. But I am pleased to record that our neighbour has subsequently read this account so is well aware of the transgression.

As the summer advanced we had noticed a number of blue butterflies about the farm. They seemed rather more of a violet, mauvish blue than the Common Blue we had been used to seeing in the past, and I was quite keen to catch one to have a closer look. I'd found an old butterfly net that we used to catch the chicks with, and I'd left it in the woodshed, where it was handy should one of these new beasties reappear.

One afternoon Mama was snoozing in a chair outside her front door and I was fussing with her sunshade when one of these blue-shot-with-mauve butterflies hovered over the bleached cotton material of the brolly. I had a brief look at it as it paused before taking off again – and calling to Brian, who was in the workshop, to find the catching net, I kept an eye on it until he returned.

It had an undulating, erratic flight and we had a number of swipes at it without avail.

A tumbler, half full of juice, by Mama's chair, came to grief, and Mama herself was batted on the ankles, as we made repeated attempts to catch the creature. It managed to escape the net however and moved down into the yard.

We chased it around the barn, flapping with our net and getting more and more irritated with each other. Several times when Brian seemed to have a superb opportunity to net the insect, it evaded him – and there were times when I couldn't quite see how I had missed – it had looked to be a sure thing.

It moved again, out towards the chicken house, where a row of hens had settled themselves down on a plank for forty winks in the shade of an rowan tree.

It landed briefly on a nettle and as I positioned my net to strike, one of the chickens stepped neatly forward and ate it. A sad end to the story. We never saw another.

In July 1984 we also had our earthquake.

It was just after eight and we were sitting on the patio drinking coffee. It was one of those magic summer mornings with a blue, blue sky, absolute silence except for the birdsong, and Mama quietly crooning to herself in her bedroom.

From afar, there started a long, low rumble. I thought it started in the west, but Brian thought it was rather more to the north.

It got louder and louder until it was quite deafening, and at the peak of the noise, the ground seemed to rise a few inches and move eastwards for about a foot.

Indoors, on the sitting room cupboards, the bric-a-brac slid about, and one or two things fell onto the floor. Then the noise slowly decreased, until there was a hollow, echoing quiet – except for the crash of boulders and stones cascading down the open rocky hillside, about a mile away. Even the birds stopped singing for a few moments.

After the initial shock, most people seemed to have enjoyed it. They all had some story telling how it had caught them, and the holidaymakers sent letters home telling of their experiences in this unpredictable place.

It was also the summer that Brian had a little embarrassment in our local supermarket. Our campsite visitors are mainly very nice folk and we've got to know many of them very well. However, the camping can be something of a pain, since it wastes so much time, and we are occasionally tight-lipped about the constant interruptions. Most of the visitors try really hard not to be a nuisance, but in many cases they cannot help it. They tread on weaver fish and come up to the house in a panic to know the antidote. They want the harness for the two ponies who lodge with us. They want to know the height of the tide or about some flower, bird or snake that they've seen – and there are so many, many more reasons for coming up to the farmhouse to have a chat – not to mention the coffee and bun that invariably accompanies the chat.

One of our regulars is a policeman. He and his family have been coming here for donkeys' years – and this part of Wales has become a magic place for him, his wife, and their teenage children. They spend hours in their small boat, fishing for mackerel and flatties, and they walk miles over the golden sand searching for the cockles that lie just below the surface of the sand, in the shallow pools, or the mussels clinging to the outcrops in the rock pools. At nightfall they build a fire on the beach – under the overhanging oaks – and cook their day's catch to wash it down with homemade wine. The sun will perhaps be sinking over the sea, and a white moon rising, turning their feast into an enchanted, mystical revel – over which owls hoot and screech – joined by the oystercatchers whose penetrating shrieks echo along the lapping shoreline. In the background, the slow curtain of night settles over the mountains, returning them to their primitive secrecy. And all is at peace.

What an antidote to walking the beat in Leicestershire.

Well, to get back to the tale. This policeman seems to be issued with a new uniform long before the last one has worn out, and thus his wardrobe is stuffed with trousers that he no longer wears. I suppose, once the pristine glory of Her Majesty's police uniform has worn off, it cannot be used to maintain law and order, and thus it has to be thrown out.

Now Brian must hold the world record for the speed with which he can get his knees through a pair of jeans, or indeed any other sort of trousers, and as he invariably walks about the farm with air-conditioning slits, where the knees should be, Chris, the policeman, offered to bring him some of these old ex-police service trousers.

When they arrived, they proved to be superior to most of the pairs of pants in Brian's wardrobe, so they became his second best – the sort of thing he wore into town for those bottles of Scotch or to go into the post office, the bank, the farmers' co-op, or the dentist's. Brian rarely goes into town for anything else.

On this particular occasion, however, he had been persuaded to call at the supermarket for a small list of groceries, after he'd been to the post office. He had his list, his basket, and a pile of pound coins, and off he went.

He had finished his calls about town, driven to the supermarket, selected his shopping and stood in the queue at the cash desk, waiting to pay. His goods were totted up, and he put his hand in his pocket for those £1 coins.

They had disappeared.

Yet he could feel the weight of them, somewhere halfway down his thigh. Then he discovered what all policemen must already know. The £1 coins will fit into a truncheon pocket like a snail in a shell, and will not come out until the trousers are removed and shaken vigorously. The truncheon pocket is only an inch or so wide but quite deep and as the material is stiff, it is difficult to work the coins up to the top.

So there we have our reluctant shopper with a choice of removing his pants by the till and giving them a shake, or putting the goods back on the shelves. Meanwhile, the people behind him in the queue were growing restive at the delay.

But Batman wasn't finished. He suddenly remembered he had a chequebook in the car, so off he rushed, while the queue behind him fumed and fidgeted, and he eventually departed with the shopping *and* without loss of either pants or dignity.

That was the summer of the snakes. We seemed to have lots of them. The campers were always coming up to tell us where they had seen a slow-worm, a grass snake or an adder. It was undoubtedly a pleasure to have them, but I was worried that someone may be bitten by an adder. Many of the campers liked to explore the marsh – to find some of the rarities for which it is famous – and often they only wore flip-flops or other somewhat flimsy shoes.

We spoke to the doctor about it, so that we had some idea of the course of action necessary in the event of someone suffering a bite from an adder, and it was worrying to find that there is no serum anywhere in the locality, and that a drive of over sixty miles would be necessary to the nearest large hospital.

So we warned everybody to wear boots if they were off the path or in long grass and to walk slowly and carefully, giving the snake time to slide off into the undergrowth. But the warning excited the interest of many of the visitors. They were keen to see one of these unusual wild creatures. They donned protective clothing – some of which would have stood them in good stead in the event of coming face to face with a man-eating tiger – and off they went to explore the peaty pools and under rotting trees on the marsh.

One or two of them did find their quarry but some of them also found slippery ditches where they sank to their thighs in thick peaty mud. I saw more visitors who had come to grief in a peaty pool or ditch than I did campers who had found a snake. I was sorry for their discomfort, but secretly rather glad that the wildlife was left in peace.

Weaver fish are another hazard here. They are about forty centimetres long with spines on the big dorsal fin that are filled with venom. The gill covers also have these protective, torpedo-like spines filled with poison – and this lethal little fellow buries himself in the sand just waiting for an unsuspecting foot to land on him, when he releases the nasty, and then scuttles off into the deep. The pain is severe and only slightly modified by immersion in hot water. Fortunately, however, it is all over in about an hour, and there are no lasting ill effects, but it is very unpleasant while it lasts. We usually warn visitors to wear flip-flops in the sea to prevent the problem, but either they forget, or they don't take the warning seriously, as we still get one or two cases every year.

The summer days were passing so quickly. There had been a delay with the construction of the roof for the new link block – the hallway that joined the two parts of the house together.

We had asked the firm that provided the kit for the house if they could also supply the roof trusses for the link block. These were rather complicated as the council had insisted that we have a pitched roof, rather than a flat or pent roof, and therefore the roof trusses had to be tapered to fit into the roof of the new wing, meaning that firstly, the tiles would have to be removed from the roof of the new wing in that area, and secondly, that there would be a valley on each side of the ridge. Valleys in roofs, according to Dai, are always a problem.

So, as the firm that provided the kit was aware of all the angles that were used on the main part of the roof, they could match them easily. Furthermore, they had a handy gadget for cutting them accurately.

So the roof trusses were ordered and we waited – and waited.

Brian had the two hall doors ready to hang – they were to be fully glazed so that natural light would fill the little hall, which was not big enough to sport a window.

And still we waited.

But one late summer evening, a man turned up with the trusses on a lorry, and we gratefully unloaded them. Brian and Dai set to, removing the tiles from the roof of the main wing – just in that area – attaching the trusses to the existing roof trusses, felting the whole thing, making the valleys and retiling the main roof – all within two or three days, while mercifully the weather held dry.

The remaining roof trusses were attached to the wooden plate at the top of the hall walls, and that roof too was felted and tiled. The two hall doors were hung, varnished, glazed and made lock-fast – *and the two parts of the house were at last joined together.*

Chapter Nineteen

Flash the Labrador pup had become confident of his welcome in his new home, and as his character emerged, he proved to be a very entertaining dog, with a sense of humour too. He was a long-legged, bouncing creature who adored everybody and was totally happy with life. He particularly loved the sea, and spent ages digging vast holes in the sand – sploshing in and out of the shallow sandy pools with the campsite children, or with the boating fraternity. He swam strongly, with the mobility of a seal and unlimited energy.

He was a menace with spades, however. Infantile roars of rage from the bucket and spade brigade were as often as not because Flash had picked up the spade and wouldn't give it back. I suppose he felt it was just another stick. He would stand on the sand with his black coat glistening with the salt sea – his tail wagging furiously – the baby wrinkles on his face flopping down to cover the part of the spade held in his teeth so that only the handle and the blade were visible – eyes and ears alert in the hope that you would be foolish enough to chase him. He seemed to grin with the joy of life.

During the day he was supposed to stay untethered in the yard with the sheepdogs, and great was the excitement when anyone called. If we did not happen to be at hand to restrain him, off he would go with the callers in the hope that they were making for the campsite beach. Whenever he was missing we knew exactly where to find him. He would be playing on the sand or cadging titbits from the campers.

He was extremely popular with almost everybody – children would come up to the house to ask if Flash could come out to play and off they'd all go – hopefully to keep each other amused for the rest of the day. For children whose homes gave them no close access to an animal, it was a great treat. I would put one of the older, seemingly more responsible, children in charge of him, with a few basic instructions regarding his behaviour and for the time of his return – and at peak holiday times, his services were sometimes booked for several days in advance. It was interesting that this rent-a-dog service was very important to some of the children – it made their holiday more enjoyable. They were put in charge of a living creature who, for a few hours, was dependant on them and subordinate to them. Some reacted differently. I recall at least one child who had long begged for a dog finding that it became tiresome after a few hours. But for many it was a rewarding experience. Flash, of course, was the major beneficiary. Surely the happiest dog in the west, and one of the cleanest since he spent so much time in the water.

Flash had been equipped with his own frying pan, and every evening this was filled with cereal, out-of-date faggots, pâté, meat pies and other delicacies passed on to us by a local butcher, who would otherwise have put them out for the dustman.

Faggots were his favourite – he swallowed them with big gulps like someone taking aspirins – but garlic pâté came a close second. One had to remember not to stand downwind of him next day, however, as the garlic tended to make him very antisocial.

He ate anything and everything and then retired into his fibreglass bed in the stable to sleep the sleep of the just.

But the following morning he would be awake at crack of dawn and wish to be released from the stable. To this end, he had chewed a large hole in the bottom of the stable door so that he could see who was passing, what the day was like, and when to woof if he thought it would bring early release.

Now the cats spent their nights in the kitchen of the old part of the house and whichever one of us was up first would open the back door so that they could go out to attend to their toilette.

The stable where the dogs slept is a short way down the lane, so they were not normally released until one of us was dressed and bewellied, or at least fit to be seen in public.

On the odd occasion, Brian and I would enjoy an early morning coffee on the patio – all was still and quiet like the inside of a cathedral except for the birds having an ecstasy of choral rejoicing on the excellence of the day. The sun was perhaps shimmering through a diaphanous gauze mist draped over the hills, its golden warmth bathing the landscape, when into this peaceful moment would burst a frenzy of barking from the doghouse.

On inspecting the cause of the trouble, one was treated to a vision of a demented Labrador face pushed into the spyhole at the bottom of the stable door, and on the outside, not four feet away but well out of range, was Robertson, the marmalade cat – pulling faces at that black canine visage, and kneading the damp grass with his front feet.

This little show of superiority appeared to give Robertson immense pleasure since he did it frequently, and it never failed to drive Flash into a trumpet voluntary of fury.

Once released, however, Flash was able to ignore the whole episode and had a very good relationship with Robbie.

All the dogs enjoyed a bone and on Saturdays when the bags of dog food arrived from the butcher, they were each presented with a fresh one. Usually the old ones were collected up to be burned – unless they were too big to get on the fire, in which case they seemed to find their way into a canine museum of ancient relics in a private area behind the barn.

We seldom wasted anything in this establishment.

The smaller, old bones were put on the Rayburn fire, helping to heat the water and cook the food. The consequent potash-cum-bonemeal was put on the garden, helping to grow the vegetables. The fat and suet from the butcher's bags was cut up and helped to feed the wild birds. And the lean raw meat was cooked on the Rayburn and fed to the dogs with their cereal after the stale cooked meats had been used up. This economy suited my purse and my view of the excesses of the human race.

Each of the dogs had a different technique with a bone.

Flash would finish his treat in next to no time. His strong young teeth could strip off every vestige of edible material so that it looked like ivory. Then he would bury the remains in a leafy grave or perhaps place it in his museum behind the barn, and it was all over very quickly.

Ben carried his bone down to his bed in the stable and sat and looked at it for several minutes, savouring the pleasure of a possession. He cast an exploratory tongue over it to assess its fragrance, and having established its bouquet, he would methodically work at it until there was little left.

Dear old Spot would sink down with his prize in his mouth and worry and chew at it until it was revolting. Then he abandoned it and Flash would take it on.

Flash appeared to have a higher degree of intelligence than the sheepdogs. This gave him the advantage on many occasions, but it also led to trouble.

When he had finished his Saturday bone, and disposed of it, he would go and sit by Ben – watching every move. He would do his utmost to distract Ben and steal the bone. It was interesting to note his strategy. On a number of occasions I watched him operating different techniques to create the distraction.

For example, he would go and stand by the barn door, out of Ben's sight. Then he would woof the excited bark, which is otherwise reserved for the occasions when the motorbike is being wheeled out of the barn.

The motorbike was not, of course, being wheeled out of the barn, but Ben, hearing the usual outcry of excitement, thought it was, and his devotion to motorbikes being as powerful as it was, he would leave the bone and race up into the yard – meeting Flash going in the opposite direction down to the doghouse to steal the unattended bone.

There were other equally cunning ways by which poor, simple Ben could be parted from his bone and Flash didn't hesitate to use them. Intelligence undoubtedly can make crime more likely and more successful.

Blooey was still trailing her lambs about the campsite and begging for titbits. Every day she brought them up to the yard where we were permitted to admire them, while we fed all three of them with choice morsels from the greengrocery bags.

The bags of leftovers from the greengrocer had been coming thick and fast as the holidaymakers swelled the number of shoppers, and the retailer took in more goods to satisfy the greater demand.

We'd stopped the pig-keeping activities, at least for the summer, but we still collected the bags of fruit and vegetables, as the chickens did well from them, as did the sheep. Blooey particularly loved peaches and didn't mind a bit about the bruised parts. She also loved bananas provided you peeled them for her, and many other items from the bags. She was fat, well, and produced good lambs, so her unusual diet couldn't have had any adverse effects.

We had to make sure she didn't overdo the peaches, the plums or the soft fruit, but otherwise she ate what she fancied, and this proved to be as much as possible of everything on offer.

Cauliflowers were another favourite, but you had to hold them for her while she chewed from the far side.

To Flash, a cauliflower was a ball encased in green leaves, and I have the most heart-warming and happy recollection of that big black puppy standing with a large speckled cauliflower in his mouth, while Blooey chewed off the far side of it.

Flash and Blooey were very fond of each other, but Flash really could not understand why she was so fond of fruit and vegetables. He'd tried all sorts of things – cabbage and carrots, apples and plums – and although he had eaten them, largely to stop somebody else from having them, you could see they were not really to his taste.

It was nearly time for the lambs to be weaned. Many of them were still feeding from their mothers and this couldn't be allowed to continue. Of all jobs on the sheep farming calendar, weaning is the noisiest and probably one of the most unpleasant. The lambs are distraught to be parted from their mothers, and the ewes are pretty well as bad. But they *have* to be separated so the ewes, the lambs and I all gritted our teeth and the parting was made. The lambs were confined to the lambing meadow and the ewes left out on the remainder of the land.

Blooey and the twins were probably less stressed than most, as for some weeks, Bloo had been in competition with her lambs for the scraps, whereas she was now queen of the campsite rounds *and* the alms given out in the yard.

Her lambs, too, had at least got each other, so did not feel totally abandoned when they were deprived of their mother. But, all in all, it is not a happy time for us or the sheep.

When Mama was sitting out of doors, Blooey could be a nuisance. She'd imagine that Mama must have some comestible hidden about her person or under the chair and she'd spend ages pushing and shoving to find it. In fact, there often were bits of biscuit, cake, apple or chocolate hidden down the sides of the armchair, dropped on the floor, gammed on the arms or stuck to Mama, so Bloo often did herself well from this intimate body search.

Mama enjoyed it too. I think she felt that Bloo was a child looking for comfort. Mama wasn't able to give very much away, but love and cuddles she could give. She threw her old arms about Blooey's neck, comforting and caressing the silly old sheep, who would meanwhile have her nose busy with an exploration under Mama's chin or up behind her ears.

But unless Blooey could smell something edible, she wasn't going to tolerate confinement, so she would pull away. Mama's arthritic old fingers would hang on to that white woolly fleece as if her life depended on it, and there would be a tug of war until Mama was practically pulled out of her chair.

Flash was also a nuisance with Mama. He hung about her, licking the biscuit crumbs from her lap and casting a long wet tongue over her face. There was no saying where he had last cast his tongue, as he had some fairly revolting habits, but I don't think she ever suffered from his attentions.

She adored him too, and spent a lot of time fondling his head, trying to encourage him to sit down by her. But he didn't spend much time just sitting down. He was a restless bundle of energy.

Indeed, far from having a delicate digestive system, Mama's gastric arrangements seemed extraordinarily accommodating.

We'd had rather a bad time with her one morning at the end of summer. If you happen to have a queasy tummy, you'd do well to skip the next few paragraphs. Brian was against me mentioning it, but I feel it is important, and should be included, even though it is very distasteful. No one had warned me it may happen, and when it did, I felt disinclined, even unable, to talk about it. I certainly felt that it must be a very rare occurrence, which happened to few people, and this left me with a great feeling of isolation.

One morning I went into Mama's room to take in her early tea and draw the curtains. The smell was dreadful, but this was often the case in the mornings as, unless she was restless in the night, we didn't get her up to change her incontinence pads. They were therefore always wet and smelly by morning. We restricted her liquid intake in the evenings, but as she had difficulty in swallowing anything in the least bit dry, it was impossible to impose too great a limit. Her nappy, nightie and often the bedding was always soaked as, unlike a baby, she weighed over nine stone, and passed the quantity of liquid that related to a frame of that size.

On this particular morning, I drew the curtains and as daylight flooded into the room, I turned to look at her.

My first thought was that she must have been helping herself to the chocolate kept in the tin on her bedside table. Her mouth was full of a brown substance – her face, hair, the pillow and the sheets were all stained with brown – her hands and nails were grimy with dried and drying pooh. It was pushed into the neck of her hot-water bottle and ground into the knitted cover.

My reaction was as can be imagined – but it also made me very tearful. I just could not accept that she had sunk to such depths.

A day or two later when she went into the day hospital, I managed to mention it to the Sister and asked for her advice. Apart from the obvious horror of the business, the question of infection worried us. Surely we could do something to stop it happening again?

Sister was quite bracing – reassuring as regards the infection, but was not able to offer any advice as to a course of action we could take to prevent it happening again. She gave me some plastic gloves with which I was supposed to remove it from Mama's mouth, and dispatched me on my way, with an assurance that it was quite common and may well happen again. This proved to be the case.

My reasons for mentioning it are twofold. Firstly, I feel it is important to be warned that it may happen, and to be made to understand that it is a common, and almost a natural, occurrence. To feel that the experience is shared by many other carers and nursing staff is helpful – it does remove some of the horror – and it avoids the feeling of isolation produced by the experience of an almost unmentionable personal problem. Secondly, it is a part of the rich pattern of life – plant, animal and human – as affected by natural laws. It is *real* life, which is changing all the time. The lithe, tanned, beautiful bodies of the young will one day be old and wrinkled, their think tanks will have muddled wires and the disposal of their waste products may give cause for embarrassment. Does this not teach us to live each present moment to the full – to extract full flavour from all the different circumstances that life offers – to build up a stock of personal philosophical rules to protect us from the brickbats and to enjoy every moment of every day safe in the knowledge that it will not come again?

Having made that sound like sage counsel, I am very well aware that it is sometimes difficult to remember to enjoy life when you have lost perhaps a husband, wife, child, a good friend, a job, your health – and your heart, or even your feet, ache with the load you feel you are carrying. Nevertheless, is it not important to strive for the positive angles – to glean growth from the depths – even if your mind sometimes slips back into the morass?

So, having accepted Mama's little aberrations, I can now regard the whole matter with tolerance. In some small way, I am even joyful that we are able to cope with it. So although Flash was admonished for licking Mama, every time we caught him enjoying a slurp, no other course of action was taken, and they continued to be very fond of each other.

One night we nearly set fire to the poor old girl. It was a clear September evening and we'd decided to cook our supper on the barbecue. This is not one of those flashy mass-produced affairs, but a design of Brian's constructed of breeze blocks, big rocks, and with a fire that will toast your toes on a chilly night, as well as cooking the bangers.

On this particular occasion Brian had made a good blaze, and we were waiting for it to die down into nice smouldering hot embers – just ideal for cooking – when, without any warning, one piece of wood spat out a shower of blazing sparks.

Mama was ensconced in a low armchair with her shawl over her shoulders and a blanket over her legs. As the sparks landed, we sprang forward and picked up the blackened splinters, shaking her blanket, and checking her cardigan for still-burning chips of wood. Then we settled back to cook our meal.

I kept thinking I could smell burning wool. Several times I ran a hand down between Mama and the side of the chair, but found nothing. We were burning all sorts of odds and ends of wood – some from the building work and some from the beach or nearby trees – so it was easy to be mistaken. However, when we had finished our supper, and heaved Mother to her feet to take her to bed, there was a large hole burned in the side of her skirt, just below her waist, and it had gone through to her vest. She must have felt it but she never uttered a word.

As the summer days began to shorten, Flash found himself in trouble. As I've already said, some way away at the back of us, there is another house – formerly a barn belonging to this farm. A few years ago the farmer sold it off, and it has since been rebuilt as an interesting stone family home. This was the property through which all our heavy transport passed when our new wing was under construction.

We had come to know these neighbours quite well and they often walked down the path through the wood for a gossip over a cup of tea on our patio. The husband was a jeweller, and he had a big leather case full of samples, which, in common with many other local ladies, I liked to go through from time to time.

Much of the jewellery was handmade and unusual, with a good selection and prices that were not unreasonable. It also saved the long journey into the nearest big town for that special gift, so our neighbour must have enjoyed quite a brisk trade with the local people, who were permitted the luxury of a private viewing of the contents of the case. As often as not, there was a cup of tea over an exchange of local news as well.

On this particular occasion, Audrey, my friend from the village, was looking for a gold necklace and I had arranged a viewing with our neighbour.

It was a bit like making a hair appointment – you were given a time and asked what you were particularly interested in so that a good selection of those items featured in the case. I loved it.

So one dripping wet morning Audrey turned up in the yard, and with the dogs bounding along ahead, we both walked up through the wood and knocked on our neighbour's door.

We had a super time. Sitting at the big table in our stockinged feet, having left our wellies on the doorstep, drinking tea and sorting out the Aladdin's cave – or perhaps Aladdin's case would be more appropriate.

Audrey took ages to decide on which necklace she would have, and as I had to get home to be with Mama while Brian went to the dentist, I left her there and walked back down the path through the wood with the dogs.

An hour later Audrey arrived in the yard in fits of laughter with one welly boot missing, having been obliged to walk down the path in the mud with only a sock on her left foot. Apparently, when she left our neighbour, who had been called to the telephone, only one welly had remained on the doorstep.

I lent her a pair of old shoes, and we both walked back to look for the missing boot, but in spite of a thorough search, it did not come to light.

A few days later we found Flash with the remains of the left welly. He'd eaten all but the heel part of the sole, and he finished that off the same day. I didn't know whether to tell Audrey or not.

Then, one morning, both Mama and Flash were in trouble and it was serious.

I returned home from work to find Brian standing in the yard, purple with rage and roaring thunderous imprecations at Flash, who was cowering in fright, his shoulders huddled into his chest and his head hanging low.

Mama stood at the open window of her bedroom, gazing out at her son as he fumed and raged. There was an amused twinkle in her eyes and a complacent grin on her face. She was obviously enjoying herself.

What on earth was the matter?

The tale was soon told.

Mama had thrown her false teeth out of the window and Flash had eaten them.

Chapter Twenty

It was so lovely to be able to walk from the old cottage to the new wing in privacy and without going out of doors. To get up at night and be able to get to Mama's room in slippers, rather than finding the wellies and struggling into them.

The only hazard now was the milk-crate-and-breeze-block staircase at the end of the passageway through the wall of the old cottage. Just occasionally this would fall over as you were halfway up it. Your foot would dislodge one of the breeze blocks or the milk crate, and before you could stop yourself, the whole lot had collapsed, and you with it. One evening, the breeze blocks fell apart, and a heavy cast-iron casserole dish full of beef stew came to grief as I smashed it against one of the walls at the top of the makeshift staircase in an effort to regain my equilibrium. In spite of a thorough scrubbing, the ensuing gravy stain stayed on the wall for about two years until the new staircase was built.

The new wing was warm, light and airy. The big windows gave lovely views in all directions. They filled the home with sunlight, making it seem a buoyant, hopeful place. The pine ceilings, the red-brick floor and the pine-clad or red-brick walls reflected a soft copper glow that seemed to enfold you in a genial embrace. It had a very welcoming atmosphere that made it a home in several different senses. It still has.

The old cottage was dark and sombre, damp and musty. It was easy to understand why so many of its residents had suffered with bronchial problems. The main room, where for centuries the family had lived, was dominated by a huge inglenook fireplace. The solid oak beam over the fireplace was massive, and black with the smoke of countless fires. It had been crudely hewn and still shows the knots where the branches had been hacked back to the trunk of the tree. I wonder where that oak had grown and in which year it had first raised leaf as a seedling.

Regimented lines of heavy black beams held the ceiling and helped to cast a gloom over the room. The floor was laid with old brown tiles. No doubt they had seemed the ideal surface a century ago when they would have replaced the stone flags, with their nooks and crannies which were difficult to clean. These tiles had been laid on the bare earth, and water oozed up through the joints and the cracks when it was very wet. The walls had been rendered and papered with a thatch-like covering. This undoubtedly secreted a multitude of troubles. On one wall an electric socket about eighteen inches from the floor seeped water in even modest rainfall. When it had rained heavily for some hours, this seep became a trickle, indicating that the water was penetrating the wall – three feet thick – perhaps even from roof level. What a fire hazard – electricity and water do *not* mix safely.

The room was lit by one tiny window through which the sun had little chance to cast its warmth or cheer. But perhaps the farmers of old had sun, wind and rain enough with their labours on the land. They were, no doubt, content to leave the views and the elements outside the house and be cocooned in this damp, dark haven when the work for the day was over.

Or perhaps it was cheaper and easier to restrict the size of the windows. Originally they would have been unglazed so the attraction of a small window was obvious and maybe when glass became available, they were disinclined, even unable, to make the change.

Our forebears undoubtedly suffered with a lack of the basic facilities that we take for granted today. For the masses, poverty and illness were the great enemy and respectability the great aim. Bigger windows and a dry floor in their homes would probably have been quite low on their list of priorities. A silk dress for the ladies and a gold watch and chain for the men to display on a Sunday would perhaps have been far more important. At least the bulk of the human race must surely have overcome this particular vanity, so perhaps we *are* growing up to a better understanding of life. But we still have a long way to go.

I have wandered from the point. When looking at the old cottage in detail, it is tempting to people it in your mind's eye with families, with furniture, with hopes, disappointments, joys, tragedies and all the things that made up everyday life for the people who have spent their lives on this small patch of soil – and of whom I am the current participant, soon – all too soon – to be succeeded by someone else.

Suffice it to say that the difference between the two parts of the house was really dramatic but the plans for the old cottage were drastic. It was to be completely gutted and rebuilt with a new roof. Without doubt, I'd be wringing my hands over more catastrophes before we were finally satisfied with our new home.

We had already made some paths around the new wing, built a ramp up to Mother's front door and sundry other conveniences. The muddy bank up which we had struggled for so long – between the two parts of the house – was to be built up into a wall. The top was to be filled in to make a level platform leading to the hall door, and a flight of stone steps would be built in the wall to lead from the yard up to the house.

The garden around the enlarged house had to be fenced, the rubbish would be removed and masses of top soil had to be tipped on to the otherwise bare rocks. Then the garden would have to be built and stocked. I was particularly looking forward to this.

It was all very exciting, especially as there was now no hurry. It didn't matter if the rest of the development took many years – it probably would. The worst was over, and we were now only titivating and making it homely and convenient.

For a few weeks over that summer, we rested on our laurels and reduced the working day to more acceptable levels. We planned to make modest sorties back to the civilised world. Into Shrewsbury for a day's shopping – in particular, to drool over the food hall in Marks and Spencer's and other big stores; into a Laura Ashley shop, where I'd perhaps buy a new dress; into tool shops for bits that Brian had long wanted; into bookshops and dozens more.

I looked forward to this trip for days beforehand. It was to be a brief taste of the old life – with a coffee and something super from a high-street patisserie in the morning, a shandy and a bar snack at lunchtime in some nice old pub, and a cup of tea and some elegant confection from a cake shop before we left for home.

In the event it was a dreadful anticlimax. The prices seemed astronomic and the streets and the shops so crowded and noisy. My recollection of the pleasures of a shopping spree had been quite false – the grass was *not* greener on the other side of the fence. After several hours, I discovered there was nothing I wanted. Even the bookshops couldn't hold me. It all seemed drab, uninteresting and divorced from reality as we had come to know it.

The dress that was to lift my morale made me look like a society hostess or the career woman I had long since ceased to be. An artificial me looked gravely back from the mirror – seeming to tell me that I looked really rather foolish. I slipped it off, put it back on the hanger, and left the shop with an inexplicable feeling of gratefulness.

It was such a relief to return home to the peace and quiet of the mountains and the seashore – to the smell of the soothing, healing, wet earth. Mama had been to the day hospital and Audrey, our friend from the village, had kindly picked her up and was looking after her until we returned. It was *really* pleasing to be back in harness after our so-called treat. Mama grinned back at me as she lay in bed late that night. There was real affection in her eyes. Perhaps she had realised the change in her routine and it had worried her. There was something indescribably satisfying in sharing our home with her. She held up her arms to me – as would a baby who wishes to be picked up. It was a special moment.

Another day we went to Aberystwyth, taking Mama with us, as it was only a relatively short drive.

It was one of her particularly noisy days – she sang snatches from a very comprehensive range, including opera, musicals, hymns and sea shanties as we bowled along.

We picked up the timber from the builders' merchant's – the reason for the trip – and then we went and parked in the town. We bought hot doughnuts and ate them in the car – after which I went off for an hour's shopping while Brian sat with Mama.

Then Brian went off while I sat in the car with Mama.

Some months after our move to Wales, the doctor had suggested that we apply for one of the discs available to disabled people, or drivers of disabled people, enabling them to park their cars in specially selected central places in an urban area. We had done so and it really had been useful. We could park outside the chemist's or the grocer's shop and leave Mama in the car on her own for a few moments, while we collected a prescription or a bag of sugar. We certainly couldn't have left her on her own in the car if it was parked in a car park, which would have meant that Mama didn't go out in the car that day, or that two of us would need to go. We both felt it was important for her to go out if a trip into town became necessary on one of her good days.

On this particular occasion, Brian had returned from his sortie into Aberystwyth, full of details about a computer he'd found in one of the high-street shops. For months he had toyed with thoughts of buying a computer. His engineering drawings were often in a dreadful state, even if he managed to find the one he wanted, when he wanted it, so if they could be stored on disc and resurrected as and when required, then this would be the cat's whiskers. Coupled with that, all his regular orders could be typed and left on a disc, meaning that mistakes were less likely to be made and it was easy to reorder when further parts were required. I do not know why it should be so but every small part required by these people who buy obscure electrical bits seems to have a long complicated order number. It is *painfully* easy, so I am constantly assured, to make a mistake with those order numbers so that something the size of a wheelbarrow is delivered, rather than the something the size of a matchbox that you were expecting. Often the numbers are far bigger than the electrical part, even if the printing is small.

So with thoughts of our own computer in mind, he had read the relevant magazines and had already made a decision on which type would be most suitable. Not having a head for mechanical or electrical gadgets, I would have nothing to say to a computer but if we were to have to live with such a device, then my only stipulation was that it should have a word processor facility.

Hence Brian's excitement at having found the actual animal – the one he would have preferred against all others, in its real-life plastic case or string of cases – *and* being offered at a discount on the usual price.

Even more fortunately there was a disabled persons' parking place immediately outside this shop, so we could leave Mama on her own for a moment or so while we made the final decision.

So there we were – having our eyes and ears filled with stories of the capabilities of the computer (mere goggling in my case), when the most awful hullaballoo started in the street outside the shop.

We rushed out. Mama had collected a small group of well-wishers about the car and had been serenading them with a selection from her repertoire. One of them – thinking, presumably, that she was in pain – some of her songs did sound like that – had slid his hand though the partially opened window and had opened the door.

Mama had not approved – she had not approved at all – and she had, very, very loudly, made her disapproval known.

A few weeks previously we had bought Naomi, the black ewe with the foghorn voice, and she now lived with us permanently. Being a total glutton, she spent most of her day haunting the farmyard hoping for titbits. Several times when Mama had been sitting out of doors and had heard Naomi's vocal capabilities at close quarters, she had tried to copy, or perhaps reply to the ewe, with the same sort of bellow. She had practised it quite a lot but didn't seem satisfied with the timbre. However, in the busy high street of Aberystwyth, surrounded by a crowd of people, she finally got the crescendo fortissimo at the correct pitch – and it was very, very impressive. Even Mama was dumbfounded with her effort and her rage changed to pleasure as she gazed at her audience with a grin on her face.

Brian and I got into the car and made off home as fast as possible leaving the computer where it was.

Another day in mid September – as warm and pleasant as any in June – Mama was again in the day hospital for a few hours. Brian launched the dinghy and with Spotty in the middle, we motored slowly up the coast. Flash and Ben splashed along the beach or swam behind us. The sea was gin-clear and very calm. Hanging over the side of the boat I could see the sandy bottom and fish darting in and out of the gentle current. Here and there, patches of weed on the seabed hid crabs, which scuttled off as the dark shadow of the boat drifted overhead. Plaice and dabs dozed on the bottom – sometimes coming rapidly to life with a burst of speed that sent the sand up in a small cloud, if they became aware of our presence.

We drifted along in the autumn sunshine in a private world of our own, to stop on a distant sandy beach and paddle in flip-flops through the warm shallow water, picking up an unusual shell or an interesting piece of driftwood. We watched a shag catch an eel. The snake-like fish put up a good fight for survival. It coiled its mobile length around the bird's throat in several spirals, and even though it had been partially swallowed, it still wriggled, and tried to cling to the feathered neck.

It was a magic, dreamlike time of immense contentment.

That evening when Mama was in bed, I walked down to check that the cowshed door was properly closed. I had left it open earlier in the day. It was twilight – warm, still and quiet. The bats flickered silently through the soft air.

Flash picked up a stick and brought it to me, hoping that I may be persuaded to throw it into the sea for him. I obliged and he dived in after it – to return a moment later and place it at my feet.

I sat down on the dry grass at the top of the beach by the harbour and looked out at the water. Spotty nudged my right arm for a cuddle and Ben was propped on my left side – warm pulsating bodies sharing this peaceful moment with me, while the rest of the world seemed a long way away.

Flash dug hopefully in the shallow water. He seemed to have found something interesting. It was a huge sand-washed bone. He struggled with it until it was free, got a good grip on it and carried it proudly up the beach, his wet, wagging tail sending droplets of seawater to right and left.

The boats pulled gently at their moorings, the ropes creaking with the movement as the tide slid round each bow and along the hull. Big trading boats had used this harbour in times past. We have a photograph of a painting showing a large sailing ship anchored where our small cruiser now lay on the ripples.

I thought of the old farmer who was born on 29th November 1900 in the cowshed just behind me. In those days, it had been two cottages – each with a tiny living room on the ground floor and one small bedroom in the roof. A wooden ladder of wide steps, one side of the living room, had extended through a hole in the ceiling, enabling the occupants to reach the bedroom.

On the day of the birth, all those years ago, the young mother, I believe only eighteen years old, had been Jane Edwards, formerly Roberts – favourite daughter of a farmer living on a farm a mile distant.

It was her first child and perhaps she was apprehensive. No National Health doctor or hospital was at hand and only modest complications could be rectified successfully. She was to be attended by Mrs Grice, a local lady of large proportions who acted as midwife and helped at many of the births occurring in the district.

The telephone network was still a distant dream but jungle telegraph would meet the need to summon assistance for the lying-in. A white flag, or piece of cloth, was to be hoisted to the top of a tree on the highest part of the farm when the birth was imminent. This would notify the grandparents of the impending arrival and call them to the birth bed.

Jane's baby started his journey into the world. The flag was hoisted – but the grandparents were not at hand. Maybe the babe was early and had caught his family unprepared – history does not tell me.

The grandfather returned home, saw the flag, and hurried across the marshy ground to be with his daughter at her childbed. But the baby – a boy, to be called Ioerwerth Cadwaladr Edwards – had already arrived and lay cosseted in blankets in his basket by the stair hole in the bedroom floor.

Grandpapa arrived at the cottage and no doubt in his haste to hear the news urged his legs up the wooden slats of the staircase. He stepped into the dimly lit bedroom – putting his foot into the basket where the infant Ioerwerth lay.

Fortunately the warning cry from the midwife came quickly, and he was able to avoid any hurt to the child – who grew up to farm this land himself until 1978.

The baby – who will be eighty-six in a few weeks' time – speaks of this story with pleasure. Fond remembrances of past times – when at his mother's knee, he was first told of his near escape on the day of his birth.

How life has changed since the day when that white flag was hoisted. Or has it?

Our technology has altered the peripheral things of life. We have choices now that were unheard of in 1900. But have the things that matter changed for the better – the love, the caring, the trust, the loyalty and the justice? The sharing of the work and of the goodies of life?

Are we nicer, happier people, better able to live in peace with each other and the natural world, for the benefits of improved education, medical care, adequate food and almost a frenzy of offerings to occupy our idle moments?

Sadly it seems not. If anything our world is more uncertain, more stressed, and under greater threat than it was all those years ago. Two world wars and countless other bloody confrontations have apparently taught us little. We continue to tear ourselves and our planet apart in the scramble to give the egotistical 'I' a good time, often without in the least knowing what constitutes a good time.

Of course, it is marvellous to know that our life expectancy is greater. That tuberculosis and so many of the killers of the earlier years have been largely eradicated. But has the quality of life improved for the bulk of the people in this world? Have we really got to grips with the big issues? The sharing of the duties and the sharing of the resources. The respect for the views and rights of our fellows, both human and animal – and for the physical planet. And most of all, what, individually, will give us a responsibly fulfilled and enjoyable life! And if not, what is required before we do get to this desirable state?

In many ways our technologies have presented us with more problems than they have solved. No one worried about the threat of nuclear war in 1900. Tuberculosis is no longer a threat – instead we die in sophisticated warfare. Or road accidents, from drug-, alcohol- and stress-related illnesses, or diseases caused by toxic emissions. And in any number of other means induced by the so-called benefits of the modern way of life. Of course it is good that many health issues have been overcome but it seems to me that by and large, many of us worldwide are really no better off.

I talk to that old boy quite often. He shakes his head and appears to think poorly of our present generation and way of life. His own life was not easy – he worked hard for little reward. But his expectations did not exceed his attainments. He was contented with his lot. He and his like were in many ways far happier, often far more caring and concerned for the important issues of the time, than we are with our exotic and refined way of life.

Ease of transport has left many families fragmented. The mutual support of a family community has largely gone. Now we look to the council, the government or the man in the street to sort out our problems instead of looking about us to see how we can cope. And yet this does not seem to be the case in many parts of the world. The rural villages in much of Europe, and elsewhere for all I know, still have the extended family communities. Nearly everyone has an old sick granny or granddad who is still respected and venerated – encompassed in the warmth and support of family life – and it is not regarded as a penance. Sickness, bereavement, ill luck or any of the other hazards of life are dealt with on a community basis and are thereby often more quickly and naturally recovered from. Why have so many of us lost this capacity for sharing our homes and our lives for our mutual support?

To some extent perhaps advertising and popular reporting – the dreaded media – is responsible. The idyllic life is portrayed as being in an exotic location, in frivolous clothes, with limitless financial resources and with a mate with a beautiful body. Given the chance to try this lifestyle, I wonder how long it would be before the average person found it uninteresting. Look at the world's wealthiest people who can command this sort of stuff. Depression, drugs, alcohol and suicide are very common. And yet the yearning, envious rest of us never seem to see what is so obvious.

Does this not point us towards a more simple, less cluttered, mode of lifestyle? For me, it does. I have had greater pleasure and satisfaction in the mud and guts of life in this relatively unspoiled corner of Wales than I ever did in the flashpots of the world. Indeed, going back for a brief taste of the old life showed me how old hat and uninteresting it was. I felt I had grown up and left those seemingly immature pleasures behind.

We cannot protect ourselves from the hazards of life and there is no sensible umbrella to run under when life gets tough. And sooner or later it gets tough for most of us. There is nothing that will cure the pain of bereavement, a broken marriage or any other heartache.

Religious views may help some people but what of those who do not have the vital spark that enables them to take comfort from a god? With the advantages of modern education, perhaps it is unreasonable to expect the maxims laid down many centuries ago in the Bible, or similar works, to be taken on trust.

For me, and perhaps many people, the only security is an internal peace and acceptance to adapt to whatever life may send. To enjoy every day for what it offers in the way of pleasures and to try and learn from the unhappy parts. Anything else is to fight a losing battle.

While I understand that this type of life would not suit everyone – perhaps very few – I can only say that it has led me to a greater awareness of the means to attain inner contentment.

I wish everyone could find an equal foothold on their ladder to their Promised Land.

Epilogue – February 2019

When Mama first moved in to live with us in September 1979, our doctor at the time had suggested we keep a diary to record our daily experiences with her and of our reaction to them. We did, with sundry other snippets of information about our lives, and our story was written in the early months of 1986 from these diaries, bolstered up with memories from our earlier lives.

Many folk have read the account of our time with Mama and our move to Wales, to the point that the original typewritten paper sheets were falling to pieces.

Many of the readers over the years, some with medical, social services or nursing backgrounds, have suggested we try to make the story available to a wider public, some of whom may be faced with the options for the care of an elderly relative. Not everyone wishes to place a beloved mother, father or other close family member in a professional care home when they can no longer care for themselves. And to have an uncensored account of the sorts of experiences that might have to be faced could be useful.

Brian and I are now in our eighties so it seemed that efforts to make the original rather amateur account of our time with Mama available to others should be made now or never.

It was then fortunate that while we were tentatively considering the next step in this venture, two regular annual visitors to our caravan site, Mike and Marcia Woods, offered to make a digital record of the story from the original tatty paper copy. This must have been a massive task and commands our grateful thanks. It meant that it was then only a small step to turn the whole thing into a modest book.

No doubt it will be of limited interest to the general public, but for those who find themselves faced with the practicalities of caring for a beloved mentally ill person, I hope it may prove helpful. Probably few such carers will be subjected to the more extreme events we experienced, so these, as mentioned in our record, can probably be taken as the worst possible scenario. And there are perhaps other folk who are mulling the possibility of moving to a rural retreat. Our experiences will perhaps give some enlightenment on the sort of problems to be encountered.

Later in 1986 it was suggested by the doctor that Mama should be placed in the North Wales Hospital at Denbigh for a few days to assess her condition to see if some form of treatment or help could be devised. This hospital was a long way from our home and, at the time, Brian and I were unaware that it was basically for patients who were mentally ill. She stayed there for two weeks. We rang daily and were assured that she was well. But when she came home, she was completely changed. Gone was the active free spirit, the noise, the confidence. She seemed merely a silent, empty shell. I called the doctor within an hour of her arrival home. He felt that she had probably been sedated for the drive home but this should wear off in a day or two. But it didn't.

She remained a mere spectre of her former self for several months. She was sleepy and remote. And shortly after six o'clock on the evening of 7th February 1987, in the silence and peace of her bedroom here, she left us. She was seventy-nine.

Inevitably we lashed ourselves with recollections of our intolerance, impatience, sharp words and many other issues. Unless you are of a saintly nature, or trained to be more forbearing, this too is, for most of us, a penance that has to be borne if you place yourself in the position of amateur carer to someone who is unable to respond.

But over time we came to accept that, in spite of our occasional lack of empathy, we had stayed the course. And that gave us considerable satisfaction. Furthermore, Mama had seemingly enjoyed a better quality of life than had she been installed in a residential care home, in spite of our lack of experience in dealing with such a patient. Our doctor made the point on two occasions that in his opinion it was unlikely that she would have survived to an age of nearly eighty had she been in professional care since the dementia first made itself apparent.

But indeed had anyone explained to us what was in store when Mama first came to live with us, then I am sure we would have been loud in our contention that we would never cope. But, unhandy as we were, we did cope. Faced with reality, most normal folks do cope.

So: Mother, was it worth it? This was one of Mama's frequent sayings earlier in her life when she had spent time and effort on something that had not turned out as she had planned.

Yes. With hindsight we both feel that it was worth it. In our case the lifestyle we gave up – careers (often stressful), holidays, concerts, theatres, social events and so forth, was replaced by a totally different sort of existence. One that unexpectedly suited us and taught us useful lessons that would not otherwise have come our way. And given the same circumstances again we both feel strongly that we would make the same choice.

In these days when mental illness, especially amongst the elderly, is so prevalent, I hope other people who read this will heed the tale of our experiences and perhaps feel encouraged to keep their oldie in their own domestic circle. Of course, there is a downside. But in our experience, this is far outweighed by the sense of a responsibility for another human being having been seen through to its natural conclusion. We recommend it. You will probably need tolerance and patience in abundance. Also a comprehensive and reliable sense of humour. Bon Voyage.